Base of the Pyramid 3.0
Sustainable Development through Innovation
and Entrepreneurship

BASE OF THE
PYRAMID
3.0

Edited by
**Fernando Casado Cañeque
& Stuart L. Hart**

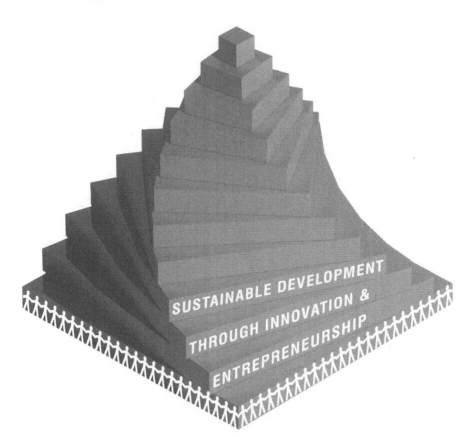

SUSTAINABLE DEVELOPMENT THROUGH INNOVATION & ENTREPRENEURSHIP

Greenleaf
PUBLISHING

© 2015 Greenleaf Publishing Limited

Published by Greenleaf Publishing Limited
Aizlewood's Mill
Nursery Street
Sheffield S3 8GG
UK
www.greenleaf-publishing.com

Cover by Arianna Osti (ariannaosti.com)
Printed and bound by Printondemand-worldwide.com, UK

British Library Cataloguing in Publication Data:
  A catalogue record for this book is available from the British Library.

    ISBN-13: 978-1-78353-203-2 [paperback]
    ISBN-13: 978-1-78353-201-8 [hardback]
    ISBN-13: 978-1-78353-202-5 [PDF ebook]
    ISBN-13: 978-1-78353-200-1 [ePub ebook]

Contents

List of figures, tables and boxes vii

Prologue: Defining the path towards a BoP 3.0 1
Stuart L. Hart

Introduction. Lessons learned: Moving the inclusive
business agenda forward 5
Fernando Casado Cañeque

PART I: BoP vision and capability:
The importance of purpose and culture 11

1 The importance of vision and purpose for BoP
business development 12
Urs Jäger and Vijay Sathe

2 Building inclusive markets from the inside out 31
Tashmia Ismail

PART II: The role of engagement, participation
and bottom-up innovation 45

3 Participatory market research for BoP innovation 46
Aline Krämer, Christina Tewes-Gradl and Claudia Knobloch

4 Open innovation and engagement platforms for
inclusive business design 59
Fernando Casado Cañeque

PART III: Building ecosystems for inclusive business

.... 79

5 Bridging the pioneer gap: Financing the missing middle 80
   Nicolas Chevrollier and Myrtille Danse

6 Creating an innovation ecosystem for inclusive
   and sustainable business 96
   Priya Dasgupta and Stuart L. Hart

PART IV: Market access for all: Solving the distribution challenge

.... 109

7 The last mile: A challenge and an opportunity 110
   Edgard Barki

8 A shared-channel model for BoP access in the Philippines 123
   Markus Dietrich and Jun Tibi

PART V: Partnership frameworks for BoP business

.... 141

9 Partnerships for poverty alleviation: Cross-sector and
   B2B collaboration in BoP markets 142
   Marjo Hietapuro and Minna Halme

10 Access2innovation: An Innovative BoP network
   partnership model 161
   Jacob Ravn

PART VI: Inclusive business models as a response to environmental sustainability challenges

.... 179

11 Urban agriculture as a strategy for addressing food
   insecurity of BoP populations 180
   María Alejandra Pineda-Escobar

12 The triple leap: Addressing poverty and environmental
   challenges both at home and abroad 190
   Tokutaro Hiramoto and Shusuke Watanabe

About the authors 202

Index 208

Figures, tables and boxes

Figures

I.1 Key sections of the book *Base of the Pyramid 3.0: Sustainable Development through Innovation and Entrepreneurship* 8

1.1 Map your enterprise on its purpose and the source of its resources 16

1.2 What drives your company's BoP vision? 27

1.3 Ambition–capability matrix 29

4.1 Principles of innovation for BoP according to Prahalad 63

5.1 Entrepreneurial steps from research to growth 83

5.2 The range of funding options 85

5.3 Position in the investment cycle 88

5.4 The BipBop approach 91

6.1 The Emergent innovation ecosystem 102

6.2 The sustainable entrepreneurship ladder 105

8.1 Example of Shared Channel Assessment Framework 129

8.2 Shared Channels Alignment Framework for the HSSi–NWTF partnership 134

8.3 Shared Channels Alignment Framework for the FVSC–ZWAP partnership 136

8.4 Shared Channel Assessment Framework for the Unilab–Hapinoy partnership 137

10.1 Phases in implementation of access2innovation partnerships 169

11.1 Rosa Poveda at "Mutualitos y Mutualitas"
     organic urban farm 185
12.1 New innovation cycle after the tsunami 192
12.2 The double leap for climate change issues 193
12.3 The Triple Leap 197
12.4 The three perspectives for new business
     from the Triple Leap 199

Tables

1.1 What is our ambition and capability for the BoP space? 28
3.1 Selected participatory methods 51
4.1 Description of grassroots innovation networks 66
4.2 Differences between closed and open innovation principles 73
4.3 Relevant innovations generating impact through
    value-chain phases 75
5.1 Overview of enterprise finance needs in the
    agricultural sector 84
8.1 Basic commodities price comparison between
    Manila and Culion 127
9.1 Cases by sector and country of origin 148
9.2 Case data 149
9.3 Types of actors used in various partner roles 154
12.1 Selected projects from a new METI feasibility study
     support policy for the acceleration of adaptation solutions 195
12.2 Benefits and challenges for companies and
     organizations making the Triple Leap 198

Boxes

3.1 About our case studies 48
3.2 The history of participatory approaches 49
5.1 About our BoPInc case studies 82
5.2 Food and nutrition sector in Africa:
    an investment perspective 84
5.3 The pioneer gap 87
5.4 Schneider Electric BipBop 91
5.5 Inclusive Business Fund 92
10.1 Extract from the DCA concept note on ICT solutions 168
11.1 Turning a dumpsite into an organic garden:
     the case of "Mutualitos y Mutualitas" initiative in Bogotá 185

Prologue
Defining the path towards
a BoP 3.0

Stuart L. Hart

University of Vermont and Enterprise for a Sustainable World, USA

Since the original publication of my article with C.K. Prahalad, "The Fortune at the Bottom of the Pyramid", in 2002, the theory and practice of bottom (base) of the pyramid (BoP) business has taken off. Thousands of new corporate initiatives, start-up ventures, development institution programmes and innovative investment funds focused on social impact have exploded onto the scene. A whole new lexicon has emerged to describe this phenomenon, including new buzzwords and catch phrases such as: "inclusive business", "opportunities for the majority", "sustainable livelihoods", "pro-poor business" and "social business". The number of conferences and summits dedicated to the premise that business and entrepreneurship (rather than just aid and philanthropy) can be brought to bear to alleviate poverty has skyrocketed. And literally thousands of books, articles, newsletters and blogs addressing this topic have appeared on the scene.

Yet despite all this activity and attention, there is still the nagging sense that we have not yet cracked the code when it comes to BoP business. The unfortunate truth is that most BoP ventures and corporate initiatives over the past decade have either failed outright, or achieved only modest success at great cost. As a consequence, a growing number of companies now simply assign this activity to their corporate social responsibility department or corporate foundation.

Such lack of traction can been explained in part by the incremental approach taken by many BoP ventures and corporate initiatives. Indeed, I and several of my colleagues have drawn a distinction between "BoP 1.0" and "BoP 2.0". The former, which has been the dominant approach to date, focuses on adapting existing products, reducing price points and extending distribution to previously under-served or unserved customers, often with non-governmental organization (NGO) partners to compensate for the lack of prior experience. And while such "business model innovation" is necessary, it has proven less than sufficient, since most such "outside-in" initiatives have been commercial failures. I liken BoP 1.0 to the pro-verbial "child with a hammer"—give a child a hammer and everything looks like a nail. Corporations know how to swing their existing hammer, and lower-income "consumers" look like a lot of new (albeit smaller) nails. Some have even suggested that this approach is nothing more than the latest form of corporate imperialism.

Over the past decade, BoP 2.0 has been advanced as a way to overcome many of the problems of simply "selling to the poor". The 2.0 approach stresses the impor-tance of co-creating products and compelling value propositions with under-served communities, innovating from the bottom up, leapfrogging to environmentally sustainable technology, and creating a dedicated set of metrics and timelines suited to the unique features of the under-served space. If the BoP 1.0 model can be summarized as "finding a fortune at the BoP" (premised on the logic of tap-ping into existing, albeit under-served, markets) then BoP 2.0 can be character-ized as "creating a fortune with the BoP" (premised on the logic of creating entirely new markets). Indeed, my earlier book with Ted London (*Next Generation Business Strategies for the Base of the Pyramid*, 2010) makes exactly this point.

The BoP Global Network has been dedicated to building the theory and acceler-ating the practice of BoP business—enterprise that is inclusive, culturally embed-ded, environmentally sustainable and profitable. Members of the network have contributed in significant ways over the past several years to moving us towards BoP 2.0. And while we are still in the midst of developing the new skills, capabilities and organizational routines necessary to execute BoP 2.0, additional challenges, complexities and opportunities are being revealed. Indeed, only by taking action does one uncover the shortcomings in the approach taken. As expected, BoP 2.0 is clearly not the end of the road. It is therefore time to press forward, towards a BoP 3.0.

This book contains contributions from members of the BoP Global Network that help stretch our thinking and point us towards BoP 3.0. How does BoP 3.0 differ from 2.0? In this book, you will find the following themes and "stretch" ideas:

- **From protected space to purpose and mind-set.** BoP 2.0 stressed the impor-tance of creating protected organizational "white space" in companies to give new BoP initiatives the time and space for creative co-creation and embed-ding. While important, creating protected organizational space is neces-sary but probably not sufficient. Looking ahead, it will become increasingly important to consider BoP ventures in the context of the larger corporation, particularly its core purpose and ambition, as revealed by past behaviour. Not all companies are equally suited to pursuit of the BoP and strategies (and effectiveness) will vary depending on the company's true purpose, mind-set and level of ambition. Part I of this book addresses these new challenges.

- **From co-creation to open innovation.** BoP 2.0 revealed the importance of co-creating solutions from the bottom up in partnership with the poor, rather than simply marketing low-cost products from the top down. We are still in the early stages of acquiring the skills necessary for effective co-creation and mutual value creation. Looking ahead, however, open innovation may represent a whole new arena for BoP innovation, drawing on the "wisdom of the crowd" to spawn previously unimagined solutions. Indeed, participatory, grassroots innovations may take BoP business to a whole new level in the years ahead. Part II of this book points us towards these new opportunities.

- **From stand alone to innovation ecosystem.** BoP 2.0 clearly recognized the importance of engagement, particularly with those in the under-served community itself. However, BoP 2.0 still tended to view the business as an island unto itself—with success or failure driven by the venture's strategy, price point, business model or value proposition. Looking ahead, it is becoming increasingly clear that for BoP ventures and initiatives to succeed, they will need to be embedded in a larger innovation ecosystem, including potential technology providers, funders, capacity-builders, on-the-ground partners and supply-chain players. Too often, good ideas have floundered because of missing puzzle pieces of the BoP innovation ecosystem. Part III of this book focuses on this larger systemic need.

- **From extended distribution to innovation for the last mile.** BoP 2.0 understood the challenge of gaining effective distribution in dangerous slums or more sparsely populated rural areas, including the high costs associated with dedicated downstream channels for single products or narrow value propositions. Indeed, the last decade is littered with the failed remains of BoP ventures with cost structures that simply could not produce competitive returns. Looking ahead, more collaborative and creative approaches may be necessary to crack the code on distribution, including wider-bandwidth value propositions and sharing channels with other complementary partners and players. Part IV of this book explores this new horizon.

- **From NGO engagement to cross-sector partnership networks.** BoP 2.0 paid considerable attention to the importance of partnering with NGOs and other key on-the-ground players especially in geographies where the company itself may have limited experience. In fact, many BoP ventures have effectively "outsourced" their customer-facing functions to NGO partners embedded in the under-served space. Looking ahead, more sophisticated and complex partnership networks, including NGOs, governments and academic partners, may be key to BoP business success. Part V of this book looks at models for such multi-sector partnerships.

- **From poverty alleviation to sustainable development.** The original motivation for BoP business was using the power of enterprise to serve the poor, create livelihoods and alleviate poverty. Looking ahead, the importance of integrating both environmental sustainability and an integrated (triple-bottom-line) perspective into the BoP space may prove critical. Potential even exists to use BoP business logic to incubate new models to better serve and include the under-served populations in the developed world. Part VI of this book examines some emerging models for enabling sustainable development.

We hope you find the contributions on the pages that follow a useful next step on the continuing quest to create opportunity for all while simultaneously conserving and sustaining natural capital ... and make money doing it.

References

London, T., and S.L. Hart (2010) *Next Generation Business Strategies for the Base of the Pyramid: New Approaches for Building Mutual Value* (Upper Saddle River, NJ: FT Press).
Prahalad, C.K., and S.L. Hart (2002) "The Fortune at the Bottom of the Pyramid", *Strategy + Business* 26: 1-14.

Introduction
Lessons learned: Moving the inclusive business agenda forward

Fernando Casado Cañeque

Center of Partnerships for Development, Spain

The base (bottom) of the pyramid (BoP) is a demographic that covers approximately four and a half billion people who live on less than US$8 per day at the base of the global economic pyramid. These low-income communities endure heavy burdens to gain access to basic services and often lack the opportunities required to facilitate their empowerment and self-sufficiency. Such circumstances often translate into a poverty penalty, which means they overpay for goods and services of low quality. Furthermore, aside from not having access to certain goods or lacking income, poverty also has social, political, emotional and even cultural aspects. To understand poverty in terms of basic needs, it is important to recognize that poverty is more than just a lack of income. In this context, it usually implies lacking food, clean water, health and education, suffering from ill health and having a low life-expectancy rate and a high mortality rate.

Since professors C.K. Prahalad and Stuart L. Hart first defined the BoP concept, great progress has been achieved in how organizations and companies are incorporating the concept and proposing solutions into their mainstream strategies. Today, governments, international organizations, civil society organizations and, in particular, companies from all over the world have adopted the concept. They are endeavouring to develop frameworks and management systems that bring them closer to the real needs of BoP communities so that they can work alongside them as partners to create social value.

However, the application of disruptive innovations and the creation of more inclusive business models can generate new innovative commercial opportunities with tremendous potential to both scale laterally and "trickle up" to the top. In fact, by developing inclusive businesses, low-income communities can potentially gain greater access to goods and services, a wider range of choices and better opportunities to improve their present and future, while companies are exposed to new growth markets that can boost their competitiveness and capacity for innovation.

Nonetheless, despite the interesting potential of BoP innovative business models, ensuring success in their implementation has proven to be challenging. There are still many methodological and management deficiencies that need to be addressed, such as developing proper co-innovation processes with BoP communities, understanding and enhancing the full potential of generating social and economic value throughout the full life-cycle of product and service processes, and exploring upscaled and replicated models of successful pilot cases.

Essentially, it must be ensured that business models are framed under specific concepts: availability—addressing challenges in distribution as BoP markets can be fragmented or non-existent; affordability—addressing low-income needs and matching the cash flows of customers who often receive their income on a daily rather than on a weekly or monthly basis; awareness building—heightening awareness and education in environments with limited media access and non-existent traditional media exposure; and acceptability, which implies adapting products and services to BoP demand and responding to socio cultural dimensions.

The BoP Global Network was established to provide responses to such challenges. Under the leadership of Stuart L. Hart, the network has brought together innovation labs in several countries to generate and transfer knowledge around socially inclusive and environmentally sustainable enterprises that generate impact at the BoP. The specific goal was to stimulate new enterprises that are economically competitive, environmentally sustainable and culturally appropriate, engaging communities in knowledge creation and dissemination as regards the theory and practice of creating sustainable businesses at the base of the economic pyramid.

The four factors for defining a "BoP business", which have been agreed on by the Global Network, are as follows:

- It concentrates on private-sector business models. While social enterprise and non-profit models are important, the focus of the Global Network partners lies on profit-making business models that engage low-income communities.

- It centres on businesses that are transformational in quality, meaning that they have a profoundly positive effect on the communities they work with. Beyond simply "selling a product", a BoP business builds local capacity and generates local livelihoods. Implicit therein is the expectation that the business will engage members of the local community as partners to achieve the greatest success.

- It considers that environmental, social and cultural impacts must be embedded in BoP business strategies. There must be motivation to improve the community's quality of life; simply creating economic activity without regard for the local environment, community or cultural impact is not consistent with BoP enterprise development as defined by the BoP Global Network.

- It should consider the potential to scale and replicate the business beyond the initial community or region within which it is launched. While local innovation and non-profit experiences are important, only through developing and expanding sustainable enterprises in BoP communities globally will we make more rapid progress towards a sustainable world.

Since its outset, the BoP Global Network's organizations have contributed in many respects to moving the inclusive business and BoP agenda forward. Its core action areas revolve around knowledge generation and dissemination as well as the incubation of innovative business models, helping to identify, design, incubate and promote innovation in business processes with companies and other stakeholders, with a view to achieving sustainable and inclusive business models that enhance BoP community lifestyles through the emerging field of BoP enterprise development. Some of the many activities developed include: fostering and developing new business enterprises; redesigning product development and creating new products and services for the BoP; implementing innovative methodologies for new business development; disseminating and building awareness of successful case studies; and fostering enabling environments for inclusive business among policymakers. In addition, the BoP Global Network has also sought to develop and implement win–win solutions that open up new opportunities for creating business value, while simultaneously boosting the development of the world's poorest people and communities.

This book is part of the efforts undertaken by the BoP Global Network to generate and disseminate knowledge, identifying the most innovative strategies that have been put in place in order to move the inclusive business agenda forward. It is divided into six specific sections that define the strategic phases of the value chain framing business models (see Fig. I.1).

Figure I.1 **Key sections of the book** *Base of the Pyramid 3.0: Sustainable Development through Innovation and Entrepreneurship*

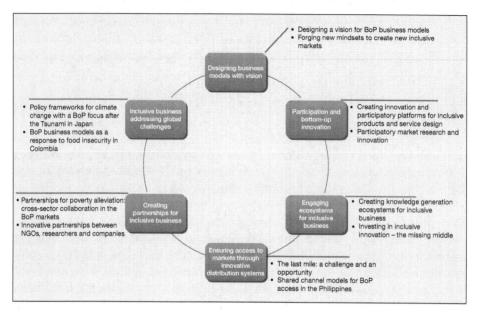

Part I of the book is focused on highlighting the need to emphasize a participatory approach and companies with a vision in business model design. In Chapter 1, "The importance of vision and purpose for BoP business development", Vijay Sathe and Urs Jäger describe some of the efforts required to gain a more in-depth understanding of the circumstances that lead to success and failure at the BoP, highlighting the reasons why it is so important to integrate the BoP space into the company's vision. Such reasoning suggests that, given the growing importance of BoP markets, companies should aim to run a successful BoP business and, as Peter Drucker asserted, every social problem is a business opportunity in disguise.

Chapter 2, "Building inclusive markets from the inside out", written by Tashmia Ismail, confirms how the BoP market in South Africa, as elsewhere, is largely underserved and under-serviced. However, it suggests that firms seeking growth opportunities in developing markets must ask themselves whether it is wise to apply models designed for middle- and upper-income consumers in markets where the bulk of the population subsist on lower incomes. Ismail concludes that as an enterprise expands into lower-income markets it needs to effect major changes in practices and processes. These changes bear an internal impact on the enterprise, potentially disrupting the resources, processes and corporate culture, and sometimes an entire industry.

Part II addresses the role of engagement, participation and bottom-up innovation. Based on research in Madagascar, Sierra Leone and Brazil, in Chapter 3, "Participatory market research for BoP innovation", Christina Tewes-Gradl, Aline Krämer and Claudia Knobloch explore how to best design market research to allow people to share their perception of the situation, preferences, challenges and solutions. The chapter describes market research as participatory when the target group has the ability to influence the perspective of the researchers.

Chapter 4, "Open innovation and engagement platforms for inclusive business design", describes how innovation has been conceived throughout different historical phases until the concept of social innovation has been embraced in an open source economy. It suggests such a concept has not fully enhanced its potential to exert an impact on BoP communities and, hence, there is a great deal to be achieved by integrating its forms into product and service design. Moreover, the article describes some of the different innovation platforms created by ecosystems to enhance social impact and achieve development goals.

Subsequently, Part III outlines the considerations for enabling proper ecosystems for inclusive business. In Chapter 5, "Bridging the pioneer gap", on the "missing middle", Myrtille Danse and Nicolas Chevrollier define how low-income groups, when seen as value-demanding consumers, hard-working producers and creative entrepreneurs, hold the potential to change their own lives by being involved in the launch of innovative business ventures that create new jobs and access to basic services. However, they emphasize that a "missing middle" is still tangible between microfinance and the regular financial instruments available to support companies in developing products and services for the BoP. The chapter describes how such a missing middle is particularly predominant in financing BoP ventures in the early stages of development.

In Chapter 6, "Creating an innovation ecosystem for inclusive and sustainable business", Priya Dasgupta and Stuart L. Hart consider why most BoP ventures of the past decade have failed or under-performed and identify the factors that create enabling ecosystems to promote initiatives at the BoP based on the experience of working with the Emergent Institute in India. The chapter highlights the need to consider an entire business ecosystem, including all its complexities, for enterprises at the Base of the Pyramid to be successful and offers a workable approach to achieve this based on experiences at the Emergent Institute of India.

Part IV addresses distribution challenges and access to markets. In Chapter 7, "The last mile: A challenge and an opportunity", Edgard Barki describes some of the major challenges organizations face in emerging markets, analysing the competition between large and local companies in the distribution arena and identifying a number of solutions to overcome these obstacles, focusing on innovation, partnerships and efficiency. Moreover, the study presents the relevance of retail as a platform for distribution and discusses the importance of distribution for access to basic services.

In Chapter 8, "A shared-channel model for BoP access in the Philippines", Markus Dietrich and Jun Tibi describe the challenges that distribution poses for scaling up BoP ventures and analyse different shared-channel models. The study ultimately proposes the Shared Channel Assessment Framework (SCAF) as a shared-channel model, offering a means of distribution that appeals to firms, as it is potentially a cost-effective means of reaching communities.

Part V of the book analyses the challenges of creating partnership frameworks for inclusive business. Marjo Hietapuro and Minna Halme, in Chapter 9, "Partnerships for poverty alleviation: Cross-sector and B2B collaboration in BoP markets", address the challenges of partnerships in companies' business models in the BoP markets. They provide an overview of the different kinds of partnerships that companies conducting business at the BoP may forge with various types of actors, such as non-governmental organizations (NGOs), local micro-entrepreneurs and companies, government agencies, intergovernmental organizations and universities. In addition, they define nine categories of roles that partners can play in BoP business: co-developers, suppliers, distributors, complementors, customers, microfinance providers, brokers, funders and impact assessors.

Following on, Jacob Ravn analyses some of the lessons learned from launching and implementing the access2innovation initiative in Chapter 10, "Access2innovation: An innovative BoP network partnership model". This initiative, carried out with the NGO DanChurchAid (DCA), in conjunction with 21 companies and five research teams, launched four partnerships that innovate market-driven solutions targeting needs within relief and development aid.

Part VI aims to provide a more practical approach to how such concepts are applied to address certain development challenges. In Chapter 11, "Urban agriculture as a strategy for addressing food insecurity of BoP populations", María Alejandra Pineda-Escobar analyses how urban agriculture has become a valid alternative for responding to the nutrition needs of urban dwellers in emerging and developing countries, with a particular focus on the implications it holds for lower-income households at the base of the pyramid. Pineda describes the framework for studying a successful and promising BoP case concerning urban agriculture in Bogotá, with the potential to both alleviate urban poverty and increase food security on a local scale. It concludes by describing the role of public policy, creating an enabling environment for urban agriculture that minimizes the risks associated with its practice, and enhances its potential for bringing food security to the urban population at the base of the pyramid.

Finally, Chapter 12 written by colleagues Tokutaro Hiramoto and Shusuke Watanabe, "The triple leap: Addressing poverty and environmental challenges both at home and abroad", outlines the challenges that arose in Japan in the wake of an earthquake, analysing how BoP products and technologies deployed by Japanese companies in developing countries have been subsequently employed in the earthquake-affected areas after the tsunami, providing access to electricity, food and water purification systems to affected communities.

Base of the Pyramid 3.0: Sustainable Development through Innovation and Entrepreneurship is the effort of the BoP Global Network's global practitioners to generate knowledge based on their applied research and expertise built through the implementation of projects worldwide. The book seeks to kindle a debate on the role innovation plays in generating value at the different levels of the BoP. It aims to contribute towards moving the inclusive business agenda forward by sharing such experiences with practitioners engaged in the global commitment to improving the lives of the BoP community by putting forward more innovative and inclusive business models.

Part I
BoP vision and capability
The importance of purpose and culture

1

The importance of vision and purpose for BoP business development

Urs Jäger
INCAE Business School, Costa Rica and Nicaragua

Vijay Sathe
Peter F. Drucker and Masatoshi Ito Graduate School of Management, USA

Ever since the work of Prahalad and Hart opened business eyes and minds to the opportunities offered by the world's four billion poor people who live on less than five dollars a day, there has been a corporate awakening and quite a few initiatives to access the base of the pyramid (BoP) space. We first describe some of these efforts to gain a deeper appreciation of the circumstances that led to success and failure. We then turn to the question of what your company's vision for this BoP space is, and what it should be.

It is both costly and difficult to succeed in the BoP space, so why should a company's vision include this space? One reason is that the purpose of the enterprise compels or at least suggests that the company should have a successful BoP business. Another reason is the Vision 2050 report, which points to the increasing importance of the BoP market. A third reason is leadership that believes in what Peter Drucker wrote many years ago, that every social problem is a business opportunity in disguise.

Even if a company wants to operate in the BoP space for these and other reasons, both ambition and capability are required to succeed. Purpose, together with ambition and capability, then determines what a company's BoP vision currently is, and what it should be.

1.1 Corporate awakening in accessing the BoP space

Ever since the work of Prahalad and Hart opened many eyes and minds to the opportunities offered by the world's four billion poor people who live on less than five dollars a day (Prahalad and Hart 2002), more and more companies have attempted to access the "BoP space". We use the term "BoP space" to refer to the complex and dynamic web of resources (tangible and intangible), rules (formal and informal) and relationships (economic, environmental, political and social) that companies doing business at the base of the pyramid (BoP) must learn to navigate if they are to be successful. In this chapter we examine how a variety of companies have attempted to do business in the BoP space, and what everyone can learn from their experience.

For instance, Khanna and Palepu (2006) show how "emerging giants" from developing countries, companies such as Tata in India and LG in Korea, have successfully accessed BoP markets based on their intimate understanding of the BoP space. Examples of other emerging giants are the Mexican company Cemex, Chile-based ENAP (Empresa Nacional de Petróleos), PDVSA (Petróleos de Venezuela SA) from Venezuela, and Petrobras from Brazil. While in 1990 the Fortune 500 rankings listed only a few companies from emerging countries, the number had already reached 52 by 2006.

Multinational companies from the developed world are also entering the BoP space. Companies such as Tetra, Puma, Danone, Coca-Cola, Nestlé and Walmart have invested millions of dollars in initiatives to explore new market opportunities in the BoP space with some success. For example, Starbucks and Nespresso have profitably integrated BoP coffee producers into their supply chains and such sourcing has become a common business practice, particularly in Europe and the United States. Fairtrade, a European non-governmental organization (NGO), reports a 52% increase in its certified coffee producer organizations worldwide between 2002 and 2011, representing more than half a million small farmers in rural areas across 28 countries.

These new business realities of emerging giants, multinationals and other companies, some of which are quite small, also find expression in new concepts to describe "doing business in the BoP space" such as social business, creating shared value, corporate social responsibility, impact investing, social entrepreneurship and social enterprise. However, despite the growing interest in doing business in the BoP space, there are still far too few examples of enterprises that have created a successful BoP business. Why?

1.2 Reasons for lack of success

Two recent studies provide insight into why so many attempts to access the BoP space have failed; each offers helpful pointers on what is needed to create a successful BoP business.

Garrett and Karnani (2010) analysed three well-known BoP ventures by multinational companies. In 2005, Essilor teamed up with two Indian not-for-profit eye hospitals to launch a BoP venture to provide inexpensive eyeglasses for India's millions of rural poor. After a few failed attempts, in 2000 Procter & Gamble launched PuR, a powder that, when mixed with water, produced clean drinking water. In 2006, Danone teamed up with Grameen Bank, the pioneering microfinance organization in Bangladesh, to create Grameen Danone, with the mission of developing a yoghurt product specifically designed to alleviate child malnutrition in Bangladesh. Procter & Gamble and Danone have failed to generate profits so far. Essilor's initiative has become profitable, but it remains marginal in terms of size and growth.

Garrett and Karnani (2010) identify four traps that one or more of these ventures fell into that led to disappointing results. The first trap is to assume that unmet needs constitute a market. For example, it is easy to estimate how many millions of Indians need eyeglasses but it is far more difficult to know how many of them can afford to buy eyeglasses at various price points. The second related trap is to assume BoP customers can afford even drastically reduced prices, even for desirable Western products that are specifically redesigned for BoP markets. The third trap is to underestimate the cost and difficulty of reaching BoP customers, and the fourth is to focus on so many BoP objectives that the project loses its focus.

Garrett and Karnani (2010) offer two basic recommendations for success in the BoP space: (1) reduce product cost and increase affordability via technological innovation, as was accomplished in the case of mobile phones in India; and (2) more controversially, reduce quality to a level that is acceptable to and affordable by BoP customers, as in the case of Nirma detergent that blisters poor hands that cannot afford a gentler but more expensive alternative. Their overriding conclusion is that success in the BoP space requires the same strategic and executive discipline as success in any other business space requires: focused objectives, understanding the customers, and appreciating the role of economies of scope and scale to bring price points down to levels that make the value proposition attractive and affordable to the poor.

Drawing on a larger database of more current experience, Simanis (2012) reaches the same basic conclusion: higher production, distribution and marketing costs, as well as a higher cost of capital (30%) than is paid by Silicon Valley entrepreneurs

(20%), make it very difficult and expensive to reach BoP customers, and success requires that good intentions be grounded in hard-headed business fundamentals.

Simanis goes further to identify the conditions under which it may be possible to lower BoP costs and increase BoP volumes to the levels needed for a successful BoP business: ability to reduce production and distribution costs by being able to leverage the existing infrastructure; lower costs to educate customers because they are already familiar with the product. Unilever could do both to enable its Wheel detergent to successfully take on BoP market leader Nimra. Simanis also challenges the conventional wisdom that business solutions for the BoP space must be based on a low-price, high-volume business model by showing that a higher-price, lower-volume model can generate the required level of profits by bundling and localizing products, offering an enabling service and cultivating customer peer groups.

But Simanis does not address the concern that some people may perceive high-price, high-margin products and services sold to the poor as exploitation of the poor. In fact, the question of whether even well-intentioned BoP ventures are actually good for the poor is not adequately addressed in the BoP literature. Two points are worth noting: First, companies might assume that customers from the BoP space will buy their products and services only if they meet their needs. "Doing good" or having impact is thus measured according to an economic logic: the more a company sells, the higher its contribution to the BoP. But second, given the conditions of life in the BoP space, what is good for the individual may not be good for the community as a whole. However, it is not easy to measure the impact of products and services on the BoP space. Articles such as Herman Leonard's "When is doing business with the poor good—for the poor?" (2007) provide an introduction to the highly complex field of social impact assessment. Methods for measuring these impacts are urgently needed in light of one of Peter Drucker's famous injunctions: To manage, one must be able to measure (Drucker 1973: 400).

The conclusions of both Garrett and Karnani (2010) and Simanis (2012) emphasize the importance of getting back to the basics: success in the BoP space requires business models and strategies that are appropriate for this market. But a more fundamental question that is rarely asked in the BoP literature is: since doing business at the base of the pyramid is so costly and difficult, why bother with it? It is important for company leaders to ask this question seriously and answer it honestly in order to decide whether their company should even have a BoP business. If the purpose of the enterprise compels or at least suggests that it should have a BoP business, what is the right model for it?

1.3 What is the right model for a BoP business?

The classic distinction between for-profits and non-profits is no longer adequate to describe the purpose of the enterprise. The former are engaged in activities that were previously the province of non-profits, and the latter are doing business to fund their operations. What then is the right business model for enterprises doing business in the BoP space?

Figure 1.1 provides a taxonomy to answer this question. The horizontal axis represents the purpose of the enterprise. For whose benefit does the enterprise exist— its owners only, society and environment only, or both? The answer of course depends on the legal structure of the enterprise and its charter, but it is also important to determine for whose benefit the enterprise exists in practice. How this can be done is explained shortly. The vertical axis represents the source of funding for the operation of the enterprise—is it from business activities only, from donations of financial and non-financial resources (houses, cars, services or the time of volunteers) only, or both? Each cell in Figure 1.1 represents a business model. Let us briefly examine each one.

Figure 1.1 **Map your enterprise on its purpose and the source of its resources**

<table>
<tr><td rowspan="3" style="writing-mode:vertical">SOURCE OF RESOURCES</td><td>Both</td><td>7
Corp
volunteering</td><td>8
Grameen
Danone</td><td>9
Hybrids</td></tr>
<tr><td>Donations
only</td><td>4
SME
development</td><td>5
Non-profits</td><td>6
Cluster
development</td></tr>
<tr><td>Business
only</td><td>1
Mobile
phone cos.</td><td>2
• NH Heart
• Aur. Eye</td><td>3
• Patagonia
• Tata</td></tr>
<tr><td></td><td></td><td>Owners
only</td><td>Society and
environment
only</td><td>Both</td></tr>
</table>

PURPOSE
For whose benefit does the enterprise exist?

Cell 1. These are classic shareholder or privately owned companies. But as the example of mobile phone companies in India shows, these for-profits can produce social and environmental benefits that match or even exceed those of the non-profits whose explicit purpose is to realize such benefits. This applies above all to BoP spaces where the creation of jobs providing regular income and social stability have high social value.

Cell 2. These are social enterprises that generate all the resources they need through their business activities and do not rely on donations. The Narayana Hrudayalaya heart hospital and the Aravind eye hospital, both in India, are world-famous examples of this type of enterprise. Both create high social value by their relatively cheap health services and fund their operations by selling those services at a very low price to the poor and a higher—but still affordable price—to the middle- and upper-class people.

Cell 3. These organizations are similar to the ones in Cell 2, but both the owners and society/environment are the intended beneficiaries. We will examine Patagonia shortly, but first consider India's Tata Group. As a senior executive of this company recently told *The Economist* (2009), "Return on capital is not at the centre of our business. Our purpose is nation-building, employment and acquiring technical skills."

Cell 4. Examples are enterprises that depend on donations to facilitate economic development by promoting business entrepreneurship and ownership and better management of small and medium-sized enterprises (SMEs).

Cell 5. These are non-profits such as World Vision, which are financed by donations only and exist for the benefit of society or the environment.

Cell 6. Examples are enterprises that depend on donations to promote cluster development. For instance, the Inter-American Development Bank and other donors support the economic development of areas (such as all of Costa Rica) and invest in companies as well as institutions designed to promote foreign investment.

Cell 7. Corporate volunteering is in vogue. Companies permit or encourage employees to work for a social or environmental cause chosen by the company or by themselves, with time either paid by the company or volunteered by the employee. The purpose of these efforts is employee growth and development as well as reputational benefits for the company from its corporate social responsibility initiatives.

Cell 8. This represents an enterprise that exists for the benefit of society and the environment and relies on revenues from its business activities as well as on donations to fund its operations. Professor Yunus, Grameen's founder, called the Grameen Danone venture a "social business" and he would probably place it in Cell 2, but since it promises to return only the principal to the shareholders and no interest or dividends on the amount invested, the investors are in fact donating the cost of capital.

Cell 9. Hybrids are combinations of for-profit and non-profit enterprises. For example, a non-profit museum with a for-profit gift shop is a hybrid.

The business models in Figure 1.1 may qualify for legal protection and tax benefits. For instance, several American state governments have recently adopted new laws authorizing the creation of the low-profit limited liability company (L3C) and the benefit corporation (B Corp). In these states, companies can now be chartered explicitly for the benefit of owners and society and/or the environment, thus offering these new enterprises with legal protection from shareholders who would otherwise be able to sue the enterprise for pursuing an objective other than shareholder value. These new legal structures are not available in many other states or countries as yet, but they may be adopted more widely in the future, even in emerging countries such as India that have a strong Western legal tradition.

While the taxonomy in Figure 1.1 is a useful way to begin to map the purpose of the enterprise, it is both possible and necessary to gain deeper insight into why, fundamentally, the enterprise exists. In order to do so, we must be clear about what we mean by purpose.

1.4 Purpose versus mission and vision

Although purpose, mission and vision are related expressions and tend to be used interchangeably, there are important differences between them that are best defined with the help of a simple analogy: America's well-known "mission to the moon"—the decision by US President John F. Kennedy in 1960 to commit America to land a man on the moon and bring him safely back to earth "before the decade is out". The mission was crystal clear—build a rocket and spaceship to land a human being on the moon and bring him safely back to Earth before 1 January 1970. But what was the purpose of this mission? Why bother given the cost and the difficulty of doing it? The purpose was to beat the Soviet Union in the space race and to keep America at the forefront of space technology.

Without an understanding of the purpose—revealed by asking the "why" question—the significance of the mission cannot be fully appreciated. The "how" question—bring the astronauts safely back to Earth—reveals the standards of behaviour, the values, by which the mission was to be accomplished. Vision, then, represents the long-term plans and possibilities for achieving the purpose, and it depends on both ambition and capability. For example, the initial vision of the US space programme of a manned lunar base was replaced later by a vision of unmanned exploration of the solar system, as both the country's space ambition and its capabilities changed over time.

In a similar vein it is important to understand why a company invests in the BoP space. Grameen Danone, for example, has been widely applauded for its pioneering social business dedicated to eliminating malnutrition among young children in Bangladesh. While acknowledging the obvious contribution, critics have pointed out that Danone has invested far too little in this venture in light of its mission. It has so far invested around US$1.3 million in this venture and eased malnutrition for around 100,000 children from a target population of roughly 8.5 million malnourished children. Since Danone's total net income in 2009 was US$2.2 billion, critics point out that the company has received a great deal of positive publicity around the world for investing a mere 0.06% of its net income in this venture—a fantastic return on its meagre investment. It is thus critical for the leaders of Danone to understand and explain the company's real purpose in investing in Grameen Danone. Is it because Danone cares for the poor and is really serious about eliminating malnutrition among young children in Bangladesh, as claimed in Grameen Danone's mission statement? Or is the real purpose to gain a better reputation in its markets or to learn how to grow market share in developing countries such as Bangladesh, or are there other reasons?

1.5 Decoding the real purpose of the enterprise

We now show why it is important to go deeper than the horizontal axis of Figure 1.1 to decode the real purpose of any enterprise. We will illustrate the diagnostic procedure with Patagonia (Cell 3 in Figure 1.1). Patagonia is a California-based clothing company founded in 1972 and focused mainly on high-end outdoor clothing. The mission of Patagonia (Reinhardt 2003), which a *Fortune* magazine cover story called "The Coolest Company on the Planet" (Casey 2007), is to:

1. Build the best-quality product

2. Cause no unnecessary harm to the environment

3. Use business to inspire and implement solutions to the environmental crisis. That is why Patagonia:
   - Must be profitable
   - Must grow (10% annual growth for next five years)

But what is the ultimate purpose of Patagonia—the fundamental reason why the firm exists? One of founder Chouinard's favourite quotes to express his concern about the environment was: "Everything we make pollutes." Well, if he felt so strongly about protecting the environment, why did he not shut the company down or sell it, thus avoiding any responsibility for its impact on the environment?

In fact, if he sold the company for $750 million (three times its sales of $250 million), kept $250 million as the family fortune, and created a $500 million foundation for the environment, this charity could contribute $25 million to environmental causes every year (at 5% annual draw on the endowment) and thus contribute ten times more to these causes than the company currently does (based on analysis from the teaching note for the Patagonia case [Reinhardt 2003]).

The answer to this line of questioning reveals the real purpose of Patagonia: to be a role model for other companies by showing them that it is possible to make money while doing minimal harm to the environment. Shutting the company down, or selling it, would not permit this ultimate purpose to be achieved. In fact, in 2012 Patagonia converted from a shareholder-owned limited liability company to a benefit corporation to legally protect this real purpose.

It is interesting to note that Patagonia's exemplary concern for the environment is not accompanied by a similar concern for the social dimension. This is typical of US companies and of US discourse in which the term "sustainability" refers to the ability to sustain both profits (company success) and the planet (environment), whereas in the rest of the world the term also includes a concern for social issues including the BoP (people), or the so-called triple bottom line.

We do not know of a company whose real purpose is to be a role model for other companies on the social dimension just as Patagonia is on the environmental dimension. But the example of Patagonia shows how it is possible to decode why, fundamentally, an enterprise exists. The basic methodology is to critically examine the most important company decisions that were made or not made in the recent past (as in why not sell Patagonia?) in order to gain insight into the real purpose of the enterprise. It could be argued that an enterprise can have more than one purpose, for example, that each of the three items on Patagonia's mission statement is its purpose. However, the analysis we just conducted clearly shows that one purpose stands above all others, and this is what we call the "ultimate" or "real" purpose of the enterprise.

Once the real purpose of the enterprise is clear, leaders can examine what their BoP vision currently is, and what it should be, by asking questions such as: What does the real purpose of our enterprise suggest about our involvement in the BoP space? Should we be involved at all? Why?

If leaders decide to be involved in the BoP space, they need to ask the following questions to develop their BoP vision: What should be our ambition in the BoP space? Do we have the capabilities to achieve our ambition? If we don't have the necessary capabilities, should we build or acquire these capabilities? Or should we scale our ambition down to match our capabilities?

What is our ambition in the BoP space?

Ambition depends on, and is limited by, both perception and motivation. If you are someone who likes equations, ambition = perception x motivation. Let us look at each more closely.

1.6 What is our perception of the BoP space?

1.6.1 Perception 1: The BoP space is filled with poor people

Leaders who have stereotypical images for the poor of slums, hunger and lack of education are likely to view them as passive customers who would be delighted with the company's products, if only they could afford them. Such an assumption may lead their companies to market their products to the BoP with a low-cost, low-price, high-volume strategy based on technology and product push versus a customer- and market-driven approach, leading to disappointing results and perhaps withdrawal from the BoP market.

Even if leaders perceive there is little or no money to be made in the BoP space, they may nevertheless support BoP projects through their corporate foundations as part of their corporate social responsibility effort. Novartis, for example, runs the Novartis Foundation for Sustainable Development, which is led by a pastor and invests in BoP projects to support "development with a human face".

1.6.2 Perception 2: The BoP space includes potential customers with their own needs

If leaders perceive the poor as customers, they are more likely to understand their specific wants and needs (Prahalad letter to Karnani, see Katz 2006). By listening to these customers, the company may be able to reduce prices, redesign packaging, open new distribution channels and collaborate with non-profit organizations to create viable business solutions for the BoP market. Simanis *et al.* (2008) call these practices "Base of the Pyramid 1.0". But it is important to understand the whole context in which BoP customers live and work in order to understand their non-economic values, which may be more important to them than money (Jäger and Rothe 2013).

1.6.3 Perception 3: The BoP space consists of informal markets that follow their own community rules in which customer needs are embedded

Business activities in the informal BoP markets are typically not taxed, monitored by any form of government or included in gross national product (GNP) calculations (Hart 2010; London and Hart 2010; Prahalad 2009). In many BoP markets negotiations are only of a verbal nature, contracts are symbolic, competition is constrained by community bonds, and money is not valued as in the formal markets (London *et al.* 2010).

Management concepts from the developed world are based on assumptions of "the money economy" (Hart 2010: 53), characterized by formal markets with enforceable contracts, rule of law, property rights, functioning market institutions and competition. But these assumptions are not applicable to the BoP space, and this makes it extremely challenging for company leaders used to the money economy to do business in the BoP space.

To address these challenges, Simanis *et al.* (2008) developed a new protocol, "Base of the Pyramid 2.0", for generating a more insightful dialogue with people in the BoP space than simply listening to them. In BoP 2.0, the focus is on creativity that merges capabilities of the company with those of the BoP communities. This work is similar to that of ethnographers—living close to local communities by "becoming a native"—but it is more complex in at least two ways.

First, while ethnographers dedicate many years of work to understanding the culture of specific communities, companies need to collect the relevant data within a few weeks. Methodologies that are both simple and cost-efficient are needed. Second, people in the field tend to look for more context-specific data, whereas people in the head office require standardized methods to enable cross-location comparisons.

The perceptions of a company's leaders about the BoP space influence their motivation for doing business there, but such motivation is also affected by a number of other factors that we now consider. Perception and motivation are both influenced by whether the company is domiciled locally or in a foreign country, and together they determine the company's level of ambition for BoP business.

1.7 What is our motivation for doing business in the BoP space?

Local companies, whether they operate in domestic markets only or are the emerging giants who conquer global markets, may be motivated to invest in their home country's BoP space for a variety of reasons. For example, research by one of the authors of this chapter obtained the following results for 33 companies operating in 12 different countries of Latin America: 60% of the companies had their headquarters in a Latin American country and were operating in international markets, and 40% were domestic only; 70% of all these companies did business in the BoP space. Their motivations for doing so were as follows:

1.7.1 Motivation 1: Expectations of civil society and governments to contribute to solving global social/environmental issues

As indicated in the World Business Council for Sustainable Development report *Vision 2050* (WBCSD 2010), the future markets for multinational companies lie in emerging countries, and their business in these countries is expected to increase from between 20% to 50% within the coming decade (Hammond *et al.*, 2007). At least some of this increase is expected to come from BoP business in these countries.

In addition, the new reality is that non-profits, NGOs, governments and the public at large increasingly expect multinationals to adhere to ethical and moral principles, including when operating in BoP space. Some civil society proponents go even further and expect multinationals to actively contribute to the resolution of global social and environmental issues.

1.7.2 Motivation 2: Knowledge of emerging giants

Leaders of multinational companies recognize the advantages that domestic international companies, including the emerging giants, have in the BoP space, and they are motivated to acquire these advantages—better access to the BoP space, greater experience with informal markets that challenge their everyday business, strong community bonds and an ability to understand BoP markets from a local perspective.

1.7.3 Motivation 3: Customer expectation and standards

Customer expectations. Customers in developed markets expect companies to support people at the base of the pyramid

International standards. Companies that move from emerging countries into international markets need to follow international standards that often include the base of the pyramid

1.7.4 Motivation 4: Need for legitimacy

In the eyes of the population at large, companies doing business in countries where inequality is high may need to legitimize their right to exist and maintain their "licence to operate" by being perceived as socially responsible. One way to do this is to undertake BoP initiatives.

In the eyes of the core and fringe stakeholders, companies have a direct impact, both positive or negative, on the communities in which they operate, for example, in job creation, providing security, land use, pollution and social disruption. As

Stuart Hart has pointed out (2010: 212), "fringe stakeholders"—those who may be affected by the firm even though they have little or no direct connection with the firm's activities—hold knowledge and perspectives that are key both to anticipating potential problems and identifying innovative opportunities and business models. Companies are motivated to respond to the expectations of not only their core stakeholders but also the fringe stakeholders concerning the company's opportunities and obligations to do business in the BoP space.

1.7.5 Motivation 5: Need to improve operational efficiency

Doing business in the BoP space may help to reduce operational cost and better distribution systems can improve BoP business having broader access to markets and increasing sales.

1.7.6 Motivation 6: Reverse innovation

Jeffrey Immelt, Chairman and CEO of General Electric, put it this way: "If we don't come up with innovations in poor countries and take them global, new competitors from the developing world—like Mindray, Suzlon, and Goldwind—will" (Govindarajan and Trimble 2012: 17).

As we have seen, a company's ambition for its BoP business depends on how its leaders perceive the BoP space and on their motivation to do business there. But a company's ambition needs to be matched by its capabilities for doing business in the BoP space.

1.8 What are our capabilities in the BoP space?

Based on the experiences of companies with a successful BoP business, we will outline six key BoP capabilities.

1.8.1 Capability 1: Incentive systems that bridge the BoP space and formal markets

All too often, companies try to manage the interface between the BoP space and formal markets with little knowledge of the former. Latincomp (pseudonym) is an example of such a corporation. It is an international company located in formal markets that buys organic fruits from small Central American producers and sells premium organic products in Western countries. An indigenous group located in a BoP space of a Central American country, producing and selling organic fruits, was considered by Latincomp to be an interesting supplier. However, these indigenous people were quite poor, with income and living conditions well below the national poverty line in their country. Latincomp thus planned the following interventions.

The company wanted to train the producers in growing fruits with modern techniques and organic fertilizers. This would increase the productivity of the suppliers, allowing the buyer as well as the suppliers to earn more money. It would also allow Latincomp to meet the social criteria set by its corporate social responsibility (CSR) standards, such as supporting producers in rural areas by raising their living standards. Latincomp even planned to build schools for the community's children. While this sounds like a smart endeavour, with the potential to meet multiple value criteria and benefit the different stakeholders, the plan could not be implemented because of differences between the CSR standards for the formal markets and the realities of local BoP spaces.

A closer look at the different cultures of Latincomp, based on a formal market, and of the indigenous group acting in the BoP space, helps to understand why the plan was not successful. There were differences in economic values. Compared to the perspective of Latincomp, many indigenous people did not consider themselves to be poor. They were living according to their natural philosophy as they had been doing for hundreds of years. Wealth was not a question of financial resources. Rather, wealth was measured in terms of being part of nature, the ability to acquire all daily needs from their land and respect for the laws of nature. Accordingly, the indigenous group of people produced its fruits in a natural way with a level of productivity that was aligned with their culture and philosophy. They neither saw a reason to change their production techniques nor had an interest in implementing Latincomp's well-developed plans.

As in the case of Latincomp, many companies follow two different logics. On the one hand, they create specific brands to meet economic, social and ecological customer values in formal markets and to set social and ecological standards for operating in BoP spaces. On the other hand, they continue to pay their managers in emerging countries according to the well-established, short-term financial indicators, restricting those managers in investing in the long-term positioning of their business in the BoP space. In this manner, corporations often avoid the systematic management of the interface of formal markets and BoP spaces at the corporate level by transferring this tension to their managers in emerging countries who are not in a position to manage it successfully. To succeed in the BoP space, companies need to develop the capability to manage this tension and bridge this gap.

1.8.2 Capability 2: Work with small suppliers to increase value-chain efficiency in the BoP space

The example of COPROCA illustrates how this can be done. COPROCA was founded in 1991 to satisfy the international demand for raw materials and finished products made of alpaca and llama in the high Andes. COPROCA currently works with 1,200 families of alpaca and llama breeders, who live in the Bolivian highlands. They are part of one of the most important agricultural sectors in Bolivia, representing approximately 54,000 families. Bolivia's per capita gross domestic product (GDP) is only US$1,000, and the llama and alpaca breeders, like small farmers in general, belong to the low-income sector.

The relatively poor living conditions of llama and alpaca fibre producers could be considered as an example of unsustainable rural development, being the consequence of important losses of cattle to agricultural self-sufficiency, an unbalanced nutrition, or a lack of motivation to do their work.

COPROCA requested support from FUNDES, an international NGO that promotes the competitive development of micro, small and medium-sized enterprises in Latin America. FUNDES proposed the development of small suppliers in order to strengthen their supply chains, decrease logistics and transportation costs and work to higher standards.

The main goal for COPROCA was to establish production standards and to ensure that these standards were met by fostering its value-chain development and the standards of its suppliers. In this manner CSR and the commercialization and production processes were integrated. COPROCA also analysed its internal processes relating to supplier management and was able to increase both the quantity and quality of raw materials.

1.8.3 Capability 3: Cross-sector collaboration in the BoP space

Companies can cooperate with non-profit organizations that have a thorough knowledge of the BoP space in order to reduce operational costs and raise product and service quality. An example of a successful public–private partnership is the Colombian company Alpina. This company has been producing dairy products, sweet food and drinks for the national market since 1950. It also exports to various countries of Latin America. The company collects milk from a large number of small producers living in remote rural areas. This involves a considerable infrastructure and well-developed logistics due to the highly perishable nature of the product and the long travel distances.

Alpina created alliances with several associations of rural producers, including Asopoleche, Asogragan and Cooaprisa. The success of these alliances enabled the company to include even more associations as partner organizations and to contract them on a long-term basis. Alpina provided technical assistance and training to the associations, with the cooperation of state agencies such as UMATA (Unidad Municipal de Asistencia Técnica Agropecuaria) to ensure the highest technical standards. Alpina was thus able to ensure a steady growth in volume by maintaining high-quality standards while the associations generated increased revenues for their members.

1.8.4 Capability 4: Build long-term relationship in insecure environments

Consider the Peruvian company Palmas del Espino. Founded in 1979, it has been involved in oil palm cultivation, palm oil extraction and the manufacture of palm oil products. The cultivation of oil palm represented a safe alternative to coca production for residents in the Upper Huallaga Valley, a region marked by high levels of insecurity during the period of control by the Shining Path guerrillas. Palmas understood the legacy of the Shining Path area. This guerrilla movement had been extremely brutal and had left surviving populations with a high level of distrust. This led to anarchy wherever land appropriation was attempted.

Palmas provided oil palm producers with the necessary knowledge and technical assistance, financial support and fair market prices. In 1987, a group of 150 people illegally occupied 3,000 hectares of Palmas property. Instead of attempting to evict them, Palmas reached a unique agreement by granting half of the property to the intruders. Palmas subsequently integrated these families into the oil palm business and provided them with the necessary initial loans that were paid back with half of the harvest over the first five years of harvesting.

Over time, Palmas was able to convince these families, and many others within the community, to cultivate palm trees instead of coca, despite the former being less lucrative. Advantages for the families were low risk, low maintenance costs, constant income, technical assistance and a guaranteed market. Palmas, aware of the region's history and anarchic tendencies, and knowing that it would not get any help from the local government, sought not only an agreement but also partnerships that have paid off.

1.8.5 Capability 5: Legitimize activities in the BoP space by following global standards

Information technology makes global transparency a reality. It is now possible to share the impact of companies in the BoP space with people around the globe using social and public media, so companies operating in the BoP space need to follow global standards in their work. Floralp, an Ecuadorian milk company, provides one example.

Founded in 1964, the family managed Floralp according to family values and implemented projects with social and environmental goals on an informal basis. In 2006, Floralp's suppliers misused their land causing its destruction and leading to a drop in milk production. If the industry had been perceived as destroying the environment, this could have affected Floralp's core business in the long term and jeopardized the company's social licence to operate.

In 2008, and under the patronage of the Nature Conservancy, Floralp signed an agreement with the Center for Dairy Industry on the responsible use of farming areas and the protection of forests. The aim of the agreement was to reduce pastureland coverage and improve the management of forest areas, through a partnership with the small producers who supply the dairy industry. As a result, Floralp has been recognized as a role model of inclusive business by international institutions. Floralp's commitment has also opened new business opportunities and given it access to preferential sources of financing. It thus made sense for the company to meet global sustainability standards.

1.8.6 Capability 6: Innovate in the BoP space

As indicated in BoP Protocol 2.0, the biggest challenge for successfully operating in the BoP space is a company's ability to innovate in this space. Magazine Luiza managed to do so. It is Brazil's third largest non-food retailer. It showed exceptional financial growth due to the pace of consumption, deep customer loyalty, a focus on low-income segments and innovative use of technology.

Luiza differentiated between high-, middle- and low-income customers. Low-income customers were illiterate, had little formal schooling and did not like changes in what they were familiar with. Luiza targeted the poor by appropriately adapting product development and marketing. It treated low-income customers in a much more personal manner than other customers. In terms of credit financing, it also recognized that customers' income stability was more important to them than income level, and both formal and informal sources of income were considered. Finally, the company realized that employee–customer relations constituted the most important connection, so they made considerable efforts to court both customers and employees. This resulted in their being recognized as Brazil's best employer in 2003.

1.9 Creating a BoP vision

Figure 1.2 is a pictorial summary of our argument in this chapter. The question of whether a company should even have a BoP business can be answered by decoding the real purpose of the enterprise—not what is written down in its mission statement but why, fundamentally, the enterprise exists. Given the costs and the difficulties of operating in the BoP space, does the real purpose of the enterprise compel or at least encourage the enterprise to have a BoP business?

If the answer is yes, the company's level of ambition in the BoP space will depend on its leaders' perceptions of the BoP space and their motivation for doing business there. And a company's BoP ambition must be matched by its BoP capabilities to achieve success. Company leaders can create a BoP vision in three steps.

Figure 1.2 **What drives your company's BoP vision?**

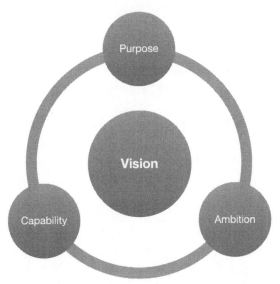

1.9.1 Step 1: What is our BoP ambition and capability?

Company leaders should answer the questions in Table 1.1 concerning their BoP ambition and BoP capability.

Table 1.1 **What is our ambition and capability for the BoP space?**

What is our BoP ambition?	What is our perception of the BoP space?	Perception 1: The BoP space has poor people
		Perception 2: The BoP space has potential customers
		Perception 3: The BoP space has informal markets that follow their community rules and in which customer needs are embedded
	What is our motivation to enter the BoP space?	Motivation 1: Expectations of civil society and governments to contribute to solving global social/ environmental issues
		Motivation 2: Knowledge of emerging giants
		Motivation 3: Customer expectation and standards
		Motivation 4: Need for legitimacy
		Motivation 5: Need to improve operational efficiency
		Motivation 6: Reverse innovation
What are our BoP capabilities?		Capability 1: Incentive systems that bridge the BoP space and formal markets
		Capability 2: Use local supplier to increase value chain efficiency in the BoP space
		Capability 3: Cross-sector collaboration in the BoP space
		Capability 4: Building long-term relations in insecure environments
		Capability 5: Legitimizing activities in the BoP space by following global standards
		Capability 6: Innovating in the BoP space

1.9.2 Step 2: Where are we located on the ambition–capability matrix?

Based on the results of Step 1, where is our company currently located in the ambition-capability matrix (Fig. 1.3) on a scale of 1 = low and 9 = high? Where should we be located in light of the real purpose of our enterprise? Should our ambition and capability change over time, given our real purpose?

Figure 1.3 **Ambition–capability matrix**

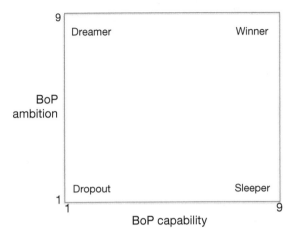

The four corners of the matrix represent four "personalities" for a company's vision:

- **Dropout vision.** Companies whose real purpose does not compel or even encourage them to be in the BoP space. These companies should not enter the BoP market or, if they have a BoP business, they should develop an exit strategy

- **Dreamer vision.** Companies that have difficulty in implementing their BoP strategy because they lack the required capabilities. These companies may be multinationals with little experience in the BoP space. They should learn from experienced domestic international companies and emerging giants

- **Sleeper vision.** Companies that have the capabilities to do business in the BoP space but lack the ambition for it. These companies may be emerging giants that do not recognize the value of their BoP capabilities. They should take note of the BoP ambitions of their multinational competitors

- **Winner vision.** Companies that have both the ambition and the capabilities to succeed in the BoP space

1.9.3 Step 3: What is our BoP vision?

With insight into where a company is currently located on the ambition–capability matrix, and where its leaders would like it to be in the future, a vision can be created to get from here to there. When fully articulated, the vision should clearly spell out what the real purpose of the enterprise is, and why this either compels or encourages the company to have a BoP business. The current and desired levels of ambition should then be described in terms of both the leaders' perceptions of the BoP space and their motivation for wanting to have a successful BoP business. Finally, the vision should specify the company's current BoP capabilities and how they will be developed or acquired over time to achieve the desired vision.

Bibliography

Casey, S. (2007) "Eminence Green", *Fortune*, 2 April: 62-70.

Drucker, P.F. (1973) *Management: Tasks, Responsibilities, Practices* (New York: Harper & Row).

Economist, The (2012) "A New Boss at Tata: From Pupil to Master", *The Economist*, 1 December 2012.

Garrett, B., and A. Karnani (2010) "Challenges in Marketing Socially Useful Goods to the Poor", *California Management Review* 52.4: 29-47.

Govindarajan, V., and C. Trimble (2012) *Reverse Innovation: Create Far From Home, Win Everywhere* (Boston, MA: Harvard Business School Press).

Hammond, A., W.J. Kramer, J. Tran, R. Katz and C. Walker (2007) *The Next 4 Billion: Market Size and Business Strategy at the Base of the Pyramid* (Washington, DC: World Resources Institute).

Hart, S. L. (2010) *Capitalism at the Crossroads: Next Generation Business Strategies for a Post-Crisis World* (Upper Saddle River, NJ: Prentice Hall Pearson, 3rd edn).

Jäger, U., and M. Rothe (2013) "Multidimensional Assessment of Poverty Alleviation in a Developing Country: A Case Study on Economic Interventions", *Nonprofit Management and Leadership* 23.4: 511-28.

Katz, R. (2006) "Prahalad Responds to 'Mirage at the Bottom of the Pyramid'", http://BoP. nextbillion.net/blog/2006/08/31/prahalad-responds-to-mirage-at-the-bottom-of-the-pyramid, last accessed 28 December 2003.

Khanna, T., and K.G. Palepu (2006) "Emerging Giants. Building World-Class Companies in Developing Countries", *Harvard Business Review* 84.10: 60-69.

Leonard, H.B. (2007) "When Is Doing Business With the Poor Good—For the Poor?" in V.K. Rangan, J.A. Quelch, G. Herrero and B. Barton (eds.), *Business Solutions for the Global Poor* (Boston, MA: Harvard Business Press: 362-73).

London, T., R. Anubindi and S. Sheth (2010) "Creating Mutual Value: Lessons Learned from Ventures Serving Base of the Pyramid Producers", *Journal of Business Research* 63: 582-94.

London, T., and S.L. Hart (2010) *Next Generation Business Strategies for the Base of the Pyramid: New Approaches for Building Mutual Value* (Upper Saddle River, NJ: FT Press).

Prahalad, C.K. (2009) *The Fortune at the Bottom of the Pyramid* (Upper Saddle River, NJ: Pearson Prentice Hall).

Prahalad, C.K., and S.L. Hart (2002) "The Fortune at the Bottom of the Pyramid", *Strategy + Business* 26: 1-14.

Reinhardt, F., R. Casadesus-Masanell and D. Freier (2003) "Patagonia", *Harvard Business School Case* 9-703-035.

Simanis, E. (2012) "Reality Check at the Bottom of the Pyramid", *Harvard Business Review* 90.6: 120-25.

Simanis, E., S. Hart and D. Duke (2008) "The Base of the Pyramid Protocol Beyond 'Basic Needs' Business Strategies", *Innovations* 3: 1: 57-83.

WBCSD (2010) *Vision 2050* (Geneva: World Business Council for Sustainable Development).

2
Building inclusive markets from the inside out

Tashmia Ismail

Gordon Institute of Business Science, University of Pretoria, South Africa

This chapter will highlight, list and describe some of the key theories and concepts which have been found to be critical in the development of successful inclusive market strategies in Sub-Saharan Africa. Important concepts are examined, including disruptive and frugal innovation, patient capital and long-term goal setting, re-organizing the organization, rethinking metrics and reporting, moving from transactional to transformational models, changing from closed to open business models, developing a partnership approach to business and reimagining products. South African companies such as MTN, Standard Bank, Capitec and Blue Label Telecoms, and other MNCs operating in Sub-Saharan Africa such as Unilever and GSK, which have embarked on this journey to the bottom of the pyramid are helping to "write the book", as well as bringing development and employment to parts of the continent that desperately need it. This chapter refers to a number of these developments.

> When I opened my account the branch manager came and shook my hand. It sounds trite and retro, but he also shook the hands of some old tatas [grandfathers] who were opening accounts. I liked that a lot.

This consumer quote was drawn from a local South African newspaper, *Business Day*, reporting on the results of the 2014 Bank of the Year survey, won by Capitec Bank (Lefifi 2014). Beating market incumbents, this bank opened its doors in 2001 with a unique low-cost focus and commitment to deliver value to the low-income consumer.

The South African low-income consumer was by and large ignored by the financial services sector, which deemed this market "not worth the effort" given the small pocket size and its relative inaccessibility. The advent of democracy in apartheid-ravaged South Africa began to shift this thinking as black consumers began entering the formal economy en masse. The Financial Sector Charter, which came into effect in 2004, marked a shift in banking strategy. It was an undertaking by the financial services sector to promote social and economic integration and access to financial services for the unbanked and under-banked. However, first-generation strategies by banks to promote financial inclusion and service this low-income segment were abysmal attempts. Banks opened millions of "Mzansi" accounts, designed with little thought given to user needs and preferences and essentially a miniaturization of the conventional account carrying the same overheads and cost. Serious design flaws, inadequate attention to usage behaviour and pricing resulted in accounts lying dormant at high cost to the bank.

Then things shifted. New market entrant Capitec Bank had a targeted strategy to capture low-income consumers. Retail principles, slick IT systems, biometric identification and a focus on low cost and building trust and strong client relationships saw this bank capturing swathes of market share in this poorly served segment. It appears to have paid off; the 2014 Bank of the Year survey conducted by Intellidex, a specialist financial services research house, showed Capitec beating the "big four" incumbent competitors for the hearts of consumers.

Today Capitec has 12.7% of the market, an increase from its 9.2% market share of 2012, and its ambitious claim is to aim for 25% of the market by 2020. This growth trajectory, which shows little sign of slowing, has caused great disruption in the financial services industry. Banks woke up to the fact that many of these lower-value consumers were on an upward economic path with promising lifetime customer value. Not only was Capitec growing market share but it was also building lifetime consumer loyalty. This disruption in the banking space came from within the sector albeit by adopting principles from retail.

The past years have seen competitors from other sectors making inroads into the delivery of financial services with a proliferation of successful mobile banking products launched by network operators across the continent. Retail checkpoints in supermarkets and "mom and pop" stores called spazas have taken on bank-teller functions, with banks clamouring for partners in the retail sector to get their products closer to consumers in this market segment.

The competitive landscape has been fundamentally altered as the firm forays into new market segments and geographies and operates across sectors. It is no longer sufficient to perfect a single game plan; continual innovation and disruption of the status quo are demanded, especially within low-income segments where the bundling of goods and services are often an efficient way to deliver cost-effective and user-friendly solutions to customers who cannot afford a myriad of products.

Kenyan insurance company UAP entered into the low-income arena with a crop insurance product called Kilimo Salama. Rather than try to convince subsistence farmers to spend on insurance, this company included the cost of the insurance in the price of a bag of seed and fertilizer, which farmers had to purchase anyway in the sowing season. Working with Syngenta and Bayer, UAP was able to subsidize the cost of the insurance to foster trial and adoption at low financial risk to the farmer. The certified, drought-resistant and high-yield seed was sold through an existing network of agro-vets trusted by local farmers and dotting the rural Kenyan countryside. By using an existing network of agents present in the rural ecosystem, the firm reduced distribution and marketing costs. Weather towers gathered and transmitted data on microclimates through to Nairobi. If poor harvest conditions were recorded in any regions covered, technology was used to make payouts via mobile money transfers straight into the pocket, or rather mobile, money account of the farmer.

This industry disruption has come with birthing pains. Bankers have had to dramatically shift company thinking in order to play in this space. When patient capital and long-term goals are required, access, cost and margins are different, and the old way of doing things is simply not sufficient to compete. A banker from a leading South African bank attempting new products in the market described his team's dilemma:

> Your [low-income] customers will be open to doing things differently because they not as vested in traditional way of doing things, and it's there where the chance for radical innovation actually opens up. Once you use that as the starting point you no longer do incremental innovation or process innovation; you are no longer just trying to take what you do and pushing it down the pyramid.
>
> It is about what the customer needs and wants and what the customer is willing to pay for it … and what that allows you to do is to make some radical shifts in the way you do business. But if you start any other place all you do is incremental stuff and that's always a mess … We need to say: OK how do we do things completely differently? (pers. comm.).

Carl Fischer, an executive at Capitec, described his bank's approach in the media as: "Simplicity plus transparency gives the client control" (Lefifi 2014). Not so long ago simplicity and transparency were unicorns in financial services; however, abiding by these tenets is what it took to drive financial inclusion and give one bank the edge over the established competition.

Learning how to serve lower-income segments successfully demands that industry embrace disruption of its metrics, systems and processes and create the organizational architecture to enable radical innovation.

2.1 Where to start?

The banker quoted above described customer needs and wants as being important to understand. For many firms, reliable data and consumer insights are scant. Business models are often built on assumptions, stereotypes and generic quantitative databases. The art of ethnography, immersion and face-to-face conversations are important starting points for firms interested in these markets. These techniques, which offer crucial insights into the consumer's life, have been neglected. Language barriers, cost, time, accessibility and infrastructure are some of the reasons behind the dearth of consumer research at the bottom of the pyramid (BoP).

Given the limited wallet size and unique challenges faced at the BoP, consumers do not have the luxury of making purchasing errors. This means that products and services that add value will be purchased, while those that waste scarce resources will be selected out of the marketplace. Word of mouth trumps elaborate marketing campaigns as the most powerful marketing tool, with consumers trusting opinions drawn from their ranks and sharing these brand experiences through peer networks in the remotest villages and alleyways of urban slums. Mass adoption of social media through mobile phones has added huge impetus to the sharing of brand experience and can both punish poor efforts and reward good brand interaction.

This makes building customer journey maps and insights into the daily pains and problems of the low-income consumer an important early marker on the innovation pathway. As with all segments, innovation must begin with solving problems for consumers; without detailed market information (both quantitative and qualitative) those insights are impossible to arrive at.

Capitec Bank identified several problems to be solved for clients on lower incomes. Affordability of financial services was a key issue. The bank realized it needed to drop overheads in order to deliver more affordable services but still make a profit; hence the efficient IT systems and biometrics that allowed for leaner and smaller branches manned by fewer staff.

The next problem to be solved involved accessibility. Customers were travelling to bank branches in urban centres paying 20 rand for transport to make a 100 rand deposit. By opening large numbers of smaller branches, Capitec was able to bring banks closer to people. They stayed open for longer hours and used supermarket tellers as alternative points for transactions. Another issue experienced was that of poor financial literacy, bureaucracy and the intimidating design of bank branches. Capitec did away with thick glass panes separating customers from tellers, allowing more human and less intimidating interaction. Additionally, relationship managers greeted customers as they came into the bank. Automatic ticket numbers were dispensed to democratize waiting times and all paperwork was written in simple language in large font size and had to fit onto a single page.

Capitec's innovators identified five kinds of cost that customers incur when they bank: direct; social and cultural; opportunity; psychological; and cost of compliance. To capture the BoP market, innovation along multiple fronts was necessary. Key among these was maximizing value to the customer and minimizing non-essential costs.

As an enterprise grows into lower-income markets, it needs to make important changes in practices and processes. These changes have an internal impact on the enterprise, potentially disrupting the resources, processes and culture of a company—and sometimes an entire industry. Learnings are absorbed across the company and again sometimes even across an industry. Middle-income customers began defecting to Capitec as they also valued the efficiency, customer centricity and lower cost of Capitec's services.

It is important to note that senior leadership buy-in is critical. The bank's executives championed innovation from the top, incorporated non-traditional elements, provided only a core of essential functions that related directly to customer needs, moved to more environmentally friendly operations, and designed their operations from the starting point of the work customers needed a bank to do for them, rather than trying to trim the elaborate structures of traditional banking.

This chapter will highlight and describe some of the key theories and concepts that have been found to be critical in the development of successful inclusive market strategies in sub-Saharan Africa such as those shown in the Capitec example.

2.2 Disruptive and frugal innovation

Important concepts to examine are those of disruptive and frugal innovation, as pioneers of inclusive market thinking and the developers of lower-cost, high-value models tend to be disruptors and learn how to innovate with less. It is interesting to note that although Capitec's retail-style banking service started by servicing BoP markets, it soon began to attract customers further up the pyramid.

According to Clayton Christensen, who developed the theory of disruptive innovation in 1997, this occurs more easily in newer firms, which are not encumbered by established routines and values. When we examine the dimensions of disruptive innovation—that is, being lower cost, lower margin and simpler, under-performing the traditional offering, needing different product architecture, attracting a new customer segment and, importantly, eventually cannibalizing the existing core products and services—we can understand why they pose a threat to the status quo and vested interests in the firm.

Frugal innovation came about in developing markets where firms were experimenting with ways in which they could design high-quality products and services to match the price points of lower-income segments. Frugal innovation demands that developers start with a "clean slate" and design from scratch to ensure that only those elements valued by the lower-income consumer are included with all the fat trimmed from the offering.

We note some famous examples of frugal innovation across sectors: in the automotive industry, the Tata Nano car or Carlos Ghosn's Dacia range; in fast-moving consumer goods (FMCG), Procter & Gamble's Tide Naturals and single blade razor or Unilever's Lifebuoy soap, and Hindustan Lever's Shakti model; in financial services, mobile money products such as Vodafone M-Pesa (of which more below), Capitec Bank and UAP's Kilimo Salama crop insurance for smallholder farmers; and in healthcare, GE's electrocardiogram machine for rural India and Dr Shetty's

Narayana Health, which has innovated successful cardiac surgery for less than US$800.

Frugal innovation demands that innovators go back into the supply chain and manufacturing process to ensure that the templates and costs of production are also lower. It is impossible to achieve high quality at low cost with superficial or incremental tweaks to products and services. If firms wish to service the consumer with a small wallet, they need to abandon a deep-pocket mind-set of throwing resources at a problem. To innovate for the poor the firm must think like the poor.

2.3 Costs and benefits: patient capital and the long endgame

Firms must be prepared to invest resources and put in before they get anything out, and this can take years.

- The disruptive and frugal innovation described above exacts a cost on the organization that is often felt early in the process, while the benefits become evident at much later points in the development of the business model. Managing this trade-off is an important skill and process to manage if the inclusive model is to survive

- Building local networks, transferring skills, investing in communities and embedding the firm into the local ecosystem are necessary to gain acceptance and to market, educate and learn about the local consumer. The firm needs to lose its "foreignness" in order to be accepted

- New market offerings may depend on resources and technologies that are, themselves, innovative and still in development

- Champions of new markets and products often have to struggle to convince others of the benefits, and lengthy trials can be costly and frustrating

Well-documented examples of intrapreneurs who persisted with inclusive business models despite strong organizational push back include that of intrapreneur Nick Hughes, previous Head of International Mobile Payment Solutions at Vodafone Group, who worked tirelessly toward the acceptance of the M-Pesa mobile money model in Kenya, a mobile payment service that was the start of a mobile banking revolution in Africa. This disrupted conventional financial service models and carried Vodafone's Safaricom from telecommunications into financial services, an uncomfortable shift. Another pioneer who warrants mention is Israel Moreno, who took multinational, B2B (business to business) cement giant Cemex into urban slums to become home builders rather than purely cement salespeople, disrupting the convention around bulk cement sales and home building (see Cemex case by Ted London [2012]).

To survive, these mass-market or low-income teams require leadership support, resources, autonomy and a relevant set of metrics. One of the strategies that forward-thinking firms employ is the creation of "skunkworks", incubators and independent teams to develop these disruptive ideas beyond the reach of "institutional antibodies" that resist these seedling ideas.

To achieve this, companies such as Philips and Ericsson set up innovation labs in countries such as Kenya, employing local developers and engineers. Banks such as Standard Bank create "skunkworks" operations to incubate early ideas around what they described as "community banking", which today has been reincorporated into the main bank as the Inclusive Banking division. Others partner with companies that already have deep experience in their market segment, such as Hollard Insurance with retail player Pep Stores.

It is clear that firms attempting to access the new arena of the low-income market must consider new products to add value to consumers who have distinct tastes, preferences, aspirations and wallet sizes. However successful, inclusive business requires new ways of thinking, a mind-set shift towards a model defined by low margin, scale and volume, high risk, patient capital and long-term goals. Internal firm shifts in structure and mind-set in addition to an ecosystem-based approach and embeddedness in communities is demanded to drive acceptability, availability and brand loyalty. None of this will be possible without a fundamental reorganization of the company, a disruption of the status quo that functions in the old market with old products.

2.4 Reorganizing the organization

In *New Markets, New Mindsets* Ismail and Kleyn (2012) offer useful guidelines drawn from multiple case studies on the internal processes, structures and systems that assist in meeting the goals of inclusive business strategies.

They write that flexibility of roles, good interdepartmental communication, and fast response times are important. Additionally there must be an emphasis on multi-skilling, which means there must be training not only for staff, but also for local partners. No room exists for the siloed organization or the "not invented here" syndrome.

Frugal engineering author Vikram Sehgal and his colleagues observed,

> Typically the more mature an organization, the more rigid the functional silos. There tends to be little coordination between functions without an explicit effort from top management, which must either create a new structure for the team or use brute force to encourage communication (Sehgal *et al.* 2010).

Ismail and Kleyn (2012: 194) summarize Christensen and Overdorf's (2000) suggestions for improving a firm's ability to innovate and move away from the lethargic and hierarchical organization that struggles to react to market demands with alacrity:

- In the existing organization, create new capabilities internally by pulling the relevant people out and drawing a new boundary around a new group.
- Create a spinout organization (which doesn't need a different physical location). The primary requirement is that the project not be forced to compete with projects in the main organization.
- Acquire a new company with the strengths you need. But don't "vaporize" the capabilities of the new company into the acquiring organization's culture. A better strategy is to let the business stand alone and to infuse the parent's resources into the acquired company's processes and values (Ismail and Kleyn 2012: 194).

2.5 Rethinking metrics and reporting

Another critical shift for the firm interested in successfully pursuing inclusive strategies concerns metrics and reporting. The old business school adage, "You get what you measure", holds true for low-income segment reporting. If scale, low margin and long-term payoffs are expected and necessary, it is disingenuous to hold inclusive business teams to the same standards and metrics applied to higher margin and more established divisions within the firm. Firms such as Nestlé and Unilever have incorporated inclusive goals into their key performance indicators in order to incentivize and drive more inclusive and sustainable decision-making in their managerial ranks.

What makes low-income opportunities particularly unpalatable within a firm are the high research, set-up and distribution costs as firms try to operate in markets with structural holes, infrastructural liabilities and institutional instability. These daunting external factors, when coupled with the lower margins of BoP products, often dissuade managers from experimenting with suitable models for fear of failure and punishment from shareholders in the short term.

Relevant metrics are therefore critical to prevent disillusionment and to support the activities of managers experimenting with new inclusive business models.

Ismail and Kleyn (2012: 200) explain that

> because building business with low-income communities is a developmental process that unfolds over time, financial planning should follow the same pattern. There needs to be consideration of the likely margins at different volume intervals, not only to assist with scaling decisions ... but also as part of making the case for embarking on and sustaining low-income market offerings.

Metrics are not only internal and profit/loss related. It is also important to consider external metrics to judge the impact of the business model on the environment, community, local partners and local economy. These metrics can be used to motivate employees and to bolster institutional and sometimes funding support.

A good set of metrics can act as a roadmap for growth and allows for objective decision-making going forward. Judging the project through a fair lens can also help build the business case and convert sceptics within the firm.

2.6 The philosophy of business: moving from transactional to transformational models

Many scholars have documented the institutional and infrastructural dysfunctions that low-income communities face in developing markets. Poverty, inequality, lack of basic healthcare and clean water, and poor educational systems continue to plague many communities. Firms with long-term growth plans cannot ignore the economic and social realities of the markets they operate in, as this has implications for the progress and transaction costs faced by the firm. The idea of conventional business where firms see themselves merely as traders, transaction-oriented, rather than an important contributor to the ecosystem is short-termist. By embracing strategies that develop the local market the firm ensures a more stable and prosperous future for itself.

The GlaxoSmithKline (GSK) team based in Johannesburg, under the leadership of Vice President Dave Thomas, is embracing a more transformational style of business by thinking about the long-term development of its brands in township markets. One of GSK's mainstay brands in the FMCG space is a headache powder called GrandPa. This brand was used to name a business training school, the GrandPa Spaza Academy. Partnering with a top-ranked South African business school, Gordon Institute of Business Science (GIBS), GSK understood the value of open innovation and building non-traditional partnerships. GIBS, with its experience and knowledge of low-income market dynamics, was able to design a practical and relevant training programme for the township micro-entrepreneurs enrolled in the course.

GSK's low-income brands are sold through small spaza stores. Many of the owners of these micro-enterprises have not finished school, lack basic business training and struggle to grow their businesses. They are, however, an important part of the township economy, offering employment and supporting an extended network of dependents. They are also a widely distributed customer-facing retail point, giving the brands an enviable footprint into the "last mile" to the end-consumer.

By allowing these micro-entrepreneurs access and enrolment into a business basics programme several longer-term goals may be achieved. First, these businesses are more likely to maintain consistent inventory of the GSK product and will market, price and sell stock better. Second, by growing and scaling their micro-enterprises, the township economy becomes more prosperous and stable, increasing market potential. Third, and very importantly, by making this investment in local capacity building, GSK embeds itself as a brand that belongs in this space, overcoming the liability of foreignness. By building this network of loyal agents across communities the firm also has an avenue to draw valuable market learning and consumer intelligence, creating a feedback loop through which it can deliver even greater value innovations to market.

The immediate payoffs for a project such as this are not big, despite the substantial upfront investment and resource pull required. Certainly there is a degree of marketing benefit accrued, as GSK receives favourable press for investing in low-income communities. The real benefits, however, cannot be measured as a line item in quarterly reports but will be felt in the long term. This type of business strategy can only be made to work if there is senior leadership buy-in and commitment to the long-term play and the willingness to deeply engage with and shift local economies through a transformational mind-set around the role of business in society.

2.7 Moving from closed to open business models

It has gradually become clear that, given the fast-changing consumer landscape and external environment and the explosion of communication devices and social media, firms will struggle to innovate using solely current internal resources and people. The closed, internally focused firm may find itself struggling to compete. Solutions are to be found in the network of consumers, competitors, suppliers and institutions that surrounds the firm. Knowledgeable and connected local staff and partners at every level are vital. Many authors (Busch 2014; Ernst *et al.* 2014; Schuster and Holtbrugge 2014) have suggested that engaging in networks external to the firm, embedding in local economies, co-creation and embracing non-traditional partnerships are critical to the success of the firm in low-income market spaces and to the development of what Ernst *et al.* (2014) refer to as "affordable value innovations".

Firms manage this challenge in various ways. Dutch multinational Philips has set up innovation labs in Africa to develop and nurture not just more local ideas but also local talent. Pharmaceutical firms such as Roche and Merck send global executives on immersion experiences in low-income communities where executives engage in close-up conversations with households and businesses in slums and townships. Increasingly, we note that global executive leadership conferences are held in emerging markets, including local faculty and emerging and developing market case studies into these programmes.

Mechell Chetty, Vice President of Human Resources at Unilever, explains that Unilever has an entrenched global Future Leaders programme with globally applied standards. However, in African markets Unilever has gone beyond convention to develop a grass-roots strategy for talent development by engaging government and universities. In Ethiopia, Unilever has offered to work with universities on developing work-relevant curricula especially within the marketing space, which is an area of particular expertise for the firm. University graduates, who are often not sufficiently prepared for the work market, are taken on accelerated learning programmes, secondments and rotations to other markets to increase their exposure and experience. According to Chetty, talent will only be developed to quality and scale through a mind-set of co-creation and partnerships with local institutions and bodies.

Standard Bank, one of the "big four" South African banks, recruits locals from the community as first-tier agents in its Access banking model. These agents set up shop on street corners in townships, informing passers-by of banking options, and are able to open accounts in the street using hand-held devices. The bank then uses local spazas to act as mini bank branches where deposits, withdrawals and other digital goods such as airtime and electricity may be purchased. This Access banking model incorporates locals as an integral part of the banking ecosystem.

For South African multinational corporation (MNC) Blue Label Telecoms, developing partnerships has been a key priority in growing the footprint and distribution of the digital packages such as airtime and electricity. Partnerships with gospel singers, tribal chieftains and soccer clubs have been an integral part of their growth story. By nurturing partnerships with local icons, leaders and influencers, Blue Label was able to share in the social capital and trust relationships held by these agents. Sharing in social capital is only possible with reciprocation; the company reinvests a percentage of the revenue generated from these digital sales back into the community via these same agents. Blue Label also trains community members as sales agents, to solve and troubleshoot issues with mobile redemption of airtime. They are thus involved in local capacity building, and in rural areas this is often the first formal job opportunity for local youth.

Through a variety of methodologies we see an increasing appetite for open innovation and open business models as firms realize the limitations of a dependence on solely current resources internal to the organization.

2.8 Building partnerships

Developing relevant partnerships is a key component of open innovation and the interactive business model. As concepts of partnership slowly gain ground, the "imperialist mind-set" that used to abound is beginning to shift. Collaborators and partners can share knowledge, expertise and, importantly, risk, lowering resource requirements for all involved. Partnerships can occur at multiple levels, between MNC partners, with NGOs, government institutions and local partners on the ground. Partnerships can be unusual but incredibly practical. Blue Label Telecoms partnered with a bakery chain called Grupo Bimbo in Mexico! Their explanation:

"Where there's bread, there's airtime". Bimbo offered a deeply respected and trusted local brand and extensive distribution networks while Blue Label imported world-class technology, digital conversion and financial service business models, helping Bimbo deliver added value into their network of low-income retailers and small shops.

2.9 Reimagining products

It used to be acceptable for companies to use a host of tricks including jingles, film stars, images and waves of TV advertisements to convince the customer that what was being sold was what was needed. It used to be that customers believed them.

Today, savvy consumers are able to verify and validate brand claims through numerous channels. The low-income consumer is forced to be that much more selective in their choices; the cost of making a mistake is simply unaffordable. Word of mouth is the most often trusted and used source of information, and through the explosion of social media and the accessibility of information through mobile phones, word of mouth has gained virtual powers. Companies must transform to be relevant to these customers for whom value and utility are an imperative. Faking it and making false claims will be punished by the market, while a push towards authenticity and the adding of real value into the consumer's life will be rewarded with brand adoption and committed lifetime customer value.

Understanding what real value is and learning how to create it can only come from deeply and actively engaging with consumers to create a purpose brand. It is important to remember, however, that if customers are to be productive and participate in co-creation, a deep respect for context, tradition and language must be upheld. Cemex, in Mexico, only understood why their "sachetization" of cement as an entry strategy into lower-income communities failed after sending teams to immerse themselves in community life. Their great insight was that cement sales were not about cement package size but rather about fear, house-building literacy and the long-term financial commitment that house building demanded. Cemex added value by helping customers with the complexities and technicalities of home building rather than focusing solely on its product.

2.10 Lessons from the BoP

Those pioneer companies in Southern Africa that have taken the initiative to initiate or increase their business among members of South Africa's low-income communities have many valuable lessons to share.

South African companies such as MTN, Standard Bank, Capitec and Blue Label Telecoms, and other MNCs operating in sub-Saharan Africa such as Unilever and

GSK, which have embarked on this journey to the bottom of the pyramid, are help-ing to "write the book", as well as bringing development and employment to parts of the continent that desperately need it. Key lessons from these companies may be summarized as follows:

- Inclusive strategies demand that the business model is reinvented and that the firm be ready to disrupt its conventional business as usual approach

- The principles of frugal innovation must be applied in order to create a port-folio of affordable, value-adding products and services

- Internal firm structure and architecture may need to be shifted, flexible, responsive teams created and metrics developed to accommodate the devel-opment of inclusive business inside the firm

- Firms cannot focus exclusively on trade but must embed themselves into local ecosystems, taking social, political and economic considerations into account as they develop business, shifting their philosophy of business towards meeting development objectives along with shareholder objectives

- Co-creation guides the firm toward the development of market-relevant innovation

- Local capacity building and the creation of mutually beneficial partnerships helps firms to fit in, learn and grow inside a low-income market

- Firm networks must be widened and non-traditional partners sought as internal firm resources are not adequate to successfully service low-income consumers. Blockbuster innovations emerge from the mixing of ideas and know how between multiple agents

Inclusive business models allow organizations to align the human values of their employees with work, creating greater congruence between work and personal identity. This is shown to build a happier, more productive workforce, able to inte-grate their managerial roles with those of community citizenship.

Bibliography

Anderson, J. and N. Billou (2007) "Serving the World's Poor: Innovation at the Base of the Eco-nomic Pyramid", *Journal of Business Strategy* 28.2: 14-21.

Busch, C. (2014) "Substantiating Social Entrepreneurship Research: Exploring the Potential of Integrating Social Capital and Networks Approaches", *International Journal of Entrepre-neurial Venturing* 6.1: 69-84.

Cappelli, P., H. Singh, J. Singh and M. Useem (2010) *The India Way: How India's Top Business Leaders Are Revolutionizing Management* (Boston, MA: Harvard Business Press).

Christensen, C.M. (1997) *The Innovator's Dilemma: When New Technologies Cause Great Firms to Fail* (Boston, MA: Harvard Business School Press).

Christensen, C.M., and M. Overdorf (2000) "Meeting the Challenge of Disruptive Change", *Harvard Business Review*, March 2000, https://hbr.org/2000/03/meeting-the-challenge-of-disruptive-change, accessed 9 January 2015.

Ernst, H., H.N. Kahle, A. Dubiel, J. Prabhu and M. Subramaniam (2014) "The Antecedents and Consequences of Affordable Value Innovations for Emerging Markets", *Journal of Product Innovation Management* 32.1: 65-79.

Goyal, S., B.S. Sergi and A. Kapoor (2014) "Understanding the Key Characteristics of an Embedded Business Model for the Base of the Pyramid Markets", *Economics and Sociology* 7.4:26-40.

Hart, S.L., and C.M. Christensen (2002) "The Great Leap: Driving Innovation from the Base of the Pyramid", *MIT Sloan Management Review*, Fall:, 51-56.

Ismail, T., and N. Kleyn (2012) *New Markets, New Mindsets* (Auckland Park, South Africa: Stonebridge).

Johnson, M.W., C.M. Christensen and H. Kagermann (2008) "Reinventing your Business Model", *Harvard Business Review* 86.12: 50-59.

Lefifi, T.K. (2014) "Capitec Grabs the Limelight from its Bigger Competitors", *Business Day Live* http://www.bdlive.co.za/business/financial/2014/03/23/capitec-grabs-the-limelight-from-its-bigger-competitors, accessed 9 January 2015.

London, T. (2009) "Making Better Investments at the Base of the Pyramid", *Harvard Business Review* 87.5.

London, T. (2012) *Constructing a Base-of-the-Pyramid Business in a Multinational Corporation: CEMEX's Patrimonio Hoy Looks to Grow* (Case Study No. 1-429-202; Ann Arbour, MI: GlobaLens, William Davidson Institute).

London, T., and S.L. Hart (2011) *Next Generation Business Strategies for the Base of the Pyramid* (Upper Saddle River, NJ: Pearson Education FT Press).

O'Reilly, C., and M. Tushman (2013) "Organizational Ambidexterity: Past, Present, and Future", *The Academy of Management* 27.4: 324-38.

Porter, M.E., and M.R. Kramer (2011) "The Big Idea: Creating Shared Value", *Harvard Business Review* 89.1: 62-77, http://www.professoralanross.com/wp-content/uploads/2011/03/The-Big-Idea_-Creating-Shared-Value-Harvard-Business-Review.pdf, accessed 9 January 2015.

Prahalad, C.K., and A.L. Hammond (2002) "Serving the World's Poor, Profitably", *Harvard Business Review* 80.9: 48–57, https://hbr.org/2002/09/serving-the-worlds-poor-profitably, accessed 9 January 2015.

Reficco, E., and P. Marquez (2009) "Inclusive Networks for Building BOP Markets", *Business & Society* 51.3, 512-56.

Rivera-Santos, M., and C. Rufín (2010) "Global Village vs. Small Town: Understanding Networks at the Base of the Pyramid", *International Business Review*, 19.2: 126-39.

Sánchez, P., and J.E. Ricart (2010) "Business Model Innovation and Sources of Value Creation in Low-income Markets", *European Management Review*, 7.3: 138-54.

Schuster, T., and D. Holtbrügge (2014) "Resource Dependency, Innovative Strategies, and Firm Performance in BOP Markets", *Journal of Product Innovation Management* 31.S1: 43-59.

Sehgal, V., K. Dehoff and G. Panneer (2010) "The Importance of Frugal Engineering", *Strategy + Business*, 59: 1-5, http://www.strategy-business.com/article/10201?pg=all, accessed 9 January 2015.

Simanis, E., and S.L. Hart (2008) *The Base of the Pyramid Protocol: Toward Next Generation BOP Strategy* (Ithaca, NY: Cornell University, Johnson School of Management, 2nd edn, http://www.stuartlhart.com/sites/stuartlhart.com/files/BoPProtocol2ndEdition2008_0.pdf, accessed 9 January 2015.

Part II
The role of engagement, participation and bottom-up innovation

3

Participatory market research for BoP innovation

Aline Krämer, Christina Tewes-Gradl and Claudia Knobloch
Endeva, Germany

Participatory market research offers effective methods for better understanding the reality of people in low-income markets. We define market research as participatory when the target group has the ability to influence the perspective of the researchers. Participatory research presupposes that the target group is not just a source of information, but also a source of ideas and solutions. Drawing on experience from our field research in Madagascar, Sierra Leone and Brazil, we explore how best to design market research that enables people to share their perception of the situation, preferences, challenges and solutions. A participatory approach creates trust among the target group, improves the understanding of researchers and can identify practical user innovations. A variety of methods can be employed, depending on what type of information researchers seek. Self-documentation can inform about the use context; interviews and focus groups give insights into perceptions; idea competitions, toolkits and innovation workshops can be used to co-create solutions. Finally, we share lessons on how best to prepare and implement participatory market research methods and use the resulting data.

Little data about low-income markets is available. But even if there is data, it is often hard to understand—or carries the risk of misinterpretation. For example, data on spending patterns suggests that Brazilian low-income consumers invest very little in furniture for their houses. However, when we investigated this market further, we found that consumers would like to buy furniture but they simply could not find pieces of furniture that had the quality they were seeking and were adapted to their particular needs.[1] In fact, most participants in our field research showed us how they adapted old pieces of furniture: for example, by cutting in half a bed that was too big for their small room, making it a bunk bed. Some even told us they preferred to have pieces of furniture custom-made rather than paying the same price for lower-quality furniture in shops. With the local carpenter, they themselves could propose a design that suited their needs and even select the material.

To really understand the low-income markets, researchers need to better understand the reality of their target group. They need to understand the choices available and the parameters that influence these choices. Only then can facts and figures be interpreted in a meaningful way. Participatory market research offers effective methods for better understanding the reality of the target group. Through our field research in Madagascar, Sierra Leone and Brazil (see Box 3.1), we explored how best to design market research that enables people to share their perception of the situation, preferences, challenges and solutions. Indeed, we define market research as participatory when the target group has the ability to influence the perspective of the researchers. In that sense, surveys and interviews with a rigid set of questions also involve participation of the target group, but they are not participatory. Participatory research presupposes that the target group is not just a source of information, but also a source of ideas and solutions. In this chapter, we share the benefits we see in this approach, the methods we applied and the lessons learned.

---

1 Some retailers such as Casas Bahia or Magazine Luiza address low-income segments with innovative business models that give them access to credit; however, they often charge high interest rates and sell goods that are of low quality and not tailored to the needs of the consumers (e.g. products do not fit into their rooms with low ceilings).

Box 3.1 **About our case studies**

Endeva is a Berlin-based company of experts who aim to accelerate inclusive business innovations. Together with companies, we have conducted market research on the ground with the objective of informing the development of inclusive products, services and business models. In this chapter, we aim to share our lessons learned from three very different contexts:

In Brazil, we conducted research to develop **new products** that aim to improve the well-being of low-income consumers in three different sectors: housing/furniture, energy/lighting and rainwater collection. The research was conducted in three urban slums in the south of Brazil. The project was initiated by the Center for Design and Sustainability of the Federal University of Paraná in cooperation with Endeva. Other partners were the local housing agency Companhia de Habitação Paraná (COHAPAR), the Brazilian Innovation Agency Finep and the Brazilian companies Soliforte and Tigre.

Our research in Sierra Leone aims to create **new services** for food-processing entrepreneurs. It is part of a project called "Business Booster", which was initiated by the Youth Employment Network (YEN) in partnership with United Nations Industrial Development Organization (UNIDO) and Endeva. The project aims to create an organization that links food-processing companies to opportunities in premium markets both locally and abroad—and thus "boosts their business". Our market research focused on getting input from entrepreneurs on the type of support they would need.

In Madagascar, the aim of our field research was to inform the development of a **new business model**, namely a model to provide electricity to rural communities. The results informed the development of a business plan for HERi Madagascar to pilot electricity kiosks powered by solar energy. They provide customers with access to equipment such as solar lanterns, to charging phones and to information and IT services.

3.1 Benefits of participatory market research

Participatory market research employs methods known as qualitative research methods, such as focus groups, interviews or workshop formats. The approach encourages participants to express their own views, even where they go beyond the original research question. In this way, participants are empowered to shape

Box 3.2 **The history of participatory approaches**

Participatory methods have a long tradition in both development and innovation research.

In the 1970s, participatory development emerged as an alternative to "top-down" development approaches. The approach calls for a change in perspective, from viewing low-income people as mere recipients of aid, causing dependency and alienation, to seeing them as development "experts" who know what they need and what works in the context of their own lives. Giving them a voice and an active role in development projects does not only empower them; it also finds leads to solutions that are more acceptable and of value to the target group, and thus sustainable in the long run (Chambers 1983; Geilfus 2008; Waibel 2012).

Interestingly, a similar shift happened in approaches to innovation. When it comes to doing market research for new product development, companies traditionally used to see consumers merely as a source of information, who "speak only when spoken to" (Von Hippel 1988, 2005). The company's role was to capture their needs and preferences, and ultimately to develop appropriate solutions ("closed innovation"). At roughly the same time as development experts started to recognize the power of "beneficiaries" as problem-solvers, innovation experts started to realize that consumers could be "co-creators". They can help identify concrete solutions to meet their needs. As a result, companies have started to actively integrate consumers and other stakeholders into the innovation process ("open innovation", see Chesbrough 2003).

the research and, in particular, the perspective of researchers on their "subject"[2] and, where necessary, to expand or refine the research question. Some participatory methods even invite participants to create solutions themselves. Seeing the target group as an integral part of the research process helps circumvent many of the challenges commonly faced when employing more traditional research methods and thus create tangible benefits.

2 Participatory research is hence necessarily based on a constructivist epistemology. Researchers do not assume that there is an objective reality that can be revealed (while best not interfering with this reality). Rather, they assume that reality is constructed collectively and that, therefore, there can be no separation between the researchers and the reality they are interested in. This collective reality is constructed in a process, and participatory methods are the means to design this process.

3.1.1 Empowerment and creation of trust

Walking around in rural villages in Madagascar and urban slums in Brazil, we realized the obvious: one cannot observe people unrecognized as foreigners, and even locals who are not from the neighbourhood stick out. People in the community want to understand why a foreigner visits them and ask questions. Furthermore, slum dwellers or peasants hesitate to answer questions when they are interviewed by a person who has a higher education and is better off. When asked about their income or consumption habits by foreigners, people are often simply ashamed of being poor. Thus, it is crucial to win their trust.

Participatory methods create trust between researchers and the community. They involve deep interaction and dialogue. They also include a proper briefing about the objectives of the method, since the people who are usually the "object" of research have to understand the purpose of the activities in order to consider their own contribution. The farmers in Sierra Leone learned about the background and purpose of the research, and they were also told that implementation of an actual project was uncertain and depended on a solid business plan and interest from funders. Empowering participants in that way creates self-esteem and builds trust (Geilfus 2008: 4).

3.1.2 Enhanced understanding

Many products that are specifically tailored to the low-income context were developed by people who lack a deep understanding of local perceptions, aspirations, informal rules and constraints—the tacit information that is often held subconsciously. As a result, many products have failed to convince their intended users. The most striking example is solar cookstoves. They are an excellent technological solution; however, they fail to consider the reality of their target group. Most people enjoy a warm meal at night, when there is no sun. Three-stone cookstoves are also preferred for cultural reasons: the stones are inherited by the eldest daughter when she leaves the house. And food cooked over a fire just tastes differently. By personally interacting with the target group and seeking their input, participatory methods help market researchers and product developers to tap this "tacit" information—and consider it in the design of products, services or business models.

A deeper interaction with the target group also helps to find answers to questions that are difficult to ask. Rainwater collectors, for example, do not exist in the favelas in Brazil. Therefore, it was hard to ask participants about the features of the product or what it should look like. Nonetheless, deep interaction with the target group revealed the value water has for people, and that they would regard a product to collect rainwater as a symbol of status. This showed product designers that they should make it a visible attachment to the house rather than hide it under the earth or the roof.

3.1.3 Identification of practical user innovations

When researchers ask the target group what they would like to have, the answers are often unrealistic. Participatory methods can serve to identify pragmatic solutions to a given problem. When people were asked to develop their own ideas for furniture in an idea competition, they thought about how the ideas could actually be realized, how they would fit into the houses and how much they would cost. The result were solutions that reflected the realities of people much better and were more informative about preferences and priorities.

3.2 Methods for participatory market research

Methods can be categorized by different outcomes, that is, the types of information they yield (see Table 3.1). Participatory research can provide insight into the use context of the consumers, their perceptions on a certain topic, product or service and, finally, into the solutions they envision. Table 3.1 also provides a selection of methods for each of these research objectives.

Table 3.1 **Selected participatory methods**

Source: Authors' own.

Types of information obtained from consumer	Use context	Perceptions	Solutions
Methods	Self-documentation ("paparazzi")	Interview, focus group	Idea competitions, toolkits, innovation workshops
Role of target group	Document	Respond to and discuss questions	Co-create products and services
Description	Target group observes itself	Target group is asked for information or consulted for specific information	Target group engages in joint activities and "co-creates"

3.2.1 Use context

Commonly, qualitative research involves observing the context of the consumer through, for example, house visits. However, foreigners, even if they are "locals", are recognized easily, and people are often inhibited when being observed. Thus, following and watching people may create a bias. In some of the communities we visited in urban slums in Brazil, people were also ashamed to let us into their home—they believed they had nothing to show. What helped was to ask people to observe themselves over a period of time—a method called "paparazzi". The method invites people to become active researchers, documenting their activities. For our research on improved furniture solutions, for example, we gave people a disposable camera and a paper with a smiley and a sad face. We then asked them to take the camera with them and take pictures of furniture solutions in their own or other people's houses that they liked, putting the smiley on them, or that they did not like by putting the sad face on them. Those who could write also documented their thoughts during this observational task in a diary. By giving people the tools to observe themselves, they also have the freedom to document other aspects that seem relevant for them, especially if they understand the objective of the research. Besides documenting furniture, they may also describe the layout of the room or how they use the furniture.

3.2.2 Perceptions

Researchers often want to understand how the target group perceives a situation, a problem or a solution. They are interested in reconstructing the mental models of the target group to be able to better predict the choices people will make. Apart from measurable facts, such as the cash flow in a household, they also want to know how these facts are evaluated and explained, for example, when people start to feel threatened by a lack of cash.

Participatory interviews are semi-structured interviews that aim to obtain deep insight into how the target group views their needs or their experiences with certain products (Geilfus 2008: 25 ff.). These interviews do not have yes/no questions, but focus on triangulating different viewpoints from the communities. The researchers should thus remain open to input from the interviewees themselves. A good way to trigger this is to involve participants in games and activities.

For example, when aiming to identify which furniture solutions could be improved in people's dwellings, we engaged them in a visual tour through their house. The researcher and the interviewee jointly drew the dwelling of the participant, and what pieces of furniture or products were in each room. Then, we asked the interviewee to describe which tasks she or he performed in each room. This triggered very detailed input on which products were used to perform certain tasks and what could be improved.

Focus groups are usually conducted to discuss certain questions with a group (Geilfus 2008). However, when employing the method in its traditional version, outcomes can be disappointing. Cultural factors can compromise the outcome, for example, when not considering hierarchies between participants, when mixing elderly with young people or women with men. People may be ashamed to talk about culturally sensitive topics, such as how much one earns, in a group setting. Employing a more participatory version of these methods by engaging people in visualization techniques or games helps to circumvent these barriers.

In Sierra Leone, we developed a seasonal calendar with the members of a cassava cooperative to understand its cash flow. The calendar visualized when they conducted certain farm activities, which production volumes they achieved when and at what prices they sold their crops. The visualization served as a basis for our discussion with them. For example, we could identify the season when they sold products and thus had money and when they lacked money and had only a little to spend.

3.2.3 Solutions

In the sense of "co-creation", the low-income target group already has ideas about ways to meet their needs and solve persistent problems. Not only can these ideas be part of the solution, but they can also provide insight into preferences and perceived constraints of the target group.

A good way to incentivize users' own creations and to identify user innovations is idea competitions. With this method, consumers are asked to submit new ideas and solutions to a given task (Belz *et al.* 2009; Jung and Chipchase 2008). An advantage of this method is that it allows many people to participate. In the three idea competitions we conducted in Brazil, around 90 people took part, handing in their ideas on furniture solutions, rainwater collection or energy-saving solutions. As the communities we worked with had only limited Internet access, we chose to collect the ideas offline at the community centre. To incentivize submissions, people who handed in an idea received a small gift, and the three best ideas of each competition were awarded a prize.

The solutions received were far from being implementable ideas or ready prototypes. However, analysing a wealth of user-generated ideas showed us how they envision appropriate solutions, and allowed us to identify patterns in current consumer trends. For example, the competition on energy solutions revealed that consumers rarely looked for new energy sources. Rather, they suggested changes to the construction of their dwelling to make better use of natural light.

Other methods could also be adapted from the domain of "open innovation". Toolkits provide a certain set of materials or design choices and let participants play with them. They can be applied when the company already has a concept of the product or a prototype. Here, the "trial-and-error" process is entirely transferred to the participant, who is encouraged to provide feedback and concrete suggestions. Innovation workshops bring together a group of consumers, or a mixed group of consumers, experts and company professionals, to share experiences and develop ideas and concepts along a structured process.

3.3 Lessons learned

Employing the methods described above for our research purposes in Brazil, Sierra Leone and Madagascar, we could draw lessons on their preparation, implementation and use.

3.3.1 Preparation

Market research always requires proper preparation, and even more so when participatory methods are used. Since there is greater openness to responding to participant input, researchers need to think through what could happen and how to deal with different situations:

- **Become informed about the context.** Understanding the context is critical to design and implement research interventions successfully. This includes an understanding of the cultural context, the roles in society (e.g. when do older and younger people speak? when do women and men speak?) as well as the cultural frames that determine people's perception (e.g. different views on time or status). We worked in teams that were supported by local researchers who helped us navigate through the communities and make sense of our observations. Also, working in interdisciplinary teams can prove effective: product developers and anthropologists make very different observations and can benefit from each other's viewpoints.

- **Select the appropriate method or set of methods.** As Table 3.1 shows, which method to use depends on the questions being asked. Often, it makes sense to design a sequence of research interventions that build on one another. When doing our research on housing and furniture solutions, for example, we first applied methods such as the "paparazzi" and focus groups to get a better sense of the problems consumers face. We learned that our target group was most concerned with solutions that optimize space, which then served as the topic for the idea competition we conducted. The competition, in turn, helped us to identify particularly talented problem-solvers, that is, consumers who had already come up with solutions for this particular problem and were willing to share them with us. In a next step, these problem-solvers could have potentially been invited to participate in innovation workshops with company professionals to further refine their idea or even to develop prototypes.

- **Focus.** Time and resources for field research are always limited. Similarly, participants often have only limited time and attention. Thus, it is important to use time and resources effectively and identify the most important research questions that can be answered only by involving the participants. In Madagascar, we started our research by gathering all information that had been collected by other organizations previously. We received all socio-economic information from a recent census and information on the current energy supply and energy use from the Agency for Rural Electrification. Thus we could concentrate on the two crucial questions of how much people spent on energy and how much disposable income they had each month.

3.3.2 Implementation

Participatory research requires a good sense for what is appropriate during implementation. After all, researchers send signals by how they implement the method, which will in turn influence people's understanding of and reaction to the task.

- **Decide how best to select participants.** First, be clear about the information you are looking for and hence the participants you need. In Madagascar, aggregated data about energy demand in a village was collected from shop owners selling energy sources such as kerosene and batteries. For more general questions, opinion leaders such as the mayor, chief, teachers or priest may have a good overview of the community's needs or at least have a good enough overview of the community to indicate the right people to talk to. Selecting participants through existing social groups such as women's self-help groups or farmer associations can also help to identify the most suitable participants for the research question.

- **Create incentives—but don't overdo it.** Rewarding participants to take part in the research can facilitate self-selection. After all, participants spend their valuable free time to take part in the research. Rewarding their time and effort with a small gift or even monetary compensation shows appreciation and is a nice way to say "thank you". However, the incentives should be well balanced. Overdoing it may attract only participants who are incentivized by the money or material compensation and crowd out participants who are intrinsically motivated by the subject. "Giving" may also create a wrong understanding of people's roles in a project, especially where they are expected to contribute to the project themselves. In Sierra Leone, people are so used to being treated as beneficiaries that they were surprised when they were asked how much they would pay for the business services.

- **Brief participants appropriately.** Based on your understanding of the context, take enough time to explain to your participants why you are doing this research, why they are asked to participate, and what will happen with the results. Clarify what they can expect and what not. In the Brazilian low-income communities we worked in, people often confused us with politicians or non-governmental organizations since they were usually the only people from outside the community who would come and ask questions. Thus, people were often rather sceptical towards us, since much had been promised to them. Only after explaining our intentions as well as the expected outcome of our research in detail did people develop trust. They felt honoured to be part of our research project and started opening up.

- **Employ visual material to get beyond language barriers.** Words are ambiguous, and low-income people are often not used to expressing themselves verbally, especially when it comes to abstract concepts such as time or money. In fact, many people have never been in an interview or focus group situation before and are thus not used to the way questions are asked. Also, they have different educational backgrounds and are not always able to read or write fluently. Preparing visual material or encouraging them to draw maps or timelines may help to bridge that gap. Techniques include developing a map of the community, a visualization of the home of the interviewee(s) or a flowchart/timeline of daily or yearly activities. For example, in Madagascar, we wanted to know how much people spend on energy sources per week. Thus, we asked them to draw a map of the village and to include the places where they bought their energy sources. It was then very natural to ask how much they spent per visit to the shop and how often they went there each week.

- **Create a comfortable environment.** People are more willing to participate in the market research if they enjoy doing so. Thus it helps to design the research process in a playful way including games and dynamic elements and to provide a congenial environment such as a restaurant, a community or a school building. The idea competitions we organized in Brazil, for example, were all organized in the community centre, which was nicely decorated and where food and beverages were served. This raised the curiosity of people. They first came to hang around in the community centre—and being comfortable, felt encouraged to participate.

- **Allow enough time—and stay flexible!** No matter how well prepared you are, the reality will always be more complicated, different and probably less satisfactory than expected. A lot of time will be "wasted" by waiting for people, unexpected incidents such as car breakdowns, funerals, weddings or storms, and things that are not put in place even though they have been communicated well beforehand. The most important thing is to plan time generously and to be prepared for all eventualities.

3.3.3 Use

Participative research generates not only information, but also a joint reality in the making. Researchers can make use of this potential, but also need to consider what this joint constructed reality does not show.

- **Triangulate results.** The quality of qualitative research is dependent on the triangulation of results from different people and methods. A topic should not be approached by one method only. What people express during focus group discussions or interviews may not always be in line with what they are actually practising. What they say they want may not always be in line with what they suggest as a solution when asked to create one. Again, a multi-step process can build and strengthen insights over time by testing an emerging hypothesis in different ways.

- **Be aware of limitations.** Any research method has its blind spots and biases, and researchers need to be aware of them to address them. There is again an upward dynamic here: with each intervention, the understanding of how people may have interpreted the task and what might have influenced their responses is enhanced. Equally importantly, researchers must be aware of their own blind spots, of what they would like to say and would like to ignore. Participatory research enables the research "objects" to point out blind spots, but researchers need to give up their preconceptions.

- **Identify key players.** One advantage of participative methods is that they create not only insights, but also relationships. Besides relationships with the target group, this can involve relationships with community representatives, community associations, public officials, civil society organizations and local research institutes. These contacts should be well documented to be able to build on them in later stages of the project. In Madagascar we used the people most active in the research to point us to people who might be suitable operators for the energy kiosks. This worked very well because the opinion leaders were honoured that we asked for their opinion.

3.4 Conclusion

Our field research efforts in Brazil, Madagascar and Sierra Leone were conducted to inform the development of new products, services and business models for low-income consumers. Participatory methods enabled us to get a better understanding of the realities of our target groups and start to construct solutions.

Reflecting on this experience, one major lesson stands out: we realized that the process of interacting with the communities was the biggest source of insight. It was not only the outcomes of the methods—the information—that contributed to a better understanding. Rather, it made a difference that we were part of the process and experienced it first hand, preparing the methods, setting them up with local partners and the community, implementing and evaluating them. Step by step, we were able to broaden our usually quite selective perception and thus improved our capacity to absorb the new and unfamiliar. Certainly, participatory methods are a resource- and time-consuming process. However, going through this sensitization process in the field helped us to gain access to an understanding we could not have obtained otherwise.

Bibliography

Belz, F.-M., S. Silvertant, J. Füller and J. Pobisch (2009) *Ideenwettbewerbe: Konsumenten Involvieren, Ideen Generieren, Lead User Identifizieren* (Freising, Germany: Technische Universität München).

Chambers, R. (1983) *Rural Development: Putting The Last First* (Harlow, UK: Longman; New York: Earthscan).

Chambers, R. (2002) *Participatory Workshops: A Sourcebook of 21 Sets of Ideas and Activities* (Abingdon, UK: Earthscan).

Chesbrough, H. (2003) *Open Innovation: The New Imperative for Creating and Profiting from Technology* (Boston, MA: Harvard Business School Press).

Gradl, C., and Knobloch, C. (2010) *Inclusive Business Guide: How to Develop Business and Fight Poverty* (Berlin: Endeva).

Geilfus, F. (2008) *80 Tools for Participatory Development: Appraisal, Planning, Follow-up and Evaluation* (San Jose, CR: IICA).

Jung, Y., and J. Chipchase (2008) "Nokia Open Studio: Engaging Communities", http://janchipchase.com/content/essays/nokia-open-studios/, accessed 1 May 2013.

Krämer, A. (2015) "Low-income Consumers as a Source of Innovation? Insights from Idea Competitions in Brazilian Low-income Communities", PhD thesis, Technical University of Munich.

Larsen, M. L., and A. Flensborg (2011) *Market Creation Toolbox: Your Guide to Entering Developing Markets* (Copenhagen: DI International Business Development).

Simanis, E., and S.L. Hart (2008) *The Base of the Pyramid Protocol: Toward Next Generation BOP Strategy* (Ithaca, NY: Cornell University, Johnson School of Management, 2nd edn, http://www.stuartlhart.com/sites/stuartlhart.com/files/BoPProtocol2ndEdition2008_0.pdf, accessed 1 May 2013).

Simanis, E., and S.L. Hart (2011) "Innovation From the Inside Out", *MIT Sloan Management Review* 50. 4 (Winter 2011): 9-19.

Simanis, E., S.L. Hart and D. Duke (2008) "The Base of the Pyramid Protocol Beyond 'Basic Needs' Business Strategies", *Innovations* 3: 1: 57-83.

Von Hippel, E. (1988) *The Sources of Innovation* (New York: Oxford University Press).

Von Hippel, E. (2005) *Democratizing Innovation* (Cambridge, MA: MIT Press).

Waibel, P. (2012) *Putting the Poor First: How Base-of-the-Pyramid Ventures Can Learn from Development Approaches* (Sheffield, UK: Greenleaf Publishing).

Whitney, P. (2010) "Reframing Design for the Base of the Pyramid", in T. London and S.L. Hart, (eds.), *Next Generation Business Strategies for the Base of the Pyramid: New Approaches for Building Mutual Value* (Upper Saddle River, NJ: Prentice Hall Pearson, 3rd edn).

4

Open innovation and engagement platforms for inclusive business design

Fernando Casado Cañeque
Center of Partnerships for Development, Spain

This chapter describes how innovation has been conceived through different historical phases before embracing the concept of social innovation in an open source economy. It suggests such a concept has not fully reached its potential for generating an impact on BoP communities and thus there is a lot to be achieved by integrating its modalities in product and service design. The chapter also describes some of the different innovation platforms created by ecosystems to enhance social impact and achieve development goals. It concludes by asserting that new platforms and approaches need to be created in order to transform the ways in which products and services are being designed and that these new platforms need to be created through a cross-sectoral approach, engaging the participation of civil society organizations, governments and private-sector associations.

4.1 The history of a concept

Innovation holds a multiplicity of definitions and interpretations. Organizations see its implications according to different trends. Although the standard definition from the Oxford Advanced Learner's Dictionary defines it as "the introduction of new things, ideas or ways of doing something different, based on the acknowledgement that something new has been introduced", real innovation involves applying information and imagination to gain greater value from resources and other inputs, including all processes where new ideas are generated and turned into useful products or services.

It is widely held that innovation often results when ideas are applied to raise the value of products and services for customers and stakeholders, including the social and environmental value *vis-à-vis* the ecosystem. This also implies facilitating the generation of new methods for forging partnerships, joint venturing, flexible work hours, and the creation of buyers' purchasing power.[1]

Interestingly, initially, "innovation" was not a compliment but more an accusation akin to the charges of heresy. As the Canadian historian Benoît Godin documents, innovation is the embodiment of previously used terms such as imitation and invention. The concept of "novation" first appeared in 13th-century legal texts as a term for renewing contracts; it was not a term for creation, but rather it referred to newness. In the 16th and 17th centuries, patents (and their precursors in the 15th century, letters and privileges) were not granted to inventors, as they are today, but to importers of existing inventions (Godin 2008). Similarly, in the case of consumer goods in 18th-century Britain, imitation was perceived as invention because it resulted in new commodities, led to improvements in quality (design) and brought diversity and variety (Benhamou 1991; Berg 2002; Berg and Clifford 2002; Clifford 1999).

It was not until the 19th century that innovation began to take root as a term associated with science and industry, focused on technical invention in particular. The rise of consumer culture, higher numbers of patents, and a strong government focus on building laboratories for research and development, helped engender the prestigious connotation that innovation enjoys today (Godin 2010).

Later on, as Freeman documents (1974), the 1970s witnessed a new stage in research and development (R & D) and the promotion of innovation platforms. There was originally a strong focus on military innovation systems as the main source; however, given the global context of changing values (lessening of tensions between the superpowers, changes in public opinion and the emergence of new problems), Freeman (1974) predicted a transition from a "military innovation system" towards a "social innovation system". This new "innovation system" was predicted to be a shift from military to customer R & D, from producer sovereignty to customer sovereignty (Godin 2010).

---

1 http://www.businessdictionary.com/definition/innovation.html.

4.2 Defining the implications of innovation

Nevertheless, one of the most recognized theorists of conceptual innovation is Joseph Alois Schumpeter, who identified innovation as the critical dimension of economic change and asserted that innovation-originated market power could yield better results than the invisible hand and price competition. One of his proposals suggested that the successful exploitation of new ideas could lead to forms of increased social benefit and defined the concept of economic innovation as follows (Schumpeter 1912):

- The introduction of a new good—that is, one with which consumers are not yet familiar—or of a new quality of a good

- The introduction of an improved or better method of production, which need by no means be founded on a scientifically new discovery, and can also exist in a better way of handling a commodity commercially

- The opening of a new market—that is, a market into which the particular branch of manufacture of the country in question has not previously entered, whether or not this market has existed before

- The conquest of a new source of supply of raw materials or half-manufactured goods, again irrespective of whether this source already exists or whether it has first to be created

- The execution of the better organization of any industry, such as the creation of a monopoly position or the breaking up of a monopoly position

More recently, Peter Drucker has contributed to the concept by way of an extensive intellectual life dedicated to research and knowledge generation, writing more than 39 books that have been translated into more than 36 languages and making eight series of educational films on managerial topics. Part of his contribution to the conceptual definition of innovation involved defining the seven opportunities for innovation (Drucker 2006):

1. "The unexpected—the unexpected success, the unexpected failure, the unexpected outside event"

2. "The incongruity—between reality as it actually is and reality as it is assumed to be or as it 'ought to be'"

3. "Innovation based on process need"—perfecting a process that already exists, replacing a link that is weak, or supplying a link that is missing

4. "Changes in industry structure or market structure that catch everyone unawares"

5. "Demographics"—changes in a population's size, age, composition, educational level, employment status or income

6. "Changes in perception"—when the customer goes from seeing the glass as half empty to seeing it as half full

7. "New knowledge"—and not just technical or scientific breakthroughs, but the innovative use of this knowledge to create a new product or service

4.3 Innovation with a social dimension

There has been much debate concerning the social dimension of innovation and its potential to exert an impact on improving social development goals. One of the European Union definitions defines social innovation as follows:

> Social innovations are innovations that are social in both their ends and their means. Specifically, we define social innovations as new ideas (products, services and models) that simultaneously meet social needs (more effectively than alternatives) and create new social relationships or collaborations. They are innovations that are not only good for society but also enhance society's capacity to act (BEPA 2011).

Whether it is under concepts of frugal innovation, grassroots innovation or inclusive innovation, among many other concepts that have emerged lately, all of them somehow address how creativity and knowledge creation, acquisition, absorption and distribution efforts are aimed directly at meeting the needs of low-income communities, improving people's lives and their access to opportunities.

Innovation, in this sense, holds the potential to address aspects of inequality in several ways. These include bearing direct impacts on income distribution favouring the highly skilled and risk takers (social innovators); providing solutions for improving the welfare of lower- and middle-income groups (frugal innovators); innovations by lower-income groups themselves (grassroots innovators); or partnerships between corporations and local communities (inclusive innovation processes).

Prahalad defined a framework with the 12 principles of innovation for base of the pyramid (BoP) markets, emphasizing the relevance of this approach (see Fig. 4.1).

Figure 4.1 **Principles of innovation for BoP according to Prahalad**

Source: Author's own based on Prahalad and Krishnan 2008.

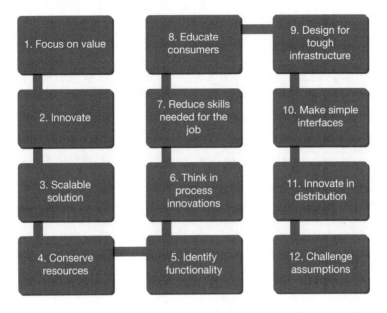

Some relevant aspects in this 12-step methodology underline major needs that are often misconceived. For example, focusing on value and on delivering performance for the price: the BoP consumer is not merely interested in cheap prices but in gaining the best possible performance for the price paid; therefore, products must be completely rethought to radically reduce the cost while at the same time having features that meet the BoP's greatest needs. Innovations in this regard should place an emphasis on conserving resources and maximizing efficiency, such as standardizing processes and adapting distribution channels and product and service design in a manner that suits low-income consumers, making them accessible to low-income communities.

Such innovation processes have brought about a series of innovative products that accomplished the goal of yielding economic profits while generating social value. For example, initiatives such as the Jaipur Leg,[2] a low-cost prosthetic developed in India, costing approximately $150 for the manufacturer, included clever improvisations such as incorporating irrigation piping into the design in order to lower costs; or the chotuKool fridge,[3] a tiny refrigerator with an innovatively designed cooling system and a creative, expanded distribution system with a process for personalizing the orders placed.

2 http://jaipurfoot.org/.
3 http://www.chotukool.com/.

Other huge innovations have created their own markets and have led to a wide variety of products and services, such as the mobile banking revolution, the micro-credit system or solar energy production for rural communities.

Regardless of the approach adopted through innovation, it is evident that the traditional ways in which the public sector, the private sector and civil society have responded to social demands no longer suffice, and social innovation represents alternatives in engaging resources in a different way to generate social value.

An interesting analysis by the Bureau of European Policy Advisers puts forward three approaches to the manner in which social innovation is being employed and the different forms of interactions established, where the output dimension of innovation, the "social", refers to the kind of value or output that innovation is expected to deliver; a value that is less concerned with mere profit and includes multiple dimensions of output measurement (BEPA 2011):

- **The social demand perspective.** Considering the social dimension to be complementary to the economic or business dimension in which "social" refers to the needs of groups, communities or segments that are more vulnerable and less able to be involved or benefit from the value generated by the market economy. In this respect, social innovation is inspired and framed by the desire to meet the social needs of BoP communities.

- **The societal challenge perspective.** Another approach suggested implies considering the creation of well-being as valued within the framework of sustainable development, adding a new dimension to economic output. In a sense, the boundary between the social and the economic domains blurs, and the "social" becomes an opportunity, rather than a constraint to generate value. As documented extensively by a Nobel Laureate in Economic Sciences, Daniel Kahneman, in the *American Economic Review* and recently by the Stiglitz Commission (Stiglitz *et al.* 2009), here, innovation is seen as a process that tackles societal challenges through new forms of relations between social actors.

- **The systemic changes perspective.** This third view is presented as the ultimate goal of social innovation, enhancing sustainable systemic change to be achieved through a process of organizational development and changes in relations between institutions and stakeholders. In this concept, the empowering/learning/network process dimension is central and the outcomes are improvements in the way people live and work. In a sense, the social dimension of innovation relates to changes in fundamental attitudes and values, strategies and policies and institutions' ways of working, and linkages between them and different types of actor.

4.4 From designing business models to enabling ecosystems

One of the core challenges behind innovating with a bottom-up approach is to be able to produce products and services that are accessible to low-income communities, maintaining quality and profitability while proposing a participatory approach with all the stakeholders engaged that enables their empowerment. With this goal in mind, one of the greatest needs that must be met is creating an enabling environment and a proactive ecosystem that fosters such a process. Engaging the ecosystem is critical, because companies often lack the resources and capabilities required to overcome the barriers to scale on their own.

Enabling ecosystems that engage innovators and entrepreneurs with other stakeholders is therefore fundamental. Given the complexity of business designs working with BoP communities, they are very unlikely to succeed if they are not built by a broad range of partners throughout the value chain that strengthen and complement one another in each of the production and distribution processes. This implies a new way of doing things, through active partnerships, sharing resources and skills as well as risks and profits throughout the process.

Enabling ecosystems holds the capacity to encourage local innovations from local groups, whether its emphasis is placed on people innovating for themselves and their community while drawing on traditional and indigenous knowledge, or on enhancing local empowerment perspectives, engaging local communities with corporations or technology developers that participate in the design, creation and production of the innovation established.

Along the broad spectrum of stakeholders in the ecosystem of innovators, one relevant group that has grown over time is what would be called grassroots innovation platforms. They come in several guises, whether in the form of networks and programmes that provide funds, training, services, capacity building or dissemination, and it serves as a crucial catalyst platform for supporting innovation. Adrien Smith and colleagues (Smith *et al.* 2012) explored facts and figures supporting grassroots innovation and identified a broad range of relevant networks that are actively promoting it at local level (see Table 4.1).

Table 4.1 **Description of grassroots innovation networks**

Source: Smith *et al.* 2012.

Network/ institution	Description	Activities and geographical focus	Examples of innovations
Prolinnova (Promoting Local Innovation in ecologically oriented agriculture and Natural Resource Management)	Promotes local innovation in ecologically oriented agriculture and natural resource management. It recognizes indigenous knowledge and informal experimentation among farmers, forest dwellers, pastoralists and fisherfolk. The intention is to develop methods, build capacity and scale up experience	International 16 country platforms in Africa and Asia, and a regional Andes platform	Farmer-led documentation using a participatory video in Ghana Participatory innovation development for climate change adaptation in Nepal Linking innovation in agriculture and management of HIV/ AIDS in Malawi Innovation in livestock-keeping by women in South Africa
International Network on Appropriate Technology; and Annual International Conference on Appropriate Technology	Developed to continue the work of annual conferences on appropriate technology	Africa, Global South and the USA Five annual conferences since 2004	Earth construction to meet urban housing needs in Africa ICTs for crop improvement and access to markets
Asia–Pacific National Innovation Systems Online Resource Centre	Provides access to resources and information amassed through projects that promote national innovation policy and practice in Asia–Pacific countries. Includes the Directory on Green Grassroots Innovation and Traditional Knowledge, which encourages policymakers in academia and R & D institutions to focus on grassroots innovation	Asia–Pacific Field visits and six workshops held in 2007–08 in China, the Philippines, Malaysia, Sri Lanka and India.	Linked with the Honey Bee Network (see below)

Network/ institution	Description	Activities and geographical focus	Examples of innovations
Honey Bee Network	Brings together individuals and institutions collecting, documenting and disseminating innovations and practices at grassroots level. The network receives institutional support from the Society for Research and Initiatives for Sustainable Technologies and Institutions (SRISTI) and the National Innovation Foundation (NIF)	Asia: India It has documented over 100,000 ideas, local innovations and traditional knowledge practices. Members can join the twice-annual Shodh Yatra journey, visiting rural communities to identify and document unrecognized ingenuity	Techniques for cultivating locally adapted traditional rice and fruit trees Labour/cost-saving machines, e.g. for weaving sari cloth into low-cost sanitary napkins, and processing bamboo Irrigation systems suited to local crops Gear trains for cycle rickshaws
Grassroots Innovation Augmentation Network (GIAN)	A technology and business incubator of grassroots innovations and traditional knowledge, linked to the Honey Bee Network and the NIF	Asia: India Six regions and many state-level incubators. GIAN has set up incubation centres across India to bring innovations to the market	Camel bus Film projector Groundnut digger Trench digger
Traditional Knowledge Digital Library (TKDL)	Bridges the gap between traditional knowledge and information in local languages and international patent examiners	Asia: India Over 150 books on traditional medicine have been transcribed so far	Traditional knowledge in Indian systems of medicine including Ayurveda, Unani, Siddha and Yoga
Centre of Science for Villages (CSV)	Links research scientists and rural communities through training and other initiatives	Asia: India Over 100 staff and volunteers at three demonstration campuses	Rainwater harvesting Plant-based pesticides Honey bee apiary
China Innovation Network (CHIN), Tianjin University	A twin centre to SRISTI. Plans to establish an innovation scholarship and international grassroots innovation and traditional knowledge registry	Asia: China It involves 54 universities from 30 Chinese provinces. Scouted about 6,000 innovations	Cycle-based hoe Simple lift to bring agricultural produce to a rooftop for drying
National Grassroots Innovation Databank, Malaysia	Provides institutional support in identifying, sustaining and scaling up Malaysia's grassroots innovations and traditional knowledge	Asia–Pacific: Malaysia 228 innovations listed	Preventing mosquito breeding in roof gutters Bioethanol produced from starch extracted from cassava

→

Network/ institution	Description	Activities and geographical focus	Examples of innovations
Practical Action	Uses technology to challenge poverty, working with communities on energy, agriculture, urban infrastructure, new technologies and waste management	International: UK head office; offices in Bangladesh, East Africa, Latin America, Nepal, South Asia, Southern Africa and Sudan	Nanotechnology for water filtration Gravity ropeways for transporting produce to market in mountainous areas cost-effective post-tsunami housing reconstruction
Social Technologies Network, Brazil (Rede de Tecnologias Sociais)	Supports products and techniques developed cooperatively with communities. It has inspired other networks, such as RedTISA (see below)	900 member organizations from Latin America Annual Social Technology Prize is building a database of entries and projects	Potable water storage (cisterns) Bio-digesters using cattle dung for home energy Seed fair for the exchange of traditional varieties in rural Argentina and Paraguay
Network on Technologies for Social Inclusion: RedTISA	Helps create and exchange community and techno-scientific knowledge, and shares learning for inclusive and sustainable development	Latin America: Argentina 90 institutions and projects	Cooperative recycling ventures Sugarcane harvesting machine for small-scale producers
Social Technologies Bank, Brazil (Fundação Banco Tecnologias Sociais)	This database includes social technologies certified by the Social Technology Prize of the Bank of Brazil Foundation	Latin America: Brazil Over 600 certified entries	Dryland horticulture and processing of cashew nuts and fruits into pulp Urban agroecology projects Water conservation and recycling
Uruguayan Center for Appropriate Technology	A non-profit organization working closely with the Latin American Social Ecology Center on energy, agroecology and medicinal plants	Latin America: Uruguay	Low-cost sustainable energy production Knowledge maps of local and traditional medicinal plant uses
Grassroots Innovations, UK	Provides research-based insights into grassroots innovation processes	UK; expanding to other countries	Has documented grassroots innovations in energy, food, housing and complementary currencies

Network/ institution	Description	Activities and geographical focus	Examples of innovations
Massachusetts Institute of Technology (MIT) Grassroots Invention Group (GIG)	Develops low-cost personal computation and production technologies.	USA 20 active projects	Prometheus, a Learning Independence Network being developed in Costa Rica New approaches to teaching computer programming
D-Lab, MIT	Promotes appropriate, low-cost technologies for international development	USA and international Hundreds of projects	Portable solar cooker Ceramic water filter Low-cost, pedal-powered rickshaw lighting
Ashoka	Pioneered the term "social entrepreneurs" for people solving pressing social needs, and changing society. The Ashoka Fellowship for social entrepreneurship, with over 2,000 fellows, supports networking and learning to achieve social goals	International programmes in over 60 countries; 25 regional offices in Africa, the Americas, Asia, Europe, the Middle East and North Africa	Home-based nurse training in South Africa Youth involvement in community forest management in Peru Digital inclusion in Brazil

4.5 Creating ecosystem innovation platforms for development goals

Given the increase of innovation platforms all around the world, it is worthwhile questioning how such platforms, as well as the enabling ecosystems that nourish them, can change the development mind-set and create a positive impact by achieving development goals and creating more opportunities for BoP communities. Whether it is addressing employment generation, developing inclusive businesses and partnership building or aligning efforts to tackle climate-change effects, innovation platforms are being created to unite strengths and response more effectively to such challenges.

For example, in the case of enabling ecosystems for employment generation in Tunisia, a project funded by GIZ (Deutsche Gesellschaft für Internationale Zusammenarbeit/German Federal Enterprise for International Cooperation) and implemented by CAD (Centro de Alianzas para el Desarrollo/Center of Partnerships for

Development)[4] was structured to enhance the employability potential of industrial areas of the country. In a context of democratic transition and reorganization of the national economy, industrial areas appear to be vital for Tunisia due to their great potential for economic growth and regional development. Tunisia currently has more than 150 industrial zones and the government plans to build more than 100 new industrial areas in the short term. However, most industrial areas remain non-operational and suffer from a lack of access to basic services; for example, restaurants for employees or catering for companies, transportation services, security, or technical platforms. This situation hinders their capacity to attract investment and prevents them from achieving their full development potential. At the same time, local communities from BoP neighbourhoods face very high unemployment rates, especially in the south and west of the country, and the dialogue between industrial areas and communities is very limited.

In December 2012, CAD was commissioned by GIZ to design and implement a new inclusive growth methodology aimed at creating in industrial areas new services that responded to the unsatisfied demand for services, while at the same time creating new jobs for local unemployed communities. In order to achieve these results, a three-step approach has been developed. The first phase entailed identifying the potential for services creation in one selected industrial area, from the perspective of both demand (services required from companies and their employees) and supply (potential of local micro, small and medium-sized enterprises [MSMEs] and communities).

Once the potential had been defined, the second phase involved identifying potential entrepreneurs or local MSMEs that could meet the demand for the services needed. Since the project is to be replicated nationwide, this identification process had to be performed by existing structures. Therefore, the focus was based on creating a partnership among all the stakeholders in the industrial area (structure in charge of managing the industrial area, companies, local employment structures, communities) and creating an enabling ecosystem that spurred innovation in those areas. Once the services needed were communicated widely, a series of workshops and meetings was conducted, resulting in the identification of a group of interested entrepreneurs. The selection was finalized during a workshop called "Making it Happen", which brought together the identified entrepreneurs, stakeholders, funding structures, etc. to select the final candidates.

Some of the most relevant outputs were the creation of five micro-enterprises with 20 jobs in one year, with the potential to replicate them in the country's 150 industrial zones given the national desire to replicate the methodology nationwide. Furthermore, an active and new dynamic dialogue between the members of the industrial zone and their partners was established, engaging them in the creation of a productive industrial zone ecosystem for employment generation.

4 http://www.globalcad.org.

Another relevant example was framed with the purpose of enabling ecosystems to accelerate partnerships and inclusive business. For such purpose, the Partnering Initiative[5] promoted the Business in Development Facility (BIDF), an open platform the helps countries drive the engagement of business in development by systematically promoting and supporting the development of "win–win" partnerships between companies, international agencies, government and NGOs. The BIDF has been launched in countries such as Colombia, Zambia and Mozambique, and its core added value has been to support national stakeholders in creating locally owned and run Business and Development Partnerships Hubs, platforms to engage business and to systematically promote, support and build capacity to help drive more widespread, effective public–private partnerships action.

The major functions of these platforms that enable a proactive ecosystem to enhance innovation in partnership-building and inclusive business are: raising awareness and building motivation around the role of business in development and the potential of partnership to achieve business and development goals; creating opportunities for dialogue and partnership co-creation, including innovation spaces and matchmaking services; providing capacity development for all sectors and direct support for new partnerships; and facilitating the exchange of knowledge and experience. Furthermore, the platforms are allowing more accurate measurement of the business and development impact of partnership activities in the national ecosystem, as well as building in-country capacity to broker partnerships and deliver additional partnership services in a more sustainable way.

4.6 Innovating for the BoP in an open economy

Innovation management has undergone several improvements over the years, which have eventually led to the concept of open innovation. As Rothwell stated (1994), there are several market changes that have contributed to these improvements, and he distinguishes five different generations of innovation:

- **1st generation: technology push.** From 1950 to the mid-1960s, rapid economic growth led to a "black hole demand" that brought about a strong technology push and industrial expansion in the Western world and in Japan. Companies focused predominantly on scientific breakthroughs: "the more R & D in, the more new products out". This was nicknamed the "strategy of hope": "Hire good people, give them the best affordable facilities, then leave them alone." R & D was considered to be a corporate overhead and

---

5 The Partnering Initiative (http://thepartneringinitiative.org/).

relegated to an ivory tower position. Innovation occurred in the fast-growing multinationals isolated from universities.

- **2nd generation: market pull.** The mid-1960s to early 1970s were characterized by a market shares battle that encouraged companies to shift their development focus to a needs pull. The central focus became responding to the market's needs. Cost–benefit analyses were performed for individual research projects, including systematic allocation and resource management. Stronger connections were initiated between R & D and operating units by including product engineers in scientist-run research teams in order to decrease time to market.

- **3rd generation: coupled innovation.** From the mid-1970s to the mid-1980s, rationalization efforts emerged under the pressure of inflation and stagflation. The strategic focus was on corporate consolidation and resulted in "product portfolios". Companies moved away from individual R & D projects. Marketing and R & D became more tightly coupled through structured innovation processes. Operational cost reduction was a key driving force behind this coupling model.

- **4th generation: integrated innovation.** When the Western economy recovered from the early 1980s to the mid-1990s, the central theme became a time-based struggle. The focus was on integrated processes and products to develop "total concepts". Typical of this fourth generation was the parallel and integrated nature of development processes. Externally, strong supplier linkages were established as well as close coupling with leading customers.

- **5th generation: open innovation.** From the 1990s onwards, resource constraints became central. As a result, the focus was on systems integration and networking in order to guarantee flexibility and the speed of development. Business processes were automated through enterprise resource planning and manufacturing information systems. Externally, the focus was on business ecosystems. Advanced strategic partnerships were established, as well as collaborative marketing and research arrangements such as open innovation. Added value for products was to be found in quality and other non-price factors.

Therefore, the concept of open innovation implies understanding the shift organizations have to undergo, becoming aware of the increasing openness of innovation and how ideas are increasingly developed beyond the organization's boundaries (Chesbrough 2003). In fact, closed and open innovation principles (see Table 4.2) are characterized by very different approaches.

Table 4.2 **Differences between closed and open innovation principles**

Source: Chesbrough 2003: xxvi.

Closed innovation principles	Open innovation principles
The smart people in the field work for us	Not all the smart people work for us. We need to work with smart people inside and outside our company
To profit from R&D, we must discover it, develop it, and ship it ourselves	External R&D can create significant value; internal R&D is needed to claim some portion of that value
If we discover it ourselves, we will get it to the market first	We don't have to originate the research to profit from it
The company that gets an innovation to the market first will win	Building a better business model is better than getting to the market first
If we create the most and the best ideas in the industry, we will win	If we make the best use of internal and external ideas, we will win
We should control our IP, so that our competitors don't profit from our ideas	We should profit from others' use of our IP, and we should buy others' IP whenever it advances our business model

Within this approach, cooperation and the concept of partnership adopts a broad new meaning as it becomes part of the added-value proposition life-cycle. This implies involving other parties in the process and intensifying stakeholder engagement through the ecosystem. Fundamentally, the concept of exchanging and sharing in an open economy focuses on engaging through network-enabled platforms, providing the possibility to share goods and services, ideas and concepts among participants with an agreed value. Such processes allow information to be shared on product design, service access, production of new products, access to markets, distribution or even re-use or elimination of products and services with a specialized community, maximizing synergies among them and generating greater added value as a result.

As the European Sharing Economy Coalition states,[6] the sharing economy model promotes a more efficient use of assets, giving access to more opportunities,

---

6 http://www.euro-freelancers.eu/european-sharing-economy-coalition/.

at lower cost, and adjusting to the needs of our resources. It essentially revolves around three models:

- **Product-based systems.** Users pay for the benefit of using a product without needing to own the product outright (e.g. car/bike sharing). This disrupts traditional industries based on models of individual private property.

- **Redistributing markets.** Redistribute used items from someone who does not want them to someone who does want them (e.g. exchange markets and second hand). In some markets the products can be free (Freecycle), others are exchanged (thredUP) or sold (eBay).

- **Collaborative lifestyles.** People with similar needs or interests come together to share and exchange less-tangible assets such as time, space, skills and money. This includes workspaces (Citizen Space), gardens (Landshare) or parking space (JustPark), loans between individuals (Lending Club) and home renting (Airbnb and Couchsurfing).

However, in order to enable an open innovation economy aimed at generating social impact, several concepts need to be ensured. First, a transparent and open data framework. Organizations working on innovation platforms for BoP communities need to understand that the information they access and retain will be more valuable if it is transparently available and shared with the larger community in such a way that they can manage it to generate knowledge creatively to address social challenges. Thus, open and transparent access to information enables more efficient use of products and services and provides more opportunities for co-creation, supporting more self-sufficient and resilient communities.

Second, creating in an open and sharing economy also requires establishing an environment based on trust and values of mutual self-respect with a win–win approach. This implies committing to building and validating trusted relationships between innovators, engaged organizations and groups through the value chain such as distributors and suppliers and members of the community.

There are a broad range of initiatives that have spurred the promotion of open innovation through the value-chain phases. Whether at the research or design and creation phases, or at the stages of production and distribution, several innovation platforms are contributing to help share knowledge and propose solutions in a co-creative manner with and among engaged stakeholders (see Table 4.3).

Table 4.3 **Relevant innovations generating impact through value-chain phases**
Source: Centro de Alianzas para el Desarrollo (CAD).

Value chain phase	Innovation description
Research	**Innocentive** – open innovation problem solving **TekScout** – crowdsourcing R&D solutions **IdeaConnection** – idea marketplace and problem solving **Yet2.com** – IP marketplace **PRESANS (beta)** – connect and solve R&D problems **Hypios** – online problem solving **Innoget** – research intermediary platform **One Billion Minds** – online (social) challenges **NineSigma** – technology problem solving
Design & Create	**RedesignMe** – community co-creation **Atizo** – open innovation marketplace **Innovation Exchange** – open innovation marketplace **ideaken** – collaborative crowdsourcing **Idea Bounty** – crowdsourcing ideas **crowdSPRING** – creative designs **Myoo Create** – environmental and social challenges **99designs** – pioneer in design crowdsourcing **OpenIDEO** – collaborative design platform **Challenge.gov** – crowdsourced solutions for government problems **eYeka** – the co-creation community
Produce	**Innocentive** – open innovation problem solving **TekScout** – crowdsourcing R&D solutions **IdeaConnection** – idea marketplace and problem solving **Yet2.com** – IP marketplace **PRESANS (beta)** – connect and solve R&D problems **Hypios** – online problem solving **Innoget** – research intermediary platform **One Billion Minds** – online (social) challenges **NineSigma** – technology problem solving
Distribute	**Inkling Markets** – use wisdom of the crowd for forecasting **Intrade** – global prediction markets **NewsFutures** – collective intelligence markets **Kaggle** – data mining and forecasting **Idea Crossing** – organize innovation quests **DataStation** – complete innovation platform **Fiat Mio** – create a car

4.7 Major conclusions and lessons learned

When considering developing new business models with BoP communities, innovation platforms have become an interesting system to spur creativity and engage different stakeholders working together with the same goal. Specifically, open innovation platforms allow generation of knowledge and co-creation in a cost-effective and efficient way promoting innovative solutions that address social technologies.

Such frameworks for innovation require a serious engagement of stakeholders and being able to share and create jointly in a transparent way, with a proactive engagement approach based on trust. Therefore, cross-sector partnerships are presented as new, innovative governance systems that imply changing the way projects and services are being designed and created, adopting a more hybrid and inclusive approach.

In conclusion, BoP innovation not only should promote the way business models are conceived in terms of adopting a bottom-up approach and changing hypothetical beneficiaries into strategic partners, but also could benefit by incorporating a co-creative approach engaging social innovation platforms through the open and shared economy. Such models, embedded through more participatory and collaborative engagement processes with a win–win philosophy, are starting to be used in project implementation and have the potential to generate more successful and sustainable business models generating long-lasting impact.

Bibliography

Benhamou, R. (1991) "Imitation in the Decorative Arts of the Eighteenth Century", *Journal of Design History* 4.1: 1-14.

BEPA (Bureau of European Policy Advisers, European Commission) (2011) *Empowering People, Driving Change: Social Innovation in the European Union* (Luxembourg: European Union Publications Office).

Berg, M. (2002) "From Imitation to Invention: Creating Commodities in Eighteenth-Century Britain", *Economic History Review* 30.

Berg, M., and H. Clifford (eds.) (1999) *Consumers and Luxury: Consumer Culture in Europe, 1650–1850* (Manchester: Manchester University Press).

Chesbrough, H. (2003) *Open Innovation: The New Imperative for Creating and Profiting from Technology* (Boston, MA: Harvard Business School Press).

Christensen, C.M. (1997) *The Innovator's Dilemma: When New Technologies Cause Great Firms to Fail* (Boston, MA: Harvard Business School Press).

Clifford, H. (1999) "Concepts of Invention, Identity and Imitation in the London and Provincial Metal-working Trades, 1750–1800", *Journal of Design History* 12.3: 241-55.

Drucker, P. (2006) *Innovation and Entrepreneurship* (London: HarperCollins).

Freeman, C. (1974) *The Economics of Industrial Innovation* (Harmondsworth, UK: Penguin Books).

Godin, B. (2008) *Innovation: The History of a Category* (Project on the Intellectual History of Innovation Working Paper No. 1; Montreal: INRS).

Godin, B. (2010) *Innovation Studies: the Invention of a Specialty (Part II)* (Project on the Intellectual History of Innovation, Working Paper No 8; Montreal: INRS).

Gradl, C., and B. Jenkins (2011) *Tackling Barriers to Scale: From Inclusive Business Models to Inclusive Business Ecosystems* (Boston, MA: Harvard Kennedy School CSR Initiative).

Green, E. (2014) "Innovation: The History of a Buzzword", *The Atlantic*, 13 February.

Hammond, A., W.J. Kramer, J. Tran, R. Katz and C. Walker (2007) *The Next 4 Billion: Market Size and Business Strategy at the Base of the Pyramid* (Washington, DC: World Resources Institute, http://www.wri.org/publication/the-next-4-billion).

Hart, S. L. (2010) *Capitalism at the Crossroads: Next Generation Business Strategies for a Post-Crisis World* (Upper Saddle River, NJ: Prentice Hall Pearson, 3rd edn).

Kandachar, P., and M. Halme (eds.) (2008) *Sustainability Challenges and Solutions at the Base of the Pyramid: Business, Technology and the Poor* (Sheffield, UK: Greenleaf Publishing).

London, T. (2008) "The Base-of-the-Pyramid Perspective: A New Approach to Poverty Alleviation", in G.T. Solomon (ed.), *Academy of Management Best Paper Proceedings* (Chicago, IL: Academy of Management).

London, T., and S.L. Hart (eds.) (2010) *Next Generation Business Strategies for the Base of the Pyramid: New Approaches for Building Mutual Value* (Upper Saddle River, NJ: FT Press).

Prahalad, C.K., and S.L. Hart (2002) "The Fortune at the Bottom of the Pyramid", *Strategy + Business* 26: 1-14.

Prahalad, C.K., and M.S. Krishnan (2008) *The New Age of Innovation: Driving Cocreated Value Through Global Networks* (New York: McGraw-Hill).

Rothwell, R. (1994) "Towards the Fifth-generation Innovation Process", *International Marketing Review* 11.1: 7-31.

Schumpeter, J. (1912) *Theorie der wirtschaftlichen Entwicklung* (Berlin: Duncker and Humblot).

Spruijt, J., T. Spanjaard and K. Demouge (2013) *The Golden Circle of Innovation: What Companies Can Learn from NGOs When It Comes to Innovation* (Katowice, Poland: University of Economics in Katowice Publishing House).

Smith, A., E. Arond, M. Fressoli, H. Thomas and D. Abrol (2012) "Supporting Grassroots Innovation: Facts and Figures", SciDevNet, 2 May 2012, http://www.scidev.net/global/icts/feature/supporting-grassroots-innovation-facts-and-figures-1.html, accessed 30 November 2014.

Stiglitz, J., A. Sen and J.-P. Fitoussi (2009) *Report by the Commission on the Measurement of Economic Performance and Social Progress* (http://www.stiglitz-sen-fitoussi.fr/documents/rapport_anglais.pdf, accessed 19 December 2014).

Part III
Building ecosystems for inclusive business

5

Bridging the pioneer gap
Financing the missing middle

Nicolas Chevrollier and Myrtille Danse
BoP Innovation Center, The Netherlands

Inclusive innovation is the market-driven development of something new with impact together with low-income groups. Offering significant market opportunities, inclusive innovations are developed by increasing numbers of companies worldwide. However, it is becoming clear that there is still a financing "missing middle" between microfinance and the regular financial instruments available to support companies developing products and services for the low-income groups. This missing middle is particularly predominant in financing BoP ventures in the early stages of development. This chapter explores the nature of the capital needed; the challenges for companies to obtain it; and the emerging financial instruments offered by public authorities, corporate and impact investors to fill this financial missing middle.

Worldwide, there is a strong likelihood that rapid growth and technical change will increase inequality unless explicit efforts are made to harness science, technology and innovation to address the needs of low-income groups, the so-called base of the pyramid (BoP). To develop and deliver high-performance products and solutions at an ultra-low cost for the benefit of the BoP, new approaches involving the private sector are needed.

Such approaches lead to new roles for the private sector, from multinationals and large national firms to small and medium-sized enterprises (SMEs), as well as non-governmental organizations (NGOs). There is a growing conviction that businesses can participate in alleviating poverty in economically feasible ways. The size of the overall market opportunity for essential goods and services for the BoP—housing, rural water delivery, maternal health, primary education and financial services—was estimated as representing a $400 billion to $1 trillion market opportunity over the next ten years (Hammond *et al.* 2007).

When seen as value-demanding consumers, hardworking producers and creative entrepreneurs, low-income groups have the potential to change their own lives by being involved in the launch of innovative business ventures that create new jobs and access to essential services, such as water, sanitation and food and nutrition security. Such specific and challenging BoP business ventures can offer great opportunities for a new and fast-growing class of "impact investors" that aim for a combination of social, environmental and economic impact and are willing to accept higher risk and lower returns.

However, it is becoming clear that there still is a financing "missing middle" between microfinance and the regular financial instruments available to support companies developing products and services for the BoP. This missing middle is particularly predominant in financing BoP ventures in the early stages of development. Potentially ground-breaking initiatives—from local entrepreneurs as well as innovative multinational enterprises (MNEs) and SMEs in industrialized economies—remain without financing at the early stage of entrepreneurial development, because impact investors have difficulties assessing in a satisfactory manner the risks involved, and entrepreneurs are insufficiently able to present themselves as "investment-ready". A major constraint for private parties to engage and invest in inclusive innovation is the absence of seed capital targeted at the stimulation of innovative solutions during the different stages of the innovation cycle—from the early stages of opportunity identification, through later phases of upscaling potentially successful solutions (Dalberg 2011). In order to convince investors, entrepreneurs need to bridge the "pioneer gap" (Koh *et al.* 2012).

In this chapter, after a brief note on BoPInc case studies (Box 6.1), we first look at the unmet financial needs of organizations developing products and services for the BoP. We then explore the main challenges that they are facing especially in the pioneering phase of developing and validating. Finally we provide an overview of emerging solutions to provide adequate financial mechanisms to support inclusive innovation.

Box 5.1 **About our BoPInc case studies**

> The BoP Innovation Center (BoPInc) is an independent foundation that provides services and tools to develop, learn about and accelerate inclusive businesses in BoP markets. Together with its strategic partners it has created the BoPInc alliance. The current strategic partners are: Wageningen University, The Netherlands Organization for Applied Scientific Research (TNO), ICCO Cooperation, SNV Netherlands Development Organisation, Nyenrode Business University, Global Compact Network The Netherlands, Ashoka, and Rabobank Foundation. These partners represent a worldwide network in a broad variety of industries and organization types. BoPInc makes use of the resources and networks of these strategic partners to develop inclusive business strategies.
>
> In the past three years, in developing these business strategies BoPInc has been confronted with the challenge of accessing the right financial mechanisms to start or grow inclusive business, whether it is to find appropriate start-up capital to develop a new milk cooling device in Ethiopia or to sustain a long-term business partnership in our agri-programme 2SCALE.[1] BoPInc has worked with donors such as the Dutch Ministry of Foreign Affairs, financial institutions such as Rabobank or private foundations to find the most appropriate source of finance in these various cases. Working mainly in the agriculture/food, energy and water/sanitation sectors, our case studies reflect our sector strategy and are a reflection of our day-to-day challenges to overcome the pioneer gap.

5.1 Inclusive innovation

A growing body of literature deals with innovation in developing countries. Inclusive innovation is still a relatively new concept. It is difficult to trace it back to its origins, as it has not been introduced by scholars as a new concept or specific type of innovation. The term "inclusive" has been used in other settings: inclusive business, inclusive growth, inclusive finance, etc. Inclusivity means that it also addresses a group that is commonly excluded, referring to the poor, the disabled or otherwise socially excluded.

Inclusive innovation is used to refer to pro-poor innovation. Other similar concepts include frugal innovation, BoP innovation and Gandhian innovation.

In this chapter, inclusive innovation refers to the innovation processes that specifically address the needs of the BoP and which involve the BoP not only as consumer, but also as producer, employee and entrepreneur. The outcomes of these processes are high-performance products, services and processes that combine awareness, accessibility, affordability and availability. Together these processes and

1 http://www.bopinc.org/projects-initiatives-79/2scale.

outcomes have a positive impact on the BoP in a financially sustainable way. This impact is reached by making (better) products and services available to the BoP, and/or by providing them an improved source of income.

In this chapter, we use the following definition of inclusive innovation: "Inclusive Innovation is the market-driven development of something new with impact together with low-income groups" (Van der Klein *et al.* 2012). The vehicle of impact of the inclusive innovation is restricted to the private sector.

In order to develop an inclusive innovation, an entrepreneur follows a number of steps from basic research to developing prototypes to introducing the product in the market and finally scaling the business for growth (see Fig. 5.1).

Figure 5.1 **Entrepreneurial steps from research to growth**

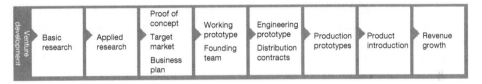

5.2 The need for financing inclusive innovations

While developing inclusive innovation, the private sector needs different types of investment and support. Some companies are seeking funding to support ideation (concept development until proof of principle and concept); others are seeking access to funding to support the realization and implementation of ideas and business plans. In general, the risk mitigation for innovating for the BoP is a key requirement of MNEs, international and local SMEs. Developing new products for new markets is the boldest but also most risky and insecure step a company can make. Initial costs are high and are hard to fund, given the internal requirements for return on investment and the lack of external parties that are willing to finance these activities.

The finance needs for inclusive innovation by individual enterprises vary significantly depending on the sector they operate in, their business model, size and maturity stage, human resource capacity and other factors. While larger enterprises may require finance of US$2 million and above, SMEs tend to have needs in the US$25,000 to US$2 million range, while micro-enterprises require less than US$25,000 (see Box 5.2 for details of the food and nutrition sector in Africa). Besides that, the needs go beyond accessing finance, as many enterprises need support to develop their ideas and create well-managed, financially sustainable operations (Dalberg 2011). A problem faced across the African continent, for instance, is a critical shortage of skilled professionals to manage and grow SMEs (UNECA 2010). A consistent message repeated in reports and interviews is the lack of managerial and financial capacity in SMEs, for which an investment package combining both capital and business development services is needed.

Box 5.2 **Food and nutrition sector in Africa: an investment perspective**

In many developing countries the agricultural sector contributes the most to GDP and is one of the main sources of income. More importantly, relative labour intensity and accessibility to jobs for marginalized populations (also contributing to social impact) tend to be high in this sector. Given the importance of agriculture, the growth of enterprises in this sector will generate not only economic but also social benefits, such as increased food security, and possibly environmental benefits if resources are sustainably managed.

Africa has the potential to increase the value of its annual agricultural output by US$200 billion in ten years (Dalberg 2011). This would increase demand for upstream products such as fertilizers, seeds, pesticides and machinery, while spurring the growth of downstream activities such as biofuel production, grain refining and other types of food processing.

Table 5.1 **Overview of enterprise finance needs in the agricultural sector**

Source: Dalberg 2011.

Types of enterprise	What they need finance for	Range of investment typically needed (US$)	Current finance options
Large-scale commercial farming	Start-up, operations, maintenance, infrastructure	LARGE (>2 million)	Private equity/ venture capital (PE/VC), commercial banks
Contract farming	Start-up, working capital	MEDIUM (e.g. 25,000 to 2 million)	PE/VC
Cooperatives	Pre-harvest finance, inputs	MEDIUM (e.g. 25,000 to 2 million)	Rural banks
Smallholder farmers	Pre-harvest finance, inputs	LOW (e.g. <25,000)	Microfinance

Table 5.1 presents the finance needs different types of business have to improve their performance in the agricultural sector in West Africa. But finance is not the only need of these enterprises. Small to medium-sized operators are often constrained by market failures and inefficiencies. These include access to markets (i.e. knowledge and information required to establish linkages with suppliers and customers) and training and mentoring to develop business leadership.

Along the different stages of developing and validating inclusive innovations, companies seek different types of funding (grant, equity, loan). This may be provided by public authorities, relatives or friends, investment firms or related organizations in the investment business such as angel investors and venture capitalists (which invest early in emerging companies) or commercial banks (see Fig. 5.2).

Figure 5.2 **The range of funding options**

The private sector, while developing products and services for the BoP, is therefore in need of capital. It is true in the agriculture sector as shown in Box 5.2 and remains valid in sectors such as waste/sanitation, health or rural electrification. However, while this need is clearly identified, it appears that it is not correctly served by the current financial sector for reasons explained in the following section.

5.3 Challenges in financing inclusive innovation

From a macro point of view, inclusive innovation benefits from the right presence of different capabilities in a country:

- Institutions (political environment, regulatory environment, etc.)

- Human capital and research

- Infrastructure (ICT, energy, general infrastructure, etc.)

- Market sophistication (credit, investment/equity market, microfinance, banks, etc.)

- Business sophistication (science, technology, innovation [STI] clusters, innovation parks, etc.)

While all these capabilities are essential for innovation in general, inclusive innovation targets the BoP and thus requires specific mechanisms to be put in place. For example, business sophistication will also include multi-stakeholder platforms where NGOs, businesses and STI converge. Building the ecosystem of innovation capabilities that will nurture inclusive innovation is an ongoing process in many countries. However, a number of constraints remain in creating a welcoming investment environment.

5.3.1 Investment constraints

There are four important long-standing constraints to investing in private-sector activities for BoP markets (see Dalberg 2011; Marr and Chiwarra 2011; UNEP 2007): (1) risks level, (2) institutional development, (3) policy and regulatory frameworks, and (4) skills and training needs.

1. **Risks barriers.** Enterprises that form the "missing middle" in the demand-side financing landscape in developing countries are generally perceived by banks and financial institutions as risky and therefore unprofitable. Further-more, differing incentives, expectations and motivations between investors and fund managers with regard to investing in entrepreneurs for the BoP market result in misalignment of the financial strategy of fund manag-ers, also becoming a reason for an incorrect perception about the sector's profitability.

2. **Institutional barriers.** Countries may appear as donor darlings and hence do not provide a suitable investment environment for private capital. Fur-thermore, the costs of identifying and developing promising investment opportunities are prohibitive for most investors. Another point of attention is the prominence of the informal sector when considering investing in BoP ventures, making the valuation of companies challenging.

3. **Policy and regulatory barriers.** From the lack of a regulatory framework con-ducive to financing BoP ventures to public policy distorting it (e.g. limitation in interest rates in a given sector), the policy and regulatory environments are often not adequately designed to support early stage investment in BoP businesses.

4. **Skills, knowledge, information and training barriers.** Inclusive innovation is a nascent sector and often fund managers or financial institutions lack the in-depth knowledge of the sector to realize suitable investments.

These constraints result in an investment climax that provides inadequate fund-ing opportunities for companies developing products and services for the BoP, especially those related to duration and size of the investment.

5.3.2 Inadequate types and duration of traditional funding

Traditional funding by banks by means of loans is often not possible in the BoP market, due to absence of collateral (especially in agriculture) and a traditional tight schedule of repayments. In traditional venture capital equity, the expected exit of shares will be on average five years (between three and seven). Since exit possibilities (on the BoP market or to the co-investors/entrepreneur) are weaker, the exit period has to be stretched. The build-up of a market position often depends on how the surrounding market is developing. This takes up to ten or more years.

Altogether there is a need for longer-term (patient) equity capital for BoP develop-ment. We estimate durations of at least five up until ten years as reasonable terms.

5.3.3 Inadequate granularity of funding available

Besides the duration of financing itself, the amount of money requested in this early stage is smaller than average as described in the previous section. Financial institutions or informal investors and impact investors tend to move to amounts higher than US$1 million and do not serve this particular area, due to an expected low return on investment.

5.3.4 The pioneer gap as a barrier to high-volume investing

It is becoming clear that there still is a financing "missing middle" between microfinance and the regular financial instruments available to established and stable SMEs in developing countries. Potentially ground-breaking initiatives—from local entrepreneurs as well as innovative MNEs and SMEs in industrialized economies—remain without financing, because investors see too many risks and entrepreneurs are insufficiently able to present themselves as "investment-ready". In order to convince investors, entrepreneurs need to bridge the "pioneer gap" (Koh *et al.* 2012) and work on their business plan, entrepreneurial skills and attitude. The pioneer gap is known in investment terms as the "valley of death" (see Box 5.3).

While this pioneer gap is clearly identified, it remains to be seen which mechanisms have been developed to provide adequate finance for entrepreneurs entering it.

Box 5.3 **The pioneer gap**

The **pioneer gap** or **valley of death** is the gap (in time and money) between the formation of the firm and the generation of a positive cash flow (see Fig. 5.3). This period is called the pre-seed/seed (financing) phase of innovation, where the firm requires an inflow of funds to offset the negative cash flow resulting from the transition from applied scientific research to proof of principle, from working prototype to engineering prototype, and then from production prototype to preparation for large-scale market introduction. In later stages (after positive cash flow is achieved) investment needs are better served by existing financial institutions and informal and formal investors. The amount of money requested in the early stages is smaller than in the later stages. Financial institutions or more traditional investors tend to invest amounts higher than US$1 million for efficiency reasons and do not serve the pre-seed and seed stages.

Figure 5.3 **Position in the investment cycle**

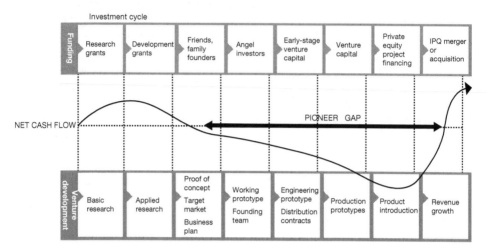

5.4 Instruments to finance inclusive innovation

As described previously, entrepreneurs developing products and services for the BoP face an ultimate challenge when entering the pioneer gap (in time and money) between the formation of the firm and the generation of a positive cash flow. Financial mechanisms developed to fill this gap require the following characteristics:

- Long-term finance (equity durations of five to ten years)

- Accepting high risk because of the lack of collateral, unstable cash flow and challenging ecosystem environment

- Covering smaller amounts of invested fund (in the order of magnitude of US$100,000)

- Besides money, a need for technical assistance and business development

5.4.1 The new wave of impact investing

There is a current rise in impact investments (Impact Assets 2011; Practitioner Hub 2012) investing for social impact and financial return. "In a world where government resources and charitable donations are insufficient to address the world's social problems, impact investing offers a new alternative for channeling large-scale private capital for social benefit" (J.P. Morgan 2010). This new type of investment aims for desired societal impact while achieving an acceptable financial return. In comparison to other alternative asset classes, the impact investment model is still immature and financial return claims have not yet been proven. Investments are made gradually and investee companies take time to realize value.

Relevant existing impact investors support local entrepreneurs in formalizing their business and realizing some scale (mezzanine financing). These entrepreneurs must have shown some market success and should be looking for additional resources to scale (e.g. Acumen, see Mohiuddin and Imtiazuddin 2007). Or fund solid business plans with social impact and acceptable financial return (e.g. FMO, the Netherlands Development Finance Company).

Furthermore, to support early-stage BoP ventures, there is an incipient but fast-growing interest among aid agencies and entrepreneurial philanthropists in supporting promising initiatives to get off the ground, based on their proven capabilities in the areas of building business skills, creating consumer awareness and improving the enabling environment. The attention should then focus on ways to harness that support towards the closing of the pioneer gap, through partnerships with private partners and participation in inclusive innovation business development efforts.

Specific financial mechanisms are then developed to fill this pioneer gap that even impact investors are not considering fully at the moment.

5.4.2 From public authorities or donors

There is a global trend from public authorities and donors to invest in a more commercially oriented way (to move from giving to supporting). These organizations also engage with specific programmes in the private sector into development-oriented projects to fill the gap between development and business. The Dutch minister in charge of development cooperation is, for instance, now called the minister for development cooperation "and trade", reinforcing the win–win situation between development and business. However, few of these bodies venture in the innovation space. Some examples are:

- Development Innovation Ventures from USAID (United States Agency for International Development) supports new applications of technology and new service delivery practices that lead to transformative improvements to development outcomes. DIV spans a large part of the pioneer gap via three stages of investment. Stage 1 is for projects in the proof of concept phase: DIV will grant these projects up to $100,000 dollars over one year so that grantees can refine prototypes and gather the evidence they need to pull in more investment and grow. Stage 2 is for larger projects, typically to expand across a country. DIV will grant Stage 2 projects up to $1 million. In exchange, Stage 2 projects will build in rigorous testing to prove whether the project is viable at its larger size. Stage 3 is for much larger projects. For grants of up to $15 million over several years, solutions that have already proven to work at a large scale will be expanded much further, and often into multiple countries.

- Innovation Against Poverty (IAP) from the Swedish International Development Cooperation Agency (SIDA) supports with small and large matching grants, and guarantees new product/service/market system development that would otherwise not have taken place due to perceived risk or uncertainty. Companies can apply for financial support from two different modules aimed at different stages of the innovation and development path. Small Grants provide a matching grant (maximum 50% of total project cost) up to €20,000 (US$25,000) for the purpose of exploring an innovation or a new market. The grant can be used for travel and pre-feasibility studies, stakeholder needs assessments, or for networking with local organizations. Large Grants provide a matching grant (maximum 50%) of between €20,000 (US$25,000) and €200,000 (US$250,000) to a company for the purpose of undertaking a project aimed at a new product, service, system, business model or a concept ready to be put to market test, or adaptation of existing products to be affordable and accessible to the poor. IAP also provides guarantees and advisory support for venture development.

Other initiatives are in gestation. For instance, the India Inclusive Innovation Fund (IIIF) will provide funding to BoP-focused companies across the venture development cycle both in early and in growth stages. This venture fund finances innovative projects that offer creative, financially sustainable solutions to developmental challenges in agriculture, education, energy, environment, food, nutrition, financial inclusion, healthcare, etc. IIIF projects combine scalable social impact with commercial returns. The fund started operating in 2014.

5.4.3 Corporate impact finance[2]

Over the past decade the approach of multinational companies has evolved when developing products and service at the BoP. Initially, multinationals followed a one-directional approach selling products and services to the poor. The value for companies was clear, but the extent to which it served the poor remained questionable. Often, strategies failed to succeed because products were not developed together with the BoP. The next-generation BoP approach came into place. People at the BoP are now embraced in the innovation process as valuable business partners in a shift from business strategies targeted at the BoP to inclusive innovation together with the BoP. Today people at the BoP are included in projects as entrepreneurs, producers and consumers. They co-create inclusive innovations partnering with companies, civil society and public authorities. The current developing view—"BoP 3.0" strategies—combines different stakeholder perspectives working collaboratively towards integrated system solutions. The strength of the company taking the lead is reinforced by smaller, more flexible, innovative local and international companies. These are strong partnerships that have collective impact on the BoP.

These trends have a direct influence on the types of mechanism multinational companies develop to address the BoP market. They still develop their own innovation with the BoP but they often provide technical and business support to BoP entrepreneurs (local or international) they invest in financially. In companies such as Danone (Danone Communities programme), GDF SUEZ (Rassembleur

---

2 Term coined by Steven Serneels (Ashoka).

d'Energies initiative) or Schneider Electric (BipBop programme), these three-legged programmes (innovation, support, investment) enable companies to create a systemic change in the BoP ecosystem they work in and ultimately accelerate their own development in the BoP market (see Box 5.4 for a description of Schneider Electric's BipBop programme and the Schneider Electric Energy Access fund).

Box 5.4 **Schneider Electric BipBop**

In early 2009, the BipBop programme was launched to contribute to access to clean energy for low-income populations through the development of a combined approach of philanthropy and business. The programme has three pillars (Vermot Desroches and André 2012):

1. **The business pillar** provides financial, technical and managerial support to SMEs and entrepreneurs in the field of access to energy through an impact investment fund

2. **The innovation pillar** develops a cost-effective portfolio of products and solutions providing access to energy for low-income populations

3. **The people pillar** creates training in energy management trades for disadvantaged youths

Figure 5.4 **The BipBop approach**

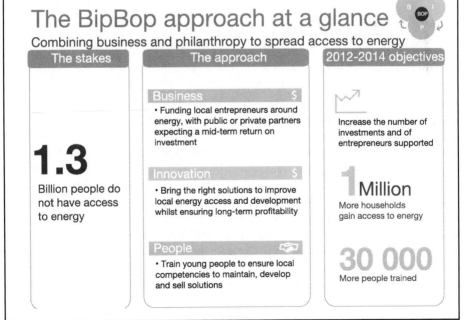

The BipBop approach at a glance

Combining business and philanthropy to spread access to energy

The stakes	The approach	2012-2014 objectives
	Business	Increase the number of investments and of entrepreneurs supported
	• Funding local entrepreneurs around energy, with public or private partners expecting a mid-term return on investment	
1.3 Billion people do not have access to energy	**Innovation**	**1** Million More households gain access to energy
	• Bring the right solutions to improve local energy access and development whilst ensuring long-term profitability	
	People	**30 000** More people trained
	• Train young people to ensure local competencies to maintain, develop and sell solutions	

The Schneider Electric Energy Access (SEEA) fund (the business pillar) works as a global sustainable venture capital fund. The fund provides support for the creation and development of enterprises and profitable entities that help the poorest to gain access to clean energy. The fund also sustains the development of entrepreneurship in electricity trades and renewable energies. Alongside its social mission, SEEA has a targeted return on investment of 5–10%. For example, SEEA invested €250,000 (US$300,000) in NICE International. NICE International builds a network of franchises providing access to energy services, and ICT (information and communications technology) in Gambia. Investments concluded by SEEA range from €100,000 to €400,000 for periods of 5 to 7 years. The fund never takes a majority shareholding in order to remain as a support for impact growth while the entrepreneur keeps hands on its activities. Employees of Schneider via a mutual find also invest into the SEEA fund.

The Inclusive Business Fund has been designed especially to bridge part of the pioneer gap described in previous sections (see Box 5.5).

Box 5.5 **Inclusive Business Fund**

Rabobank Foundation, ICCO Investments and the BoP Innovation Center have initiated a new fund called the Inclusive Business Fund. The fund aims to create access to finance in developing countries and to enhance economic development. The partnership provides the required business development support that brings investment-ready entrepreneurs and committed investors together, and thus helps launch substantial numbers of inclusive business ventures with the potential for large-scale impact.

The Inclusive Business Fund builds on the unique abilities of Rabo Foundation, ICCO and BoP Innovation Center to provide capital, expertise, TA and an extensive branch network. The strategy is to invest risk capital in sustainable and social SMEs and cooperatives with growth potential, thus generating a positive IRR (internal rate of return) to investors, over an average period of five years. The sectors addressed are: Food and Agribusiness, Health, Energy, Water and Sanitation, and Education. The fund's geographical focus is Africa, Asia and South America. In general, the fund's investments are made through medium-term debt and mezzanine instruments. The average deal size is between €100,000 and €1 million.

5.4.4 Dedicated early-stage BoP investment firms

While public authorities and multinationals provide some financial instruments to support early-stage BoP ventures as described in previous sections, dedicated financial organizations are starting to invest in early-stage BoP ventures. Organizations such as Unitus Seed Fund[3] or Accion Venture[4] provide patient seed capital and support to inclusive innovation start-ups. Another example is the Inclusive Business Fund that includes Rabobank, ICCO and the BoP Innovation Center (see Box 5.5) as shareholders. These firms/funds invest between $100,000 and $500,000 in equity or quasi-equity instruments and provide business support (to refine a given business model or operational strategies, to broker entrepreneurs to technology experts). A number of them are for-profit investment firms.

These organizations often use innovation financial schemes to deliver their services. Crowdfunding is one of these mechanisms, where equity is proposed in small shares online to a large open public. Enviu, a sustainable business developer, raised €100,000 ($120,000) using equity-based crowd funding platform Symbid. Enviu was able to attract 372 investors from all over the world who invested from as little as €20 ($25). Investors become actual owners of the company, receive a return on investment in the form of dividends and have the ability to sell their shares. Enviu will use the funds raised to invest directly in new start-ups developed.

Ultimately the financial mechanisms provided by these intermediary organizations will play a crucial role in shaping the inclusive innovation investment ecosystem.

5.5 Conclusion

There is a vibrant and resilient private sector that would like to contribute to the well-being of people at the base of the pyramid by creating job opportunities, and by offering access to quality elementary products and services at affordable prices. Practical experience reveals a demand for financial support from these companies in early stages of innovation trajectories, and currently traditional financial organizations are not providing the necessary instruments to support market-based inclusive innovations. In addition, even innovative financing (e.g. impact investing) is so far not completely addressing the demand to support the fuzzy front end of inclusive innovation that requires patient capital in small amounts. Furthermore, existing impact investing funds show that the success of funding schemes aiming at financial and social impact at the BoP depends on a combination of business development services, funding and technical assistance services within the fund. This has created a pioneer gap in time and money between the formation of a firm and the generation of a positive cash flow.

3 http://usf.vc/about/.
4 http://www.accion.org.

Responses to provide adequate solutions to mitigate this pioneer gap are starting to appear and have come from different angles providing innovative financial mechanisms to firm venturing at the BoP, from public authorities wishing to
invest public capital more efficiently to multinational companies creating a social
investment arm alongside their own innovation programmes. A new investment
ecosystem is coming to life. Intermediary organizations have a key role to play in
building this ecosystem by providing a link to social investing and providing firms
at the BoP with adequate business support to develop innovative BoP products
and services.

The challenge of the pioneer gap is clearly identified, and the nascent movement
of hybrid investment mechanisms providing finance and adequate business support holds the promise of being an accelerator for BoP firms making a larger impact
at the BoP. Over the next decade, these investments and efforts will allow the BoP
community to resolve part of the financial and business challenges that entrepreneurs face when entering BoP markets for the benefit of society at large.

Bibliography

Dalberg (2011) *Impact Investing in West Africa* (Copenhagen/New York: Dalberg).
Dutz, M.A. (2007) *Unleashing India's Innovation: Toward Sustainable and Inclusive Growth*
(Washington, DC: World Bank Publications).
George, G., A.M. McGahan and J. Prabhu (2012) "Innovation for Inclusive Growth: Towards
a Theoretical Framework and a Research Agenda", *Journal of Management Studies* 49.4:
661-83.
Hammond, A., W.J. Kramer, J. Tran, R. Katz and C. Walker (2007) *The Next 4 Billion: Market
Size and Business Strategy at the Base of the Pyramid* (Washington, DC: World Resources
Institute/International Finance Corporation).
Hilst, B.J.G. van der (2012) "Inclusive Innovation Systems: How Innovation Intermediaries
Can Strengthen the Innovation System", Master's thesis, Utrecht University.
Howells, J. (2006) "Intermediation and the Role of Intermediaries in Innovation", *Research
Policy* 35.5: 715-28.
Impact Assets (2011) "50 Impact Investment Fund Managers Managing $8.9 Billion in
Assets", http://www.impactassets.org/impactassets-50/2011-impactassets-50, accessed
30 November 2014.
J.P. Morgan (2010) *Impact Investments: An Emerging Asset Class* (New York: J.P. Morgan, www.
morganmarkets.com).
Koh, H., A. Karamchandani and R. Katz (2012) *From Blueprint to Scale: The Case for Philan-
thropy in Impact Investing* (New York: Acumen Fund/Monitor Group).
Marr, A., and C. Chiwara (2011) *Investment Supply for Small and Medium Enterprises* (New
Partnership for Africa's Development [NEPAD] Report; Johannesburg: Development
Bank of Southern Africa).
Mohiuddin, M., and O. Imtiazuddin (2007) *Socially Responsible Licensing: Model Partner-
ships for Underserved Markets* (Acumen Fund Concepts; New York: Acumen Fund).
Practitioner Hub (2012) "Database of Financial and Technical Support for Inclusive Busi-
nesses", http://businessinnovationfacility.org/page/data-of-financial-and-technical-
support-for-inclusive-businesses, accessed 30 November 2014.

UNECA (2010) *Economic Report on Africa* (Addis Ababa: United Nations Economic Commission for Africa).

UNEP (2007) *Innovative Financing for Sustainable Small and Medium Enterprises in Africa: International Workshop, Geneva, 2007 Meeting Report* (Geneva: United Nations Environment Programme Finance Initiative/African Task Force/WWF/ Geneva International Academic Network (RUIG-GIAN), International Organizations MBA, University of Geneva).

Van der Klein, W., N. Chevrollier and L. Collée (2012) *Inclusive Innovation: Shared Value at the Base of the Pyramid* (Three Pilots for Pro-poor Innovation Consortium; Utrecht, The Netherlands: BoP Innovation Center).

Vermot Desroches, G., and André, T. (2012) "The BipBop Programme: Providing Access to Reliable, Affordable and Clean Energy with a Combined Approach of Investment, Offers and Training", *Field Actions Science Reports*, Special issue 6, http://Factsreports.Revues.Org/1997#Tocfrom2n2, accessed 30 November 2014.

World Economic Forum (2011) *The Global Competitiveness Report 2011-2012* (Cologny, Switzerland: World Economic Forum).

6
Creating an innovation ecosystem for inclusive and sustainable business

Priya Dasgupta
Enterprise for a Sustainable World, USA

Stuart L. Hart
University of Vermont and Enterprise for a Sustainable World, USA

Over the past decade, most base-of-the-pyramid (BoP) ventures have either failed outright or dramatically under-performed against expectations. There are many and varied reasons for this less-than-stellar track record. Perhaps no cause for BoP failure, however, has been more ubiquitous than the mistaken belief that BoP ventures are no different from new ventures aimed at the developed markets at the top of the pyramid—the assumption that all that is required for venture success is an affordable product and an effective business model for production, marketing and distribution. Unfortunately, when it comes to the BoP, "no man is an island": in the under-served, informal and opaque settings at the bottom of the income pyramid, ventures must be embedded in larger ecosystems rather than stand-alone initiatives. To paraphrase Hillary Clinton, it "takes a village"—or an innovation ecosystem—to succeed with BoP enterprise.

6.1 The rise and fall of CleanStar Mozambique

Nowhere can the importance of building base-of-the-pyramid (BoP) business ecosystems be seen more clearly than in the domain of clean cookstoves for the poor. Indeed, despite the best of intentions, the past decade has seen scores of failed clean cookstove ventures relegated to the scrapheap of history. One initiative in this space, however, stands out from the crowd: CleanStar Mozambique.[1] From its inception, the founders of this venture understood that cookstoves must be embedded in a larger ecosystem to succeed. That is, until their original vision and business model was tragically reversed.

What began as a research experiment in India in 2005 with the support of the United States Agency for International Development (USAID), the World Resources Institute and local universities, soon morphed into an international parent holding company—CleanStar Ventures, which was incorporated in 2007. One of the ventures incubated by this group was a commercial platform to increase food and energy security of smallholder farmers while addressing the perils of charcoal-based deforestation and cooking rampant across Africa—CleanStar Mozambique (CSM).

Indeed, before clean cookstoves caught the attention of world leaders and became a global priority (the goal is to foster the adoption of clean cookstoves and fuels in 100 million households by 2020[2]), a pair of young, visionary entrepreneurs, founders Greg Murray and Segun Saxena, were thinking beyond the clean cookstove silo: a vertically integrated business model that would address the challenges of charcoal-based deforestation and improve food security, health and income for smallholder farming communities living on subsistence agriculture.

For CleanStar Mozambique, the actual cookstoves were a small part of a much larger ecosystem of value, which included the upstream production of smallholder-farmer-based biofuel from cassava, along with an integrated agro-forestry model that generated additional income—and food—for the subsistence farmers who previously subsisted on cassava and made charcoal to sell for cooking in the urban areas, accelerating the problems of deforestation and climate change.

Within five years of launch, the integrated agro-forestry model was adopted by more than 1,000 farmers, and a 2 million litre/year ethanol-based cooking fuel production facility was built near Beira, Mozambique, to replace charcoal. Over $21 million was raised from strategic corporate and institutional partners and investors such as Danish biotech powerhouse Novozymes, biofuel plant builder ICM, and financiers Bank of America Merrill Lynch, the Soros Economic Development Fund and IFU, Investment Fund for Developing Countries, to grow and scale operations not just in Mozambique but across Africa. These partners also contributed technology, project management skills, connections, credibility and financial savvy to the venture.

---

1 Parts of this section are adapted from Hart 2012.
2 http://www.cleancookstoves.org/the-alliance/.

With over 33,000 cookstoves and 1 million litres of branded, cassava-based ethanol sold to local households, CSM was clearly emerging as a game changer. It was a poster child at Rio+20 with the "Screw Business As Usual" award, recognized as Bioenergy Finance Deal of the Year 2012 by Environmental Finance, celebrated and discussed by sustainability experts, international agencies and impact investors alike. Here, it seemed, was a true triple-bottom-line BoP ecosystem that created sustainable value for all the stakeholders involved.

However, by late 2013, the story took a dramatic turn. Driven by a fresh round of investment capital, the decision was made to "focus" the business by suspending its agro-forestry and ethanol production. The company also got a new name, NewFire Africa, and was now focused on just the sale of clean cookstoves and fuel. Unfortunately, this move produced limited success and, by June 2014, a decision was made to voluntarily liquidate NewFire Africa to put an end to the continuing losses. "The company was not able to achieve the scale and retail penetration required to make this venture viable" (Novozymes 2014).

Nearly a decade of research, business model innovation and funding, among other things, had gone in to making a business case for clean technology at the base of the pyramid a reality. What went wrong? Was the business case for this venture flawed? Were there too many moving parts? Was greater focus indeed required? Could the execution have been different? Was patient capital really patient?

6.2 Thinking like a mountain

Reflecting on the CleanStar experience, and then thinking about the hundreds of failed attempts by multinational corporations, non-governmental organizations (NGOs), entrepreneurs, development agencies and multilateral organizations to create "sticky" business models further down the pyramid, why is the failure rate so high? After all, a study of household consumption of more than one million households in over 90 countries by the International Finance Corporation and the World Bank's Development Data Group valued the collective spend of the 4.5 billion poor people in developing countries at more than $5 trillion a year—higher than the middle and higher consumption segments combined.[3]

The first instinct is to search for ways to reduce the complexities inherent in the BoP enterprise space, as we saw with the CleanStar case. Unfortunately, this bias towards reducing complexity tends to lead to a more myopic view of the business opportunity—viewing this rich vibrant community as a channel to push down existing products and get a slice of the $5 trillion, flooding markets where there is limited consumer education, seeing only short-term gains - all of which ultimately leads to long-term devastation. Surely this $5 trillion market is not just a consumer

---

3 http://datatopics.worldbank.org.

base but also an economic engine to increase the earning potential of those living on less than $8 a day with minimal impact on our natural capital?

In his 1949 classic book, *A Sand County Almanac*, Aldo Leopold coined a phrase that would reverberate through history: "thinking like a mountain" (Flader 1974). He was the first to observe that the extermination of wolves, while solving problems for ranchers, led to explosions in deer populations—and trouble for the ecosystem as a whole. Focusing only on individual species in isolation, he observed, led to bad outcomes when it came to the natural environment. Better to "think like a mountain" by envisioning the holistic character of natural systems and all their intricate interconnections. Little did he know at the time that his observations about the natural world would one day provide a key insight in the development of sustainable ventures and economies at the base of the world income pyramid in the 21st century.

Like Leopold's single-minded wolf hunters, too many BoP ventures and initiatives have been "rifle shots"—business strategies premised on the design and sale of low-cost products to targeted low-income end-users. The landscape is littered with the remains of failed BoP ventures focused on the sale of such things as low-cost water filters, solar lights, clean cookstoves and myriad other household goods. The reasons for failure: product misfire, low sales penetration, high selling and distribution costs, and inability to scale (Simanis 2012).

As Khanna and Palepu at Harvard Business School observed many years ago in "Why Focused Strategies May Be Wrong for Emerging Markets" (1997), such an approach can work well in developed markets where infrastructure and institutions are well established. But in the developing world, such a "rifle shot" approach is a death sentence. That is why most successful corporations from the developing world are highly diversified "business houses"—they can supply the infrastructure and institutions (e.g. power, transport, distribution, education, healthcare) that are missing in the society itself. In short, they think (and act) like a mountain.

It is now becoming increasingly clear that the same logic applies to individual BoP ventures and initiatives—success demands that BoP enterprises create wide and compelling value propositions. For BoP innovators, thinking like a mountain means creating an entire business ecosystem that delivers value to local people and communities in multiple ways, not just through a single product (Hart 2010). It is time to reverse the bias for focus and simplicity that comes from doing business in the developed markets at the top of the pyramid. Instead, we need to embrace complexity—by building wide and deep value propositions along with the innovation ecosystems needed to deliver them (Hammond 2011; London 2015).

6.3 Building a BoP innovation ecosystem

Until about 20 years ago, the term "ecosystem" generally meant the biological ecosystem, as described by Aldo Leopold, which included all living organisms in an area as well as the physical environment functioning together as a unit to reach one or more equilibrium states (Flader 1974). However, the last decade or two has witnessed the growing use of this term in the business world, recognizing the growing interconnectedness across domains led by information technology, social media and cultural integration. In other words, there is a growing thrust towards another type of ecosystem—the innovation ecosystem—modelled on Joseph Schumpeter's ideas of entrepreneurship and creative destruction (Schumpeter 1942).

With the rapid penetration of technology into under-served markets, from over 93% of the world's population covered by cell phones to over 83% of the world having access to electricity, there has been a fundamental shift in focus towards the lower income tiers at the base of the pyramid (ITU 2014). Accordingly, over the last decade or so it has become increasingly clear that conventional business models also need to change if we are to effectively reach the BoP (Prahalad and Hart 2002).

With this changing landscape in mind, a group of individuals (which included the authors) came together in April 2011 to create an innovation ecosystem in India to accelerate the number and increase the success rate of BoP and "green leap" ventures: the incubation today of the environmentally sustainable and socially inclusive businesses of tomorrow (Hart 2011). The new initiative was called Emergent Institute, with the bold vision of being the "breeding ground for tomorrow's sustainable industries and companies". Emergent initially sought to work with promising intrapreneurs and entrepreneurs to help them build their ideas into successful BoP ventures.[4]

Emergent aimed to create nothing less than a new model of business education and entrepreneurial training appropriate to the social and environmental challenges of the 21st century. This reflected the belief that the transformation to sustainability was the biggest business challenge—and opportunity—in the history of capitalism. India was the ideal place to launch and base this new institute, given its large population size, sustained economic growth, entrepreneurial culture, poverty and environmental challenges. The vision for Emergent included the following core elements:

- **Integrated model**. Rather than creating a conventional business school with a side-initiative in sustainable enterprise and BoP, we sought instead to build the entire institute around these challenges as articulated above. Our intent was that Emergent serve as a model for institutional innovation in business education throughout the world so that we might better confront the looming challenges in population, poverty and environmental degradation.

- **"Next" practice**. An active research platform was critical to the new institute. However, rather than focusing the research enterprise primarily on the production of scholarly journal articles, we sought instead to foment a new model of action-based, applied research that was embedded in the phenomena. In so doing, our research would focus on the creation of new (next-practice) strategies rather than studies assessing the effectiveness of pre-existing

4 See www.emergentinstitute.com for further details.

models and past behaviours (best-practice). Our focus would be on achieving widespread adoption and impact through practitioner articles, books, blogs, videos and cases.

- **Co-creation**. Rather than working exclusively with people from privileged backgrounds interested in the challenges of poverty and environment, we sought also to engage directly with emerging entrepreneurs from the slums and rural villages. By mixing intrapreneurs from existing companies, both Indian and foreign, with entrepreneurs from poor and under-served communities in India, we would build a spirit of "co-creation" into the institute by design.

- **Locally embedded**. Rather than having the bulk of the training occur on campus with occasional field experiences, we sought instead to create an integrated experience with field-based work in slums and villages as a core part of the model.

- **Local and global**. Rather than building a new institute focused exclusively on the challenges and opportunities in India, we sought to create a locally embedded institution that was also globally connected—to the latest clean technologies, business models and partners. Our aim was to incubate innovation from the bottom up in India, but ultimately to share this learning globally. We sought global thought leadership in this emerging space.

- **Walk the talk**. Rather than creating only another not-for-profit educational institute focused on business and entrepreneurship, we sought also to create a for-profit entity premised on the idea of triple bottom line and win–win. We planned to take equity stakes in the new green leap ventures that we help to create so that the financial success of the institute—and its faculty—was directly tied to the success of the work we did.

6.4 The evolution of the Emergent ecosystem

During the first year of operation in 2012 we worked with seven ventures: five were led by corporate intrapreneurs and two were start-ups led by young entrepreneurs. Six of them were at the ideation stage and one in pilot. As we worked with these seven enterprises (spanning the healthcare, nutrition, industrial manufacturing and agri-products industries) for the entire course of the year, it proved to be a tremendous learning opportunity for us as well as the enterprises. The cohort included enterprises such as Udyogini, an NGO with an impressive record of building a network of more then 20,000 indigenous women-led micro-enterprises in rural India, now looking to spin off a business focused on the indigenous production of lac[5]

---

5 A resinous substance secreted by lac insects used in manufacture of shellac and other products.

into a for-profit enterprise. It also included multinational companies such as Novo Nordisk, which was piloting an integrated approach to diabetes diagnosis, treatment and prevention for the under-served BoP communities in Bihar, India.

While both ventures had very different DNA, surprisingly, both faced very similar roadblocks and challenges: long cycles of establishing the necessary partnerships and collaborations to make the enterprise both socially and financially viable. Indeed, interdependence and integration risks contributed to significant delays (Adner 2006). We soon realized that to effectively drive BoP market creation and accelerate the growth and success of ventures such as the Udyogini spin-off and the Novo Nordisk BoP initiative, we had to assemble an "innovation ecosystem" composed of several interrelated "puzzle pieces" (Figure 6.1). We identified the critical components and started building each one from the ground up. Each is described in more detail below.

Figure 6.1 **The Emergent innovation ecosystem**

6.4.1 Emergent Accelerator

The Emergent Accelerator focused on the actual development and launch of new, disruptively innovative BoP ventures and corporate initiatives. It was designed to empower and enable entrepreneurs and intrapreneurs to create the inclusive and sustainable enterprises of tomorrow, rather than manage the existing businesses of today. While basic business literacy was necessary, it was by no means sufficient.

Thus, rather than placing emphasis on functional skills and the management of existing businesses, Emergent's Accelerator focused on the next-generation knowledge, skill, and capability crucial to success in incubating clean technologies in under-served communities at the BoP. This included classroom- and field-based education and experience in tools such as participatory methods, deep dialogue, co-creation and business model innovation. The Accelerator also included mentorship and field support for the new BoP ventures and initiatives as they developed in real time.

6.4.2 Cluster Networks

Since no venture or entrepreneur can successfully launch a new BoP business alone, the Emergent Cluster Networks served as social affinity groups for cross-sectoral stakeholders in search of a sustainable solution to a particular problem. The stakeholders included, but were not limited to, entrepreneurs, corporations, government agencies, financiers and NGOs. The power of the Cluster Network lay in the fact that different actors could come together to address different needs associated with a common challenge. From food security, to energy, to building sustainable housing for the urban poor, Emergent convened the actors necessary for building effective value propositions and business ecosystems around new BoP ventures.

6.4.3 Green leap Technology Bank

Many organizations, corporations and research universities today possess substantial stocks of unused (or at least uncommercialized) clean technology literally "sitting on the shelf" (shelf technology). Frequently, these technologies are disruptive to current core businesses, are not suited to current served markets, or at least do not fit easily into existing business models.

According to a United States Patent and Trademark Office (USPTO) report, more than 3 million technology patents have been granted globally in the last 25 years, 52% of which have originated in the United States. It is estimated that around 90–95% of all patents are idle or sitting on the shelf. Both corporations and research universities therefore possess enormous stocks of under-used intellectual property. Some of these technologies may have commercial potential if viewed through a different lens—the lens of new enterprise creation focused on the vast under-served space at the base of the income pyramid.

To be effective, however, these green shelf technologies need to be optimized in new and unexpected ways, based on experience on the ground in actual under-served communities. The technology and the business model must co-evolve as the process of commercialization unfolds. Emergent Institute partnered with Cornell University to identify and help commercialize some of these technologies. This resulted initially in the creation of an inventory of more than 40 technologies that were originally intended for an up-market, developed world use but found applicability in under-served communities in India.

The objective was to continue to build this inventory into a green leap Technology Bank with shelf technology from both universities and corporations to enable entrepreneurs with local insights to apply them in under-served settings.

6.4.4 Emergent Seed Fund

The Emergent Seed Fund was designed to provide start-up capital to the promising entrepreneurs engaged in the Accelerator who needed funding to validate their business models. It is estimated that more than 70% of BoP ventures struggle at this stage and require financial and operational support. The Seed Fund sought to fill the existing gaps in the system, which include the right talent, training, development process, branding, and marketing. The Seed Fund was thus designed to take selected BoP/green leap ventures from the Accelerator to the next level, as part of the complete innovation ecosystem being assembled at Emergent Institute. The Seed Fund also looked to invest in some of the technologies from the green leap Technology Bank, which were in the proof of concept stage in order to make them "commercializeable" through the Accelerator Program.

6.4.5 Entrepreneur network

A key part of the vision at Emergent was to nurture entrepreneurs from underserved communities. We sought to develop passionate and capable individuals who were determined to create solutions to the most pressing societal needs in low-income markets, to create jobs in their communities and to bring about transformational change. As we set out to find these entrepreneurs, we soon realized there was a shortage of individuals who fitted this description and the "pipeline" was slowing drying out. Before we could nurture, we had to identify and develop potential entrepreneurs. We had to build a sustainable entrepreneurship ladder.

We knew we lacked the expertise and capabilities at Emergent to build this ladder from the ground up. Reaching remote geographies, understanding cultural sensitivities, overcoming language barriers, influencing and changing mind-sets and then identifying potential entrepreneurs seemed a mammoth undertaking. Emergent therefore decided to team up with appropriate partners on the ground that could help us build the pipeline (Figure 6.2).

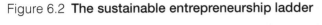

Figure 6.2 **The sustainable entrepreneurship ladder**

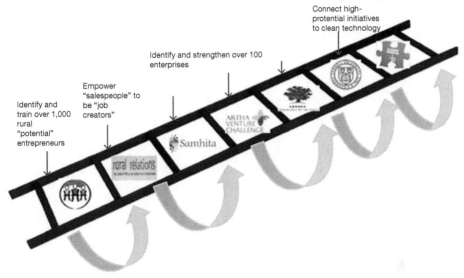

Partners such as Rural Relations and Head Held High, who had pioneered innovative training programmes to build self-confidence, knowledge and skills of youth in far-flung villages across India, were sought to help identify high potential entrepreneurs from their networks. Other partners such as Samhita, Artha Venture Partners and Ashoka had the capability to help pilot and support enterprises led by these entrepreneurs. And as noted above, technology transfer offices in universities such as the Center for Technology Licensing at Cornell University had hundreds of technologies that could be applied to some of these enterprises. Thus, the ladder was being built to create the necessary pipeline of entrepreneurs for the emergent Accelerator.

6.4.6 Action research

Finally, Emergent sought to foment a new model of action-based, applied research that was embedded in the phenomena, as noted in the previous section. Such action-based research helped to make the faculty and staff at Emergent ideal consultants and mentors for both the entrepreneurs and corporate intrapreneurs.

6.5 Lessons learned

In spite of identifying and operationalizing the necessary puzzle pieces critical to the BoP/green leap innovation ecosystem, Emergent Institute saw only modest success in the early days. Another ten ventures were selected into the Accelerator in the next year (2013) and the necessary puzzle pieces were being animated to support the ventures. Today, out of the 17 total ventures, eight are operational or have evolved into viable ventures. These eight ventures have a strong value proposition on multiple fronts, and all have a leadership team that has been able to build successful collaboration both internally as well as externally. These ventures have also been successful in securing resources to stay operational and not succumb to "pilotitis", the disease that stunts the growth of ventures such that they remain at the pilot stage indefinitely. While 8 out of 17 represents a high success rate in the field of entrepreneurship, the question still arises as to why the others fizzled out in a year.

It would be easy to blame it on the business climate in India. After all, out of 189 countries ranked by the World Bank, India, the world's largest democracy (slated to be the next manufacturing powerhouse), is way down on the list at 142 in terms of ease of doing business.[6] Still, the Indian economy has grown rapidly in the last 20 years, since the reform process began in 1991. The size of the Union (federal) Government's budget has grown fivefold in that time. Vast (and increasing) sums of money are being spent by the government on education, infrastructure, health and public employment programmes. Increasingly, the responsibility for managing these expenditures is being devolved to local government officials across India, partly in an attempt to reduce "leakage" of funds through corruption as funds are transmitted from higher levels.

However, most local government officials, especially at the village council level (Panchayats) have no background in governance, management or finance. There is a pressing need to educate them in these and related areas to improve the quality of local governance in India as the responsibilities of local government continue to grow. Indeed, Emergent sought to add a Panchayat Development Program to its innovation ecosystem, but a lack of political support at the state level prevented this programme from going forward. Despite this failure, including government, especially local government, in the innovation ecosystem appears to be critical to success.

In addition, the recent passage of a provision mandating that companies spend 2% of average net profit on corporate social responsibility (CSR) activities has sparked significant debate and action on CSR and sustainability in India. However, most businesses have failed to seize this opportunity: myopic vision, a need for quick wins, failure to collaborate, lack of a visionary champion, "herd mentality" and fear of leading the way have all been barriers in our experience with Indian companies and Indian subsidiaries of multinational companies.

Rather than using this new CSR law to fuel the creation of new inclusive and sustainable business experiments, most Indian corporates have instead simply allocated the necessary funds to the corporate foundation or donated the money to NGOs—effectively separating their core business operations from the challenges of poverty and environment. CSR has thus been framed more as a compliance act than

6 http://www.doingbusiness.org/data/exploreeconomies/india.

an innovation opportunity. In fact, eight out of nine ventures at Emergent that failed to launch were corporate initiatives. There is still much work to be done to enable corporations to effectively realize the opportunity at the base of the income pyramid.

Indeed, one of the other key reasons why the corporate intrapreneurs saw minimal success was that they were typically lone mavericks in behemoth systems and did not have the necessary internal support to effectively build the venture. The champion for these intrapreneurs was usually a senior executive who had often failed to build the necessary support coalition or create the necessary "white space" to protect the fledgling venture. Creating cross-functional teams and identifying champions across the organization willing and able to protect such BoP ventures thus appears to be key to success.

A final recurring challenge was the resource commitment required for a BoP venture to flourish in a large company. Tinkering on the side after hours, cobbling together expertise wherever the intrapreneur can find it in the company, and force-fitting "innovation" into the existing structure were all detrimental to success. Indeed, without empowering intrapreneurs to function with a different set of metrics and incentives, the possibility of building BoP ecosystems within existing large corporations will remain elusive. Companies need to invest in dedicated resources over a three- to five-year window to allow the venture the time to develop the value proposition and full ecosystem needed to be successful—and transformational— over the long term.

6.6 Conclusions

Despite its tragic reversal of fortune, CleanStar Mozambique (CSM) provided a dramatic illustration—and model—for the type of wide value proposition and innovation ecosystem required to succeed at the base of the income pyramid. The company included partnerships with Novozymes, ICM, Bank of America Merrill Lynch, Soros Economic Development Fund and IFU.[7]

The CSM ecosystem sought to: (1) Bring clean cooking solutions that eliminated indoor air pollution in urban households, which were (2) Fuelled by affordable biofuel, which was (3) Produced in rural Mozambique by subsistence farmers who (4) Converted to a multi-crop system of sustainable agriculture, which (5) Dramatically raised farmers' incomes and food security while (6) Producing excess cassava, which was used as the feedstock in the (7) Bio-refinery that was constructed near the small city of Beira, which (8) Had the potential to dramatically reduce the production of charcoal used in cookstoves, which (9) Accounted for a significant share of the deforestation and greenhouse gas emissions in the region. This is an innovation ecosystem for inclusive and sustainable business!

7 Parts of this concluding section are adapted from Hart 2012.

However, conventional wisdom would suggest that CSM was too complicated and had too many moving parts to be successful. But this conventional wisdom comes from the established markets at the top of the pyramid. Indeed, this was the logic for later "focusing" the venture solely on cookstoves and fuel—which ultimately led to its demise. Such logic does not apply when it comes to the BoP. The truth is that natural systems are complex but resilient at the same time: stress in one part of the system can be compensated for in other parts. The whole is greater than the sum of the parts.

Building innovation ecosystems for inclusive and sustainable business is therefore crucially important for the successful development and scaling of BoP enterprise everywhere in the world. The early experience with the Emergent Institute in India suggests that it is possible to construct such ecosystem incubators and support systems, despite significant structural barriers and roadblocks. Let us now aim to take this to the next level in the years ahead.

Bibliography

Adner, R. (2006) "Match Your Innovation Strategy to Your Innovation Ecosystem", *Harvard Business Review*, 83.4: 98-107.

Flader, S. (1974) *Thinking Like a Mountain: Aldo Leopold and the Evolution of an Ecological Attitude toward Deer, Wolves, and Forests* (Columbia, MO: University of Missouri Press).

Hammond, A. (2011) "BoP Venture Formation for Scale", in T. London and S. Hart (eds.) *Next Generation Business Strategies for the Base of the Pyramid* (Upper Saddle River, NJ: Financial Times Press).

Hart, S.L. (2010) *Capitalism at the Crossroads* (Upper Saddle River, NJ: Wharton School Publishing, 3rd edn).

Hart, S.L. (2011) "Taking the Green Leap to the Base of the Pyramid", in T. London and S. Hart (eds.) *Next Generation Business Strategies for the Base of the Pyramid* (Upper Saddle River, NJ: Financial Times Press).

Hart, S.L. (2012) "Create Business Ecosystem: Think Like a Mountain", Voice of the Planet (blog), 20 November 2012, http://stuartlhart.com/blog/2012/11/create-a-business-ecosystem-think-like-a-mountain.html, accessed 7 February 2015.

ITU (2014) *Measuring the Information Society Report* (Geneva: International Telecommunication Union, http://www.itu.int/en/ITU-D/Statistics/Documents/publications/mis2014/MIS2014_without_Annex_4.pdf, accessed 7 February 2015).

Khanna, T., and K. Palepu (1997) "Why Focused Strategies May Be Wrong for Emerging Markets", *Harvard Business Review* 75: 41-54.

Leopold, A. (1949) *A Sand County Almanac* (New York: Oxford University Press).

London, T. (2015) *Fulfilling the Base of the Pyramid Promise* (Palo Alto, CA: Stanford University Press).

Novozymes (2014) "NewFire Africa Files for Voluntary Liquidation", 20 June 2014, http://www.novozymes.com/en/news/news-archive/Pages/NewFire-Africa-files-for-voluntary-liquidation.aspx, accessed 7 February 2015.

Prahalad, C.K., and S.L. Hart (2002) "The Fortune at the Bottom of the Pyramid", *Strategy+Business* 26: 54-67.

Schumpeter, J. (1942) *Capitalism, Socialism, and Democracy* (New York: Harper and Brothers).

Simanis, E. (2012) "Reality Check at the Bottom of the Pyramid", *Harvard Business Review* 90.6: 120-125.

Part IV
Market access for all
Solving the distribution challenge

7

The last mile
A challenge and an opportunity

Edgard Barki
FGV-EAESP, Brazil

There are many challenges in accessing the base of the pyramid. Most of this population is found in rural areas or in places that are difficult to reach and sometimes even dangerous. Moreover, infrastructure and modern retailing are not always available. It is therefore very important to find new ways to reach this population. Innovation, partnerships and efficiency in the distribution strategy are some of the possible approaches to access this market. Furthermore, distribution is key to offering the population access to basic services, reducing its vulnerability.

Access has been one of the main difficulties companies have faced in emerging markets (Prahalad 2005). The capillarity and extension of the market, the existence of small, non-professionalized and sometimes informal retailers, the lack of infrastructure and high transportation costs are some of the distribution challenges companies face in poorer regions.

If the challenges are huge, the opportunities are also enormous. Many examples around the world show that success in distribution is associated with innovation, partnership and relationship. Some companies are able to create innovative solutions to access the bottom of the pyramid (BoP) market, offering a more suitable service for the population and creating a competitive advantage in a clear win–win proposition.

However, local organizations often have a competitive advantage over multinational companies (MNCs). Even large companies with intensive distribution have a hard time reaching the BoP because of the several obstacles faced in emerging markets.

The difficulties in reaching the BoP population have been studied since at least the 1940s. The fact that low-income people usually buy from small and inefficient retailers in the community is one of the main reasons for the poverty penalty, which means that besides being poor, this population pays more for the same products. If it were possible to create a more efficient distribution network, BoP consumers could get basic products at a better price, diminishing the poverty penalty.

Moreover, distribution might also be a bottleneck for offering basic services such as health and education. Basic needs are not always accessible for the BoP population at the right place, at the right moment and with high quality.

This chapter is therefore divided into eight sections. The first describes some of the most important challenges organizations face in emerging markets. The second discusses the competition between large and local companies in the distribution arena. The third, fourth and fifth sections identify some solutions to overcome these obstacles, focusing on innovation, partnerships and efficiency. The sixth section presents the relevance of retail as a platform for distribution and the seventh discusses the importance of distribution for access to basic services. Lastly, the eighth part highlights some final considerations.

7.1 Challenges of the last mile

Emerging markets have many peculiarities and differences between countries. As a simple example, while 85% of the Brazilian population lives in urban areas, in India this drops to 32%.[1] Even within one country there are huge differences in income and infrastructure availability; therefore, a solution for one locality might not be feasible in another place. The distribution strategy has to be defined according to the needs, resources and conditions of each area.

One of the challenges in some emerging markets is to reach the rural population. Usually this population is scattered, has a lower formal education and is difficult to reach by modern retailing, and therefore different marketing channels should be used. One of the most famous concepts is door-to-door distribution as it was developed by Unilever in India or Grameen Danone in Bangladesh.

However, door-to-door is not a simple and cheap channel. It needs a complex organization to hire, train and develop salespeople. The logistics are also complicated. For instance, in the case of Unilever in India, salespeople sometimes had one year of income as inventory in their houses.

---

1 Source: World Bank indicators for 2012 at http://data.worldbank.org/indicator/SP.URB.TOTL.IN.ZS, accessed 3 March 2014.

Even in urban areas some difficulties in approaching the BoP arise. Although not scattered, a great number of people live in slums. These neighbourhoods have their own logic and sometimes their own law. If an organization wants to enter a slum, it has to have permission from the community. For safety reasons, organizations do not often enter slums, and if they do, it is only during predetermined hours of the day. Moreover, as the streets are narrow, organizations need to have a specific fleet. Safety concerns are not restricted to slums. There are certain routes for which it is difficult to find drivers to deliver products, owing to the lack of safety.

One characteristic of emerging markets is the lower concentration of modern retailing and the predominance of small traditional shops. On one side this is positive: there are many small entrepreneurs that survive through owning those shops. On the other side, the capillarity of those stores and their informality and lack of professionalism usually make it difficult to create more efficient distribution. Furthermore, there is a tendency in emerging markets to have a longer marketing channel. To reach more distant, difficult or unsafe places, manufacturers sell to wholesalers, who sell to mini-wholesalers and these to smaller wholesalers or distributors until the products reach the small retailers. Besides that, in emerging markets, the infrastructure is another obstacle. Damaged roads, deficiency in energy supply and old technology are some of the difficulties organizations face.

All the characteristics discussed in this section—scattered population, unsafe neighbourhoods, lack of infrastructure and channel length—make the cost of delivering products higher in emerging markets, which increases the transaction costs and puts more pressure on the poverty penalty. Alternatives to reduce these transaction costs and increase efficiency are needed to diminish the cost of being poor and to create possibilities of access to basic needs and services.

7.2 Competition between MNCs and small companies

In a first approach to reach emerging markets, many MNCs failed. Although they had good business models and good products, there was still something missing: full understanding of the importance of relationship and the difficulty of access with the right product, at the right time and with the right price for BoP communities.

Countless MNCs have encountered fierce competitors in emerging markets. These competitors were not necessarily large companies or emerging giants (Khanna and Palepu 2006). On the contrary, they were small companies from the BoP that had some important competitive advantages. Although not having products with higher quality, these companies usually had good prices and, more importantly, an excellent distribution strategy. Four aspects can better explain the appropriateness of their business model:

- **Cost structure.** As small manufacturers are close to their market they do not need great investments to deliver their merchandise. These companies might even deliver in their own car rather than investing in drivers, insurance or new trucks.

- **Logistics.** Although small manufacturers do not have a high investment in logistics, they are able to maintain good logistics because of their proximity to the market. In that way, if a small retailer is missing a product, the manufacturer might deliver on the same day without any bureaucracy.

- **Flexibility.** Small companies are flexible. Besides their flexibility in delivery, these companies are flexible in commercial policies. For example, small manufacturers will sometimes accept third-party cheques from small retailers. Moreover, if the retailer has some difficulties, small manufacturers may be understanding and give more time for the retailer to pay. This would be very difficult with a large company.

- **Relationship.** The flexibility pointed to before comes from the relationship built between parties. The small manufacturers and small retailers are very close. It is common for them to join in the same celebrations. In the same way, small retailers have a good relationship with consumers. Most of the time they know their names and can talk about personal matters.

7.3 Innovation in distribution

Innovation is usually related to new products and services. However, the distribution challenges that emerging markets pose demand innovative models to reach customers. Organizations have to think outside the box to access BoP populations.

For instance, in Africa it is difficult for the population to access banks, and most citizens do not have bank accounts. One interesting initiative to overcome this obstacle is mobile banking. As most of the population has a mobile phone, one solution for the unbanked is to create a service in which people can access some bank services by mobile phone. It is possible to make money transfers and pay bills through the mobile in a simple way. To create this service, organizations such as Safaricom and Wizzit have to use high technology and be cost effective.

In Brazil the dilemma of the unbanked population is similar. However, instead of creating mobile banking, finance organizations developed correspondent banking, where it is possible to offer banking services in small grocery stores or drugstores in places where there is not a bank branch. Through that service, the population has access to almost all the services of a bank and the small retailers have a differential to offer to their clients.

Those innovations might appear to be similar to the concept of reverse innovation, which brings the idea of developing products in emerging countries and then distributing them globally (Govindarajan and Trimble 2012). However, instead of thinking of new products, the idea here is how new distribution models might be a success in emerging markets and afterwards how these models might be used in the developed world.

Innovation does not necessarily mean using technology. Some companies innovate using different means to reach the consumer. Door-to-door is an example. Although this model is not new, and has been used for years, mainly by cosmetic companies, the novelty is its use by other sectors. Nestlé in Brazil, Hindustan Lever in India and Grameen Danone in Bangladesh are some examples of MNCs using this model for different kinds of product.

Nestlé has a project in Brazil called "Nestlé até Você"[2] that aims to reach the BoP population in scattered places through door-to-door selling. In 2013, the company had almost 8,000 people selling their products in the outskirts of many cities, reaching more than 250,000 households every fortnight. The products are not sold individually, but in small kits. Nestlé also has a boat that crosses the Amazon river and reaches small communities. One criticism of this last initiative is that, instead of encouraging the local economy, the boat takes the money from the municipalities to Nestlé, instead of stimulating transactions inside the city. Some banks such as Bradesco and Caixa Econômica also use boats to offer their services in the Amazon.

In the same way, Hindustan Lever (HUL) has the Shakti Project in India in order to reach small rural communities. The project started in a few pilot villages in Andhra Pradesh in 2000. In 2012, the programme had 45,000 Shakti women entrepreneurs across 15 states in India. Although it has had some success, the turnover of the women who sell the products is very high, owing to the lack of embeddedness created throughout the programme (Simanis 2012).

The criticisms of those initiatives lead to new approaches with a higher social impact. Besides its innovative perspective, another important element is the concept of partnerships and embeddedness presented in the next section.

7.4 Partnerships and embeddedness

Some researchers (Austin 2002; Brugmann and Prahalad 2007) have discussed the evolution in the relationship between private enterprise and non-governmental organizations (NGOs). If some decades ago organizations on both sides appeared to be enemies, in recent years a greater coming together can be perceived. NGOs might use the managerial competences of companies, which in their term can understand the goals and the strong relationship that NGOs have with some communities.

For distribution, these partnerships are very important, since they create the possibility of engaging in a different kind of relationship that is much more embedded.

2 "Nestlé up to you", https://www.nestle.com.br/portalnestle/nestleatevoce/Default.aspx.

For the NGOs these partnerships might be important to help them to achieve their goals. While on the other side, large companies might achieve the means to create a differentiated relationship with the communities.

For instance, in Brazil, Coca-Cola partnered with two NGOs, Committee for Democratization of Information Systems (CDI) and Visão Mundial, to create the Projeto Coletivo. CDI aims to strengthen low-income communities through information and communication technology, and Visão Mundial works to combat the causes of poverty so that vulnerable populations may reach their full potential. These NGOs have been active in facilitating the operationalization of the project and the interaction of Coca-Cola with communities, identifying social institutions interested in hosting the project.

The purpose of the project is to offer education to young people from low-income communities to help them to get jobs. To achieve that, Coca-Cola also has partnerships with large retailers. More than just a social corporate initiative, Projeto Coletivo also has economic objectives that are measured, such as brand equity and numeric distribution in the regions reached by the programme. Therefore, it is an important initiative to improve distribution in regions that are very difficult for Coca-Cola to access.

Another example of partnership is the case of Grameenphone. On one side, Telenor, the Norwegian telecommunications company, wanted to enter the Bangladeshi market. On the other side, Grameen Bank had the objective of improving its social impact. Both organizations together created Grameenphone, which was operated by experienced Telenor managers with a strategic objective of maximizing financial returns (Seelos and Mair 2007). The technological know-how and managerial expertise of Telenor was crucial in setting up an international mobile phone operation in Bangladesh. The partnership with Grameen provides a presence throughout Bangladesh and a deep understanding of its economy.[3] In 2012, Grameenphone was the largest mobile telecommunications operator in Bangladesh in terms of revenue, coverage and subscriber base.

Both cases show the relevance of partnerships when reaching the BoP population. It is very difficult for a large company to access this population alone. As the consumers are scattered, in unsafe and difficult to reach places, partnerships are essential. In most cases, although large companies have managerial skills, they lack a personal touch with the communities. NGOs and local companies have this potential to get in touch through a differential perspective.

More than just a transactional relationship, it is important to create a partnership that seriously offers both parties a win–win situation. In fact we look for the "triple win" proposition, in which the partners win, because they are better able to reach their economic and social objectives, the consumers win because they have access to products and services in a more efficient way, diminishing the poverty penalty, and society as a whole wins owing to the social impacts created by these initiatives.

---

3 http://grameenphone.com, accessed 17 December 2012.

7.5 Efficiency in distribution

As in any market, efficiency in distribution is very relevant to reaching the BoP. The main difference is the complexity of this distribution in a multi-strand, non-structured and informal market. At the BoP, distribution has different contextual conditions that push for an even higher efficiency.

Owing to the obstacles, it is often more expensive and more difficult to get into these markets consistently, with the right frequency and still giving support to developing the marketing channel. Therefore, execution is an important resource to create competitive advantage within distribution strategies. As an executive declared during research carried out by the author:

> When you ask the small retailer what are the main attributes of a good seller, he will answer that firstly is the friendship with the salesperson. Secondly, it is the delivery. Sometimes we can understand delivery as punctuality and in other cases delivery of products in good conditions. Lastly, there are the financial conditions (pers. comm. 2010).

The main dimensions that define an efficient distribution are logistics, cost structure, sales structure and commercial policies.

7.5.1 Logistics

The capillarity of BoP markets intensifies the importance of efficient logistics. Moreover, small, distant retailers usually buy small portions and limited numbers of units of products. Manufacturers try to reach some far locations in a hostile transportation infrastructure that makes costs high and delivery late. Companies that access BoP markets also have to know exactly which are the unsafe places where they cannot go, or the right time when they can enter a slum.

Partnerships might help also in this issue. The point here is to identify which distributors or local partners can offer a better delivery. Even companies that usually have intensive distribution and deliver directly to the whole market have to use wholesalers and distributors to reach the small retailer in these BoP regions. In some remote places, companies are not able to deliver their products at all and the retailer is obliged to travel and buy stock in a larger city.

Besides being able to reach those places, companies with good distribution are able to access the market fast. In other words, how can a company deliver small orders in a reasonable timing? Large manufacturers have a very tough time accomplishing that.

7.5.2 Sales structure

Salespeople from companies operating at the BoP have to approach small retailers where people tend to lack formal education and so the situation demands simple communication. Sometimes salespeople with a high educational background are not able to talk the same language as these small retailers, who feel more comfortable with "people like them". Furthermore, as small retailers are scattered, each region or each community has its own language codes. It is therefore preferable to have salespeople from the community who might have a similar level of formal education as the small retailers. This allows greater empathy and it becomes easier to build a friendly relationship. Thus, the sales structure should consider this type of salesperson profile. This idea is similar to one of the principles Prahalad (2005) proposes for developing new products for BoP markets. According to him, the lack of formal education demands simplified work for the employees. Even though this idea was related to product development, it can be transposed to sales management. This is an important issue that might create a social benefit to the communities.

As trust depends on the timing of operation and the relationship with salespeople, successful companies try to motivate salespeople and to avoid high turnover as much as possible. Therefore, engaged employees who feel valued might be a source of competitive advantage.

7.5.3 Cost structure

As low income has, by definition, a limited budget, it is important to be cost effective to be competitive in the market. To reach the BoP it is not necessary to have the best price, but the market demands a cost-effective structure. The management of the cost structure is another challenge. To distribute to BoP markets, companies need to distribute their products in an environment of informality with a lack of infrastructure. Therefore margins are low and costs have to be kept under control.

Both logistic efficiency and cost structure are related to the argument that poor people pay more for the same products. The hurdle of infrastructure and access difficulties makes the BoP market less efficient and, consequently, low-income consumers pay the poverty penalty.

Furthermore, as the cost to serve small retailers is high, mainly when a company operates nationally, it is harder for some categories to operate efficiently in low-income markets due to their small margins. In these cases, regional and local companies are a great threat.

7.5.4 Commercial policies

Commercial policies play a key role in distribution. There are many facets to building strong commercial policies. We describe below two of the main important issues when defining commercial policies for BoP.

7.5.4.1 Credit

Credit is an essential tool for any market growth. It helps in the cash flow of the retailers and allows the availability of a larger assortment. In BoP markets, credit has another important role in financial education. If the credit is given for a short term, the retailer is unable to repay. However, if the term is too long, it is very possible that the retailer will use the money from the products for other personal needs, and he will not have money to purchase again the product he needs to supply his inventory. Therefore, credit can be a source of help to a non-professionalized and unqualified small retailer who still needs support to run his or her business. The credit has to be given for the right term for the small retailer to sell, receive and pay; otherwise the money will be mixed up with personal needs. Credit done well helps the small retailers' survival.

If we think about selling products directly to the consumers, credit is also very important because it allows them to purchase. If a low-income consumer is not able to buy a television for $300, he might pay it in many instalments with a much lower cost. Two criticisms are always made of this. The first is that consumers might be buying superfluous products, instead of focusing on more basic ones such as food and clothes. However, some researchers present the perspective of the consumer in which he or she considers a television as more important than food on some occasions (see, e.g. Banerjee and Duflo 2011). The second criticism is the ethical issue of charging interest rates to the poor. Again, many authors have already discussed the importance of the interest rates for the survival of organizations (e.g. Novogratz 2009) and that often consumers choose to get credit with interest rates, even though there were available options without it, due to unreliability, lack of privacy and lack of transparency (Collins *et al.* 2009).

7.5.4.2 Flexibility

Commercial policies are important for creating rules to be followed and often offer a fairer policy among partners. Nevertheless, sometimes they can be a straitjacket that inhibits new opportunities. When selling to BoP markets a higher degree of flexibility is required in order to meet the daily challenges of cash-flow planning. Sometimes it is important to have flexibility in the repayment conditions for credit or flexibility to allow a delivery rescheduling. Moreover, this flexibility might create a sense of trust and a more empathic relationship. This is not naivety, but just a way to understand the difficulties and needs of this market. This flexibility is valid for direct and indirect sales.

In this aspect, small manufacturers usually have a source of competitive advantage as they are more flexible over payment conditions and in their management of defaulting. Large companies are less flexible and have rigid commercial policies that do not accept delays in payment.

One example of efficient distribution is the Dabbawala organization in Mumbai. This case is unique in both its simplicity and its efficiency, but typical of a business model created by BoP people, mostly illiterate, which works because it generates income and, at the same time, makes workers proud to be part of the organization.

The objective of the *dabbawalas* is to carry and deliver freshly made food from home in lunch boxes to office workers. The *dabbawalas* get the food from the houses of the clients (usually Indian businesspeople) to their work. Between 175,000 and 200,000 lunches get moved every day by an estimated 4,500–5,000 *dabbawalas*, all with an extremely small nominal fee and with utmost punctuality.

The system has many success factors:

- **Simplicity.** Barefoot deliverymen are the prime movers of the meals. The success of the system depends on teamwork and time management. A simple colour-coding system doubles as an ID system for the destination and recipient. There are no multiple elaborate layers of management either—just three tiers.

- **Organizational structure.** Everyone who works within this system is treated as an equal. Regardless of a *dabbawala*'s function, everyone gets paid about two to four thousand rupees per month (around US$40–80).

- **Commitment.** Prince Charles visited them during a trip to India, but even he had to fit in with the *dabbawalas*' schedule, since their timing was too precise to permit any flexibility.

- **Knowledge of the consumers' needs.** Indian people's aversion to Western-style fast food outlets and their love of home-made food.

- **Execution.** The system has almost perfect punctuality and precision. According to one survey (Thomke and Sinha 2010), there is only one mistake in every 6 million deliveries. On average, every box changes hands four times and travels 60–70 km in its journey to reach its eventual destination.

7.6 Retail as a platform

Even though you might have the best technology to sell on-line or a great door-to-door programme, it is difficult to think of a world without retailing. Retail makes part of our daily lives and it is no different for the BoP.

From the rural villages in India to the slums in São Paulo, passing through the small municipalities of the banks of the Amazon or Nile rivers, retail is a place of interaction and an important network node. Besides purchasing, people meet, talk and entertain themselves in retailers. Even though in many instances the shop is no more than a tiny store, retail is much more than a place to buy and sell things.

Usually, in small towns shops do not have specialized positioning. On the contrary, they have a very general proposition, in which it is easy to find a 20 sq. m store that sells food, clothes and home appliances. The concept is to have a large variety to meet the daily needs of the customer.

In the developed world, there is a market to create segmented stores, an extreme example being Rice to Riches in New York, which sells only rice pudding. For the BoP market this is unthinkable; stores are much more general and you are not surprised by a completely irregular and broad assortment. Consequently, small retail might be a good platform for the distribution of any product or service. From soft drinks to banking services, and from clothes to insurance products, these little shops are one of the most important points to introduce and sell products. Moreover, these shops might be an important focus and locus for communicating with the community.

On the other hand, these shops present some challenges for manufacturers. The concepts of category management, positioning and marketing experience are difficult to be implemented for those retailers. Sometimes soap might be sold on the same shelf as meat. Therefore, those companies concerned with their product display and positioning should define a model that includes visiting those retailers with frequency and, more importantly, educating them in basic management principles.

7.7 Importance of distribution to give access to basic service

Distribution is not only important to offer access to products. It might also have an important role in allowing access to basic services such as health and education. One of the greatest dilemmas when dealing with poverty is how to enhance the freedom of the population (Sen 1999). Indeed, the BoP suffers from a lack of opportunities and access to opportunities to meet basic needs.

Although governments have an important role in this issue, the discussion here is how the private sector might complement those services with a good value proposition and in an efficient way. There are countless cases that innovate in product/ services operation so as to offer these services, such as Jaipur Foot, Embrace and Aravind,[4] to name just three. However, besides product innovation, there is usually a need to give access to the population, because often it is very difficult, if not impossible, for them to go to the service provider.

One interesting possibility for dealing with this problem is to use the concept of franchising, which enables a greater reach. One example is the HealthStore Foundation, which aims to improve access to essential drugs, basic healthcare and prevention services for children and families in the developing world using business models that maintain standards, are geographically scalable and achieve economies of scale. As it says on its website:

> The HealthStore Foundation has combined established micro-enterprise principles with proven franchise business practices to create a micro-franchise business model called CFWshops. Franchisees operate small drug shops or clinics strategically located to improve access to essential drugs. HealthStore clinics and shops enable trained health workers to operate their own businesses treating the diseases that cause 70–90% of illness and death in their communities while following HealthStore drug handling and distribution regulations calculated to ensure good practice.[5]

4 Jaipur: http://jaipurfoot.org/; Embrace: http://embraceglobal.org/; Aravind: http://www.aravind.org/.
5 http://www.cfwshops.org/, accessed 17 December 2012.

Besides improving access to essential drugs, the model provides economic benefits for the microfranchisee, who enjoys the benefits of owning a valuable profit-making business.

Another example in the health sector is Sorridents. Founded in São Paulo, Brazil, in 1995, the company is considered to be the largest dental clinic in Latin America, with more than 180 units in Brazil in 2013. The main goal of the organization is to offer access to oral health, with good quality and affordable prices. To scale its distribution, the company also decided to use the franchising model, ensuring quality in all the clinics. Its goal is to offer all dental treatments in one place, with safety, comfort and convenience.

Distribution might also enable scale for education services. After all, one of the main questions is how to scale a good education platform, and distribution is again a bottleneck. One possibility for solving this problem is the use of technology. If it is difficult to take the students to a school, it might be interesting to take the school to the students. That might be impossible in the real world, but technology might help to make it happen.

This is the case, for instance, of the social business Geekie. The company, founded in 2012 by two young Brazilians, offers a platform of education based on technology in which it is possible to personalize the whole process, since the education is based on the characteristics of each person, which are learnt by the interactions of the student with the website. With the information, each student has a unique experience, according to his or her profile and objectives. The content presentation, exercises, revisions and other elements are therefore defined in such a way that all can develop their maximum potential.[6]

7.8 Final considerations

Distribution is one bottleneck in reaching BoP markets and understanding its challenges and defining the best solutions and strategies are essential to be successful. Despite the challenges, some organizations are able to create a competitive advantage through innovation and partnerships. The main points when developing a strategy are to think outside the box and innovate, to create partnerships and embedded relationships and to seriously seek efficiency through all the steps of the process.

Because of differences in infrastructure, channel design and location of the population, it is necessary to design new ways to reach the population. Here we can perceive the strength of the concept of reverse innovation. Technology might be one solution for delivering services. Using simple but efficient means to reach the population, for example, boats on the Amazon, is also an innovative solution.

6 www.geekie.com.br.

The difficulty in accessing the BoP population creates the need to develop partnerships. It is very hard for an organization to get into the communities alone. Partnerships with local players and NGOs might facilitate the process. Moreover, developing a close and embedded relationship directly with the communities is a source of competitive advantage and it provides the possibilities to develop successful business models.

Finally, as the margins are low and one of the objectives is to reduce the poverty penalty, efficiency in this distribution is a must. Organizations have to carefully evaluate the logistics, sales structure, cost structure and commercial policies. These are basic dimensions that make the difference when developing a distribution strategy.

When thinking about distribution, people usually think about delivering products. However, when talking about the BoP population, it is important to consider basic services such as health and education. After all, these are the services for which the population has the most important needs and reaching this population with good-quality, on-time services makes all the difference. Therefore, creating mechanisms to offer these services through different platforms is a way of giving not only access, but also capacity and freedom.

Bibliography

Austin, J. (2002) *The Collaboration Challenge: How Nonprofits and Businesses Succeed Through Strategic Alliances* (San Francisco: Jossey-Bass).

Banerjee, A., and E. Duflo (2011) *Poor Economics: A Radical Rethinking of the Way to Fight Global Poverty* (New York: Public Affairs).

Brugmann, J., and C.K. Prahalad (2007) "Cocreating Business's New Social Compact", *Harvard Business Review*, February: 80-90.

Collins, D., J. Morduch, S. Rutherford and O. Ruthven (2009) *Portfolios of the Poor: How the World´s Poor Live on $2 a Day* (Oxford: Princeton University Press).

Govindarajan, V., and C. Trimble (2012) *Reverse Innovation: Create Far From Home, Win Everywhere* (Boston, MA: Harvard Business School Press).

Khanna, T., and K.G. Palepu (2006) "Emerging Giants. Building World-Class Companies in Developing Countries", *Harvard Business Review* 84.10: 60-69.

Novogratz, J. (2009) *The Blue Sweater: Bridging the Gap between Rich and Poor in an Interconnected World* (New York: Rodale).

Prahalad, C.K. (2005) *The Fortune at the Bottom of the Pyramid: Eradicating Poverty Through Profits* (Upper Saddle River, NJ: Prentice Hall).

Seelos, C., and J. Mair (2007) "Profitable Business Models and Market Creation in the Context of Deep Poverty: A Strategic View", *Academy of Management Perspectives* 21.4: 49-63.

Sen, A. (1999) *Development as Freedom* (New York: Alfred Knopf).

Simanis, E. (2012) "Reality Check at the Bottom of the Pyramid", *Harvard Business Review* 90.6: 120-25.

Thomke, S.H., and M. Sinha (2010) "The Dabbawala System: On-Time Delivery, Every Time", *Harvard Business School Case* 610-059, February.

8

A shared-channel model for BoP access in the Philippines

Markus Dietrich and Jun Tibi

Asian Social Enterprise Incubator, The Philippines

This chapter is based on research undertaken by Asian Social Enterprise Incubator (ASEI) in the Philippines. Working with multilateral agencies, corporates, social enterprise and NGOs, it was realized that distribution to the BoP is, on the one hand, a major challenge for scaling up BoP ventures, and, on the other hand, a major contributor to the BoP penalty. The shared-channel model offers a mode of distribution that appeals to firms as it holds the promise of being a cost-effective way to reach clients. It overcomes the need to build up a sales force, which is a resource-intensive undertaking as the clients live in difficult-to-reach areas. The application of the model will ultimately contribute to a reduction of the BoP penalty. The chapter analyses different shared-channel models and proposes the Shared Channel Assessment Framework (SCAF) for BoP ventures on evaluating and monitoring distribution partnerships.

8.1 Global perspective on the shared-channel model

Corporations, non-governmental organizations (NGOs) and social enterprises are turning their focus on serving the needs of the 4 billion people at the base of the pyramid (BoP). Ideally, these entities engage the BoP in three ways: culturally appropriate, environmentally sustainable and economically profitable (Hart 2008). The attention given to the BoP market is a result of the realization that many needs of those at the BoP are unmet and can be met in a profitable way thus ensuring future growth. Of the three ways of engaging the BoP market identified above, being economically profitable is the most complex.

A study of BoP marketing identified five dimensions that should be understood in serving the untapped markets of the BoP: development, design, distribution, demand and dignity (Bhan 2009). According to the study, companies engaging in the BoP market have to develop products or services that must either fill an "unmet" need or provide a way for them to enhance their livelihood or quality of life. Both of these can only be ensured if the products and services reach the BoP and the last mile can be conquered in an efficient and effective way.

Since infrastructure—the backbones of logistics and transportation—is less developed, innovative distribution becomes a critical factor to reach the BoP. Many companies whose products reach the BoP, such as Coca-Cola, have built their own supply chain. However, most of these companies still do not directly engage the BoP. Products pass through wholesalers and from there move through informal distribution channels to the BoP.

An example is Nokia, which experienced significant success in the vast hinterlands of rural China, which are characterized by uneven development and rudimentary infrastructure. The success can be attributed to local salespeople, who brought the products to the remotest villages to sell. Nokia products were able to reach rural China through this informal (and unexpected) distribution network in addition to the conventional dealers and retailers (Bhan 2009). Those examples indicate that it is possible to reach the BoP at scale through formal and informal channels with innovative models.

8.2 Distribution channels as one of the major challenges in serving the BoP market

Widespread infrastructural constraints prevail in reaching the BoP market in the developing world. These areas are inadequately connected by roads and poorly served by appropriate and affordable transport, which poses a physical barrier to markets (Vachani and Smith 2007). This is one reason why establishing cost-effective distribution channels proves to be a major challenge for companies targeting the BoP market.

Thus, innovative distribution channels are as critical for developing the BoP market as innovations in product and process (Prahalad 2005). To fully exploit this market's potential, companies serving it have to establish distribution channels that work.

Due to the challenging distribution channels, companies consider disruptive ways to reach the BoP market. One emerging practice is establishing common or shared distribution partnerships wherein companies trying to penetrate the BoP market work with organizations that already have an established network in the area. These organizations include corporate partners from another industry, microfinance institutions (MFIs), NGOs, social enterprises and cooperatives.

8.3 Emergence of the shared-channel business model

The Monitor Group, a multinational management consulting firm, conducted a study about emerging markets and identified four business models focused on serving the poor as customers. One of the business models was called "shared channels" (Karamchandani *et al.* 2009).

According to the study, in a shared-channel model, companies piggyback on the distribution channels of other enterprises, thus reducing costs and increasing reach through:

- The use of existing distribution platforms that may already be functioning

- Increased field force responsibility to carry multiple products from a single hub

- Going deeper into the rural areas

- Proper incentives to all participants in the distribution chain

- New alliances to allow specialization by task or capability

As an emerging business model to address the distribution challenges of companies attempting to reach the BoP market, shared channels, according to Monitor, have a high scalability potential as multiple companies can share the costs of distribution that would otherwise be too expensive for any single company. Shared channels also offer the potential to reduce the time and the cost in reaching the market compared to building a distribution channel from scratch.

8.4 Shared-channel model in the Philippines

According to the *Inclusive Business Study: Philippines* commissioned by the Asian Development Bank and conducted by ASEI (Asian Development Bank 2013), only 7% of inclusive businesses in the Philippines engage the BoP as distributors, thus revealing a shortage of established distribution channels that companies use to reach the BoP. In general, the inclusive business sector was found to be in a "nascent state" with only a limited number of companies engaging the BoP as a core business activity. However, the sector is expected to increase with the entry of existing companies into the BoP market and start-up social enterprises.

The proliferation of these companies led to the identification of various distribution challenges. The BoP markets in the Philippines—an archipelago of 7,107 islands—are mostly concentrated in the rural areas; 70% of the poor population resides outside the urban centres. Reaching these areas is one of the distribution challenges that companies need to address.

This is made even more challenging by the underdeveloped infrastructure, particularly in the rural areas. About half of the rural villages in the Philippines lack all-weather access to the main transport system. Only 14% of the road network in the country is paved. Gravel roads make up about 78% of the total network and the rest are earthen roads (Donnges 2006). There is also no efficient inter-island transport system.

8.5 Distribution challenges in the Philippines

Owing to the Philippines' geographical features, distribution channels for the BoP market experience the following challenges:

- Delivery of goods to far-flung areas such as mountain *barangays* (villages) where roads do not exist

- Delivery of services to the same areas where, as well as the lack of roads, there is a lack of facilities for provision of services such as an efficient hospital to provide basic healthcare

- Lack of commercial facilities to support economic activities such as warehouses for safe and efficient distribution, offices for business operations and banks or cash dispensers to conduct financial transactions

- Delivery of products to island-communities where regular water transport services are not yet available

- Where these water transport services are available, most are not conducive to businesses because fares and shipping rates are expensive and schedules are weather-dependent, affecting the timely and cost-efficient delivery of goods and services

- Lack of facilities in remote areas to promote commercial or entrepreneurial endeavours such as power supply, water supply and internet services

8.6 Distribution challenges and the "BoP penalty"

All the distribution challenges contribute to the "BoP penalty". According to the World Resources Institute (Hammond *et al.* 2007) the BoP often pays higher prices for basic goods and services than wealthier consumers, either in financial or transaction costs, and often receives lower quality. The BoP penalty is expressed in multiple forms:

- Lack of access to essential goods and services
- Higher prices for goods and services
- Poor quality of goods and services

An illustration of the BoP penalty is the municipality of Culion in Palawan province. The municipality is composed of 37 islands, with Culion Island the biggest and most inhabited. Most of the basic commodities in Culion are shipped from Manila by boat. A sole shipping line services the Manila–Culion route with trips leaving Manila usually thrice per week. Travel time for this route is two days. The BoP penalty in the pricing of basic commodities for Culion can be as high as 67% as the price comparison between prices in Manila and in Culion in Table 8.1 indicates.

Table 8.1 **Basic commodities price comparison between Manila and Culion**

Basic commodities	Manila	Culion	Difference
Canned sardines, reg. size	12.75	18.00	41.18%
Powdered filled milk, 150 g	48.00	53.00	10.42%
Evaporated filled milk, 370 ml	34.00	43.00	26.47%
Powdered coffee, 50 g	39.00	45.00	15.38%
Detergent/laundry soap, 400 g	43.00	72.00	67.44%
Instant noodles, 55 g	7.00	10.00	42.86%
Vinegar, 350 ml	12.00	16.00	33.33%
Soy sauce, 350 ml	13.00	18.00	38.46%
Toilet soap, 135 g	35.00	40.00	14.29%
Hard flour, 1st class, 25 kg	930.00	1,125.00	20.97%
Soft flour, 3rd class, 25 kg	790.00	950.00	20.25%
Cement, 40 kg	205.00	300.00	46.34%
Kerosene, per litre	47.93	63.49	32.47%
Diesel, per litre	40.00	52.91	32.28%

Notes: Manila prices, with the exception of petroleum products are based on the report on Monitored Prices of Basic Commodities by the Department of Trade and Industry, November 2012; Culion prices are based on actual retail prices as of December 2012. Prices of petroleum products in Manila are based on prevailing retail prices by the Department of Energy, December 2012. Prices in Culion are based on a per US gallon retail volume (1 US gallon is equal to 3.78 litres).

Owing to bad weather, delayed trips of ships and other factors that affect delivery of products, prices in Culion also tend to be volatile when deliveries are delayed and product supplies are running low.

Additionally, Culion has very limited access to basic commodities that require cold-chain logistics and refrigeration. This is due to the limited power supply in the

lso low availability of after-sales services due to Culion's distance
ther urban areas.

8.7 The Shared Channel Assessment Framework (SCAF)

To overcome the distribution challenges four models are employed in the Philippines. First, formal distribution channels such as supermarkets and convenience stores have established supply chains for fast-moving consumer goods, hardware and agricultural supplies. However, their geographical presence is still limited and the focus on fast-moving high-volume goods makes it challenging for distributing products to the BoP market owing to the level of revenues necessary to keep the channel operating. Specific products and services for the BoP also often require substantial consumer awareness raising, which the formal distribution channels are found to be unwilling to undertake.

Direct sales forces, or direct selling, are the second mode of distribution used in the country. Although this is an effective model since direct sellers immediately interact and influence a buyer's decision, it is also a costly undertaking for the company in training, compensation and expenses, further contributing to the BoP penalty for the customers.

Third, multilevel marketing has become popular for specific products such as herbal supplements. However, when used for products aimed at the BoP it was found that the cost of the product increases to untenable levels for the end-user because of the various margins that have to be integrated at the different levels.

Fourth, the shared-channel distribution model is used, which stands out as it addresses some of the shortcomings of the other models. Companies partner with commercial partners, MFIs, NGOs and cooperatives—organizations that have a strong presence in the rural areas—in engaging the BoP market. In the Philippines, especially, there are about 22,000 cooperatives,[1] 330,000 NGOs, and about 15,000 MFIs.[2]

The widespread presence of these organizations and their established network with the BoP enable companies to gain access to the BoP market. Companies can piggyback on the networks of these organizations to deliver their products and services to the BoP market while reducing distribution costs, increasing consumer awareness, improving after-sales services and so on.

Based on ASEI's consulting work and interviews with key stakeholders, the Shared Channel Assessment Framework (SCAF) was developed as a tool for companies in

1 Cooperative Development Authority Masterlist of Cooperatives as of November 2012.
2 Microfinance Sector Data by Microfinance Council of the Philippines as of June 2010; data includes NGOs, banks, and cooperatives with microfinance services.

evaluating shared-channel partnerships. The framework is based on three main categories: alignment between the partners, value add by the channel partner and market development status, each evaluated on three dimensions.

It is proposed that the level of alignment along three dimensions—product/service, organizational skills and values, and supply-chain management—between the shared-channel partners is an important indicator for the partnership's success and highlights areas to which time and resources have to be allocated to achieve better alignment.

The value-add dimensions—financing support, business location and market access of the distribution partner—are indicators in how far the partner brings additional value to the partnership to make it worthwhile cooperating.

The market-development dimensions—market readiness, customer awareness and geography—influence on a more general level the appropriateness of a shared-channel business model to reach the BoP market.

An example of the SCAF is shown in Figure 8.1.

Figure 8.1 **Example of Shared Channel Assessment Framework**

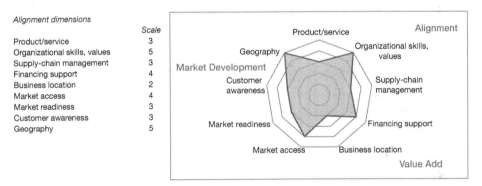

8.7.1 Alignment dimensions

8.7.1.1 Product and service dimension

Evaluating the alignment of products and services is the most important alignment dimension. It has been shown that the closer the new product or service is aligned with the existing offering of the proposed shared-channel partner, the easier the integration will be, increasing the likelihood of a successful partnership.

MFIs that deal primarily with credit and savings services have a good chance of successfully integrating other financial products such as insurance services into their product range since they are closely aligned. Distributing physical products, for example, solar lanterns, poses challenges to an MFI, such as the capacity of the field or sales officers, or the lack of physical distribution logistics and management information system. To achieve a successful partnership, these challenges need to be addressed and considered in terms of time and financial resources.

8.7.1.2 Organizational skills and values dimension

Organizations have different skills and values embodied in their DNA. As an example, a city-based, multinational company can be very fast-paced and aggressive, while a rural-based NGO may opt for a relaxed stance in doing business. In addition, a company cannot penetrate a BoP market without considering how the BoP and the partner transact. Otherwise, there will be a wide misalignment between the two that will affect the entire engagement.

The alignment in this dimension can be addressed by both the company and its shared-channel partner being open and adaptive about each other's strengths and weaknesses. Since direct interactions will be made with the BoP, it is important for a company to understand how its partner engages the BoP market and focus not only on the products or services delivery.

8.7.1.3 Supply-chain management dimension

Managing the supply chain is a complex task wherein both the company and shared channel partner have to work hand in hand. This is the part where the partnership itself operates, from acquiring the products to delivering them to the BoP market and providing after-sales services.

The alignment of this dimension has to be evaluated to determine which specific areas along the value chain the partners have to focus on and which partner is responsible or better equipped for which task. For example, when an MFI sells physical products, the after-sales service might have to be managed by the company instead of relying on the shared-channel partner due to its lack of a proper tracking system.

8.7.2 Value-add dimensions

8.7.2.1 Financing support

The ability of a shared-channel partner to provide access to financial products for the BoP as its added value is important to make products accessible and affordable and thereby the partnership successful. This is especially the case when the cost of the product is above the BoP's financial capacity for outright cash purchases. In this situation it is beneficial when a company partners with an MFI since these organizations can develop specialized financial products for the new products and services or can integrate them into their standard portfolio.

8.7.2.2 Business location

Companies have to evaluate a shared-channel partner in terms of the location and geographic areas of activities of the partner. The physical presence of a shared-channel partner in the specific BoP market is often assumed; however, its constituency might not have a need that the company can fill, for example, an MFI operating in a poor but electrified area is not a good choice to distribute solar lanterns.

8.7.2.3 Market access

The ability to access the market as a trusted partner of the BoP is an important dimension for the choice of a distribution partner. MFIs, NGOs, cooperatives and social enterprises, the premier organizations to serve as shared-channel partners, have staff or employees working directly, often on a long-term basis, with the BoP market. This helps the partnership to introduce new products to the BoP because of the leverage brought by the shared-channel partner's identity, which has been established already in the BoP. The company has to understand the profile of the distribution partner's clients and beneficiaries and determine the potential of its products and services for them.

8.7.3 Market development dimensions

8.7.3.1 Market readiness

The framework also considers the conditions of the BoP market itself. The BoP's readiness for new products is an important success factor for the products and services to be distributed by the partnership. The need of the market does not establish automatically the fact that there is a demand.

8.7.3.2 Customer awareness

The awareness of BoP consumers of the product or service has to be considered in evaluating a shared-channel partnership. The remoteness of location of rural BoP markets and the lack of information often contributes to a lack of awareness of the benefits of products and services a company wants to deliver to the BoP. When there is low customer awareness of the product or service to be offered, the partners have to determine activities to raise its awareness. Hybrid Solar Solutions, Inc. (HSSi), which distributes solar lanterns through MFIs and NGOs, discovered that solar lanterns were not well known in the rural and off-grid communities of the Philippines. It therefore conducts market awareness campaigns with its partner. To fund the costs of such campaigns, HSSi developed innovative financing facilities via its corporate foundation.

8.7.3.3 Geography

Evaluating the geography of the BoP market and aligning it with the coverage of the distribution partner is essential for a successful partnership. This evaluation helps the partnership to determine how to plan and execute the distribution plans as, for example, an extremely far-flung BoP market will require a great deal of resources from the partnership for the products to reach it.

The degree of the alignment, value add and market development dimensions contributes to the success of the shared-channel partnership. The SCAF can be used to identify the best partner and to evaluate an existing partnership in case of misalignments or shortcomings in the dimensions that are inevitable in a shared-channel model. Misalignments, low levels of value add or low state of market development do not necessarily indicate that a partnership is not feasible. Rather, they highlight the areas where actions need to be designed and implemented in order to enhance the partnership.

Rating the dimensions to fill in the SCAF has to be done objectively and in partnership, with consideration to the parameters that apply to each shared-channel partnership. These parameters may vary according to the partners, products and services.

8.8 Shared-channel distribution as a business model

Case studies on three organizations in the Philippines were developed to discuss the potentials of using shared channel as the distribution model and test the Shared Channel Assessment Framework.

1. **Partnership with a microfinance institution (MFI).** HSSi is a company primarily engaged in selling solar products to the BoP market, particularly the off-grid areas where electric services are not yet available. It partners with Negros Women for Tomorrow Foundation (NWTF) in selling solar lanterns on instalment basis

2. **Partnership with a social enterprise.** Unilab is the Philippines' largest pharmaceutical company. It partners with Hapinoy (managed by Microventures, Inc.) for the Hapinoy Botika Project. It enables Hapinoy's network of small stores (locally referred to as sari-sari stores) to sell over-the-counter medicines and also helps Unilab to establish a direct touch point with the BoP market

3. **Partnership with an NGO.** Family Vaccine and Specialty Clinics, Inc. (FVSC) is the Philippines' largest operator of animal-bite clinics. It partners with Zambales War Against Poverty (ZWAP) in operating clinics in the province served by the NGO

8.8.1 Opportunities and challenges of using shared channels

8.8.1.1 HSSi–NWTF Partnership

According to the Philippine government's latest statistics, 25% of Filipinos lack access to electricity.[3] Most of these people without electricity are located in isolated villages in coastal or mountainous areas. After sunset, productive activities in these

---

3 Partner's Briefer for the ACCESS Program by Hybrid Social Solutions, Inc.

communities slow down or cease. People resort to batteries (including car batteries), kerosene-fuelled lamps and candles as sources of light.

Seeing the need for a safer and more economical source of light, HSSi took this opportunity to market its solar lantern products. The SunTransfer is a durable, high-capacity solar lamp designed for off-grid use. It enables users to safely light their houses without any risk of fire, save money spent on kerosene and batteries, and generate income through enhanced productivity.[4] But since the target markets are in the off-grid rural areas, HSSi recognized the challenge of making the products available and affordable for the BoP in a profitable way.

HSSi partnered with NWTF to distribute its solar lanterns. Although there was a need for NWTF to equip its staff with knowledge about solar products, selling non-financial products for NWTF was already established business practice. The cooperation between the organizations went smoothly as well since both are experienced in dealing with the BoP.

In order to make the products accessible and affordable for the BoP, NWTF sells the solar lanterns by instalment, particularly to its members. Non-members who are interested may purchase in cash. Using their MFI practices, NWTF was able to integrate the solar lanterns in their financial offerings.

NWTF sends its loan officers to the BoP communities to support the selling of solar lanterns. This strengthens the presence of the partnership in the BoP market through remote front-line employees who implement programmes conducted by both NWTF and HSSi. This is a very strategic move for the partnership because the product is new to the market.

The ACCESS programme was conceived as HSSi's way of establishing and nurturing partnerships that involves its shared-channel partner and the BoP market. ACCESS stands for Advancing Citizen and Community Empowerment through Sustained Solutions.

Through the ACCESS programme, HSSi was able to solve the distribution challenges in bringing solar lanterns to the rural unelectrified BoP market. HSSi ensures that the buyers understand what they are about to buy, how they will be assisted at the point of purchase and about after-sales support. The programme is the partnership's solution to raising market readiness and awareness for the solar lanterns and the entire concept of solar energy.

The implementation of the programme works but it is costly and time consuming. It runs for 3–4 months and includes training about the product, sales and branch management for the HSSi partners. Solar caravan outreach activities and solar user forums are also conducted to raise the level of awareness about the solar products. Nevertheless, the time and resources spent on the programme help HSSi and its partner in establishing a lasting and self-sustaining partnership. ACCESS is financed through HSSi's partner, the Solar Energy Foundation (SEF). Figure 8.2 shows the SCAF for the HSSi–NWTF partnership.

---

4 http://www.hybridsolutions.moonfruit.com/-/suntransfer/4553662505, accessed 31 December 2014.

Figure 8.2 **Shared Channels Alignment Framework for the HSSi–NWTF partnership**

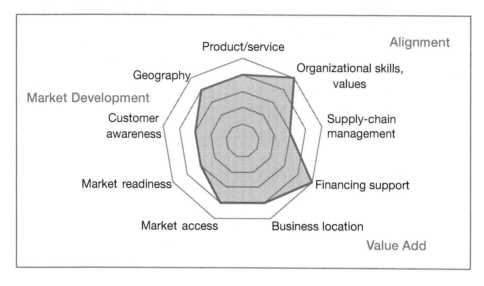

8.8.1.2 FVSC–ZWAP partnership

Family Vaccine and Specialty Clinics, Inc. is the Philippines' largest operator of privately run animal-bite treatment centres and vaccination clinics with 41 branches across the Philippines. Whereas the government provides early childhood immunization programmes, it does not cover vaccination for rabies and other diseases.

This BoP vaccine market has been a previously untapped market, which was primarily due to the fact that vaccines in the Philippines are expensive and there is very low awareness about the importance of vaccination. In order to distribute vaccines to the BoP, FVSC partners with government hospitals and NGOs to help the company in setting up vaccine clinics. FVSC decided to share channels with government hospitals and NGOs since these organizations cater to the needs of the poor and are situated mostly in the rural areas. The BoP market relies heavily on government hospitals for healthcare needs because of the unaffordable rates charged by better-equipped private hospitals.

FVSC operates its clinics inside the premises of its shared-channel partners. In government hospitals, FVSC uses free of charge a hospital room/office that serves as FVSC's clinic. Most of the time a clinic is situated near the Emergency Room. The company also partners with NGOs where the FVSC clinic is located within the NGO's premises. In return, FVSC offers free vaccine shots to patients (usually two out of the eight-shot regimen). Thus patients only need to pay for the remaining six, which are specifically priced for the BoP market. These free shots are subsidized by the partner organization.

FVSC's partnership with ZWAP enabled the company to open clinics in Zambales Province where the NGO operates. FVSC has three branches there, which are located in ZWAP-operated community stores where various public services have been integrated. The partnership is beneficial for FVSC since the company does not need to go through the process of opening and operating its own place. FVSC focuses on the distribution of vaccines, which require cold chain logistics. Vaccines have to be maintained within a specific temperature thus the distribution itself relies on FVSC.

Since government hospitals are already familiar with vaccines and NGOs such as ZWAP are also well oriented to providing services to the public, the product/service alignment is no longer a concern for the partnership. Besides, even though the FVSC clinics are located within the premises of the shared-channel partners, it is still the company that handles almost everything from product deliveries, administering vaccines, to managing the value chain. The only area for misalignment in the partnership is the low financing support for the BoP.

The very low awareness about vaccines particularly in the BoP is one of the challenges that FVSC and its partners need to solve. This is currently addressed through various information drives that FVSC and ZWAP have implemented. These include radio programmes (ZWAP operates its own public-service radio station), community engagement and information drives done by other ZWAP stores. FVSC also continuously trains its nurses in public speaking and other necessary skills to use them beyond the typical nursing duties. The misalignment in the dimensions of market readiness and awareness shows that in order to establish an ideal partnership, the organizations need to constantly address this to achieve alignment and make the partnership more stable and successful.

With this kind of partnership, FVSC was able to treat more than 271,700 patients after six years of operation and has lowered the cost of rabies preventive treatment by at least 70%.

Figure 8.3 shows the SCAF for the FVSC–ZWAP partnership.

Figure 8.3 **Shared Channels Alignment Framework for the FVSC–ZWAP partnership**

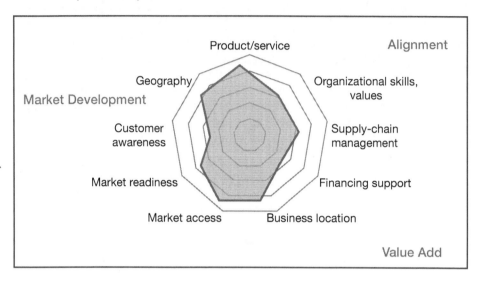

8.8.1.3 Unilab–Hapinoy partnership

Unilab is the largest pharmaceutical company in the Philippines. Its portfolio includes some of the biggest prescription and consumer healthcare brands in the country. Despite this, Unilab lacked controlled reach in the BoP market. Through the typical distribution model, Unilab only monitored its market reach to the level of drugstores/pharmacies. The sari-sari stores, which according to Unilab contribute 18–20% of sales of over the-counter (OTC) medicines, get their OTC medicine supplies from the drugstores and from this point Unilab loses control over the market reach.

This led to Unilab's partnership with Hapinoy, which is managed by Microventures, Inc., an internationally recognized and pioneering social enterprise in the Philippines. The partnership resulted in the creation of the Hapinoy Botika Project (*botika* is the Filipino word for pharmacy or drugstore). Hapinoy manages a network of almost 8,000 sari-sari stores in the country. Currently 4,000 stores benefit from the Hapinoy Botika Project.

The partnership is an almost perfect fit in terms of alignment dimensions except for some areas where action points have to be taken. Once the medicines have been delivered by Unilab to Hapinoy, it is the latter's responsibility to deliver the medicines to its chain of sari-sari stores.

Market awareness needs to be addressed as well. Mostly, the BoP market is not very knowledgeable about OTC medicines. There is a danger that without proper guidance, buyers will commit errors in purchasing the right medicines and in taking the right dosage. This is addressed by Unilab conducting training and other support services to the sari-sari store owners so that they can effectively sell OTC medicines.

For Unilab, the partnership with Hapinoy did not result in just an increase in sales. The pharmaceutical giant was able to establish a touch point with the BoP market that could not be attained through the conventional distribution systems. The touch point enabled Unilab to fully understand the BoP market and improve services, and at the same time it provided it with the controlled market reach that it had wanted to establish. On the part of Hapinoy, the partnership helped it attain its mission of bringing affordable medicines to the BoP and enabled its sari-sari stores to expand their portfolios and sales.

Figure 8.4 shows the SCAF for the Unilab–Hapinoy partnership.

Figure 8.4 **Shared Channel Assessment Framework for the Unilab–Hapinoy partnership**

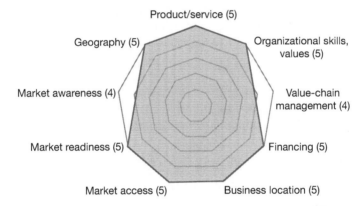

8.9 Assessment of shared-channel partnerships

It is important for companies planning to engage the BoP market through shared channels to carefully review and determine the best partner to engage with. Every shared-channel partner (corporates, NGOs, MFIs and social enterprises) has its own pros and cons. And every company seeking to share channel with an organiza- tion has its own set of strengths and weaknesses. Since there is no perfect shared-channel partnership, the Shared Channel Assessment Framework is proposed to give guidance on what to expect and consider when discussing different possible shared-channel partners. The framework enables companies and shared-chan- nel partners to establish a well-rounded partnership with a multi-dimensional approach evaluating all aspects of delivering products to the BoP. Considerations should not be limited to whether a shared channel partner can be a good distribu- tion partner and can go along with the "corporate" attitude of urban area-based companies and whether the company can provide leverage for shared-channel partners to fully widen their portfolios and strengthen their presence in the BoP market.

8.10 Conclusions

The BoP market in the Philippines is still greatly untapped, but there are a number of organizations that have taken up the challenge and obtained positive results. As stated by the Asian Development Bank (Dietrich 2013), the inclusive business sector in the Philippines is still in the nascent stage.

Given the poor infrastructure conditions in the rural areas, engaging the BoP is posing a considerable distribution challenge. Based on the experience and the case studies presented, it can be concluded that the shared-channel distribution model is a viable and scalable option for organizations engaging the BoP market.

The Shared Channels Assessment Framework is suggested to serve as a decision-making tool for companies and shared-channel partners. The framework provides an instrument for these organizations to evaluate an existing or a future partnership. Possible pitfalls can be identified so that remedies can be prepared beforehand or the pitfall itself be avoided. The aim of the framework is to lead decision-makers towards cost-efficient solutions in their engagement with the BoP market and ultimately in a reduction in the BoP penalty, making products and services more accessible and affordable for the BoP. As SCAF is still in its infancy more research is required to test and improve the framework.

Bibliography

Asian Development Bank (2013) "Inclusive Business Study for the Philippines. Prepared by ASEI, Inc. for the Asian Development Bank", ADB Poverty, http://www.scribd.com/doc/142734216/ASEI-23-Apr-2013-IB-in-PHI-Final-Report-with-Disclamer, ADB Poverty, accessed 30 November 2014.

Bhan, N. (2009) "The 5Ds of BoP Marketing: Touchpoints for a Holistic, Human-Centered Strategy", http://www.core77.com/blog/featured_items/the_5ds_of_bop_marketing_touchpoints_for_a_holistic_humancentered_strategy_12233.asp, accessed on 30 November 2014.

Donnges, C., M. Espano and N. Palarca (2006) *Philippines Infrastructure for Rural Productivity Enhancement* (Rural Access Technical Papers [RATP] No. 14; Geneva: International Labour Organization).

Hammond, A., W.J Kramer, J. Tran, R. Katz and C. Walker (2007) *The Next 4 Billion: Market Size and Business Strategy at the Base of the Pyramid* (Washington, DC: World Resources Institute).

Hart, S.L. (2007) *Capitalism at the Crossroads: Aligning Business, Earth, and Humanity* (Upper Saddle River, NJ: Prentice Hall, 2nd edn).

Karamchandani, A., M. Kubzansky and P. Frandano (2009) *Emerging Markets, Emerging Models* (Cambridge, MA: Monitor Group)

Prahalad, C.K. (2005) *The Fortune at the Bottom of the Pyramid* (Upper Saddle River, NJ: Prentice Hall/Wharton School Publishing).

Vachani S., and N.C. Smith (2007) *Socially Responsible Distribution: Distribution Strategies for Reaching the Bottom of the Pyramid* (Working Papers Series; Fontainebleau, France: INSEAD).

Part V
Partnership frameworks for BoP business

9

Partnerships for poverty alleviation

Cross-sector and B2B collaboration in BoP markets

Marjo Hietapuro
EY, Finland

Minna Halme
Aalto University School of Business, Finland

Poverty alleviation is arguably the most burning social sustain-ability problem globally, and business innovation for market-based means of poverty alleviation has proliferated in recent years. Base of the pyramid (BoP) and inclusive market streams of research emphasize that such innovation calls for companies' collaboration with untypical allies, in particular with non-govern-mental organizations (NGOs) and local micro-entrepreneurs. Yet the research of partnerships and partner roles in BoP business models has relied predominantly on piecemeal and anecdotal evidence. To start filling the gap, this study addresses partner-ships in the business models of companies in the BoP markets through a literature review and an analysis of 20 BoP business models. We provide an overview of the different kinds of partner-ships that companies doing business at the BoP may form with various types of actors, such as NGOs, local micro-entrepreneurs and companies, government agencies, intergovernmental organizations and universities. We identify nine categories of roles that partners can take in BoP business: co-developers, suppliers, distributors, complementors, customers, microfinance providers, brokers, funders and impact assessors. Contrary to much of the BoP literature, our findings indicate that traditional partnerships with governmental organizations are also of importance for companies conducting business in BoP markets. In addition, it turns out that not only foreign but also local companies equally need partnerships with actors that are close to the BoP.

In recent years, there has been growing interest in the base of the pyramid (BoP) approach, according to which companies can help eradicate poverty by entering the market of the 4 billion under-served people at the base of the world economic pyramid, and make profits at the same time (Hahn 2009; Prahalad and Hart 2002). Despite attractive market potential, succeeding in these markets is not easy, and thus the need for complete rethinking of business models has been repeatedly emphasized in BoP literature. In particular, there has been a call for companies to build new kinds of partnerships with actors that are familiar with the BoP, such as citizen-sector organizations and local micro-entrepreneurs. These non-traditional partnerships are considered important because very few companies have traditionally been operating in the BoP markets, and thus companies tend to be very unfamiliar with them (e.g. Hart 2005; Klein 2008; London and Hart 2004; Prahalad 2005).

Although partnerships have been frequently promoted in BoP literature, the evidence is fragmentary. A literature review by Rivera-Santos and Rufin (2010) on networks in the BoP context suggests that networks differ significantly from the ones at the top of the pyramid in terms of structural characteristics, boundaries, ties, partner diversity and dynamics. Many authors have focused on describing BoP ventures' partnerships especially with non-governmental organizations (NGOs) or poor communities. It is argued that the capabilities needed by companies when operating at the BoP can be best provided by NGOs rather than traditional partners such as national governments, since these actors rarely have necessary knowledge about, or embeddedness in, the BoP (e.g. Hart 2005; Klein 2008; London and Hart 2004; Prahalad 2005; Rondinelli and London 2003). From the perspective of poverty alleviation NGOs are seen to safeguard that the solutions are pro-poor.

However, an integrated approach to the types of partners that are used in BoP business and the roles that various partners fulfil is still missing. This study aims to bridge that gap by analysing from an empirical vantage point what kinds of partners companies collaborate with in BoP business, and what kinds of roles different partners have in the BoP business models. To that end, we systematically analyse 20 BoP business models. As our aim is particularly to provide knowledge on partnerships needed for business-based innovation of poverty alleviation, we selected BoP business models that have a company as the central actor.

The term partnership is used in this study in a broad sense, referring to any type of arrangement that a company can make to collaborate with another entity. Partnerships can be, for example, joint ventures or strategic alliances with other companies, cross-sector partnerships with governments or non-profits, or partnerships with the individuals and communities at the BoP.

In the remainder of this chapter we first review the relevant literature, then briefly describe the data and method, and finally discuss the main contributions of this study to the literature and to BoP business practice.

9.1 Partnerships of business firms at the BoP: why and with whom?

This section reviews the previous literature in order to shed light on why companies may want to form partnerships and which types of actors they collaborate with when doing business at the BoP.

9.1.1 Partnerships as a way to gain resources in BoP business

According to the resource-based view of networks and strategic alliances, firms essentially use alliances to gain access to valuable resources of their partners (e.g. Das and Teng 2000; Gulati *et al*. 2000; Uzzi 1996). The rate of alliance formation is likely to increase when market conditions are difficult and when firm strategies are risky or innovative. In such situations, alliances can provide critical resources, both concrete ones such as specific skills and financial resources and more abstract ones such as legitimacy (Eisenhardt 1989).

Alliances may help firms overcome various challenges at the BoP. One of these challenges is the underdeveloped state of business ecosystems in BoP environments. When entering BoP markets, firms may find that the suppliers, distributors or support services that are taken for granted in "top of the pyramid" markets do not exist at the BoP. For example, there can be gaps in the economic infrastructure, such as electricity or water supply, in support activities, such as financing or distribution, and in the information infrastructure (Rivera-Santos and Rufin 2010). Consequently, companies operating at the BoP increasingly reach out to external collaborators who can "fill in pieces of the (value) system that they themselves cannot" (Jenkins and Ishikawa 2009). Such collaborators may include companies in complementary lines of business, government agencies, civil society organizations, microfinance institutions, international development agencies and international financial institutions (ibid.). In addition, challenges imposed, for example, by dispersed locations, unfamiliarity of the markets, limited market information, mistrust of BoP individuals towards business firms, inadequate knowledge and skills of BoP individuals, ineffective regulatory environments, and the great costs and risks involved, may all further contribute to the need to form partnerships at the BoP (Klein 2008; Sánchez *et al.* 2005; UNDP 2008).

Moreover, operating at the BoP may require new capabilities that can be fuelled through partnerships. London and Hart (2004) emphasize the need for social embeddedness or the ability to integrate with the local BoP environment. This involves the ability to create a web of trusted connections with a diversity of organizations and institutions.

The BoP literature frequently argues that the challenges of the BoP environment and the need for new capabilities cannot be met through cooperation with traditional partners, such as national governments and large companies, since these actors rarely have necessary knowledge about, or embeddedness in, the BoP (Hart 2005; Klein 2008; London and Hart 2004). Therefore, the BoP literature emphasizes the need to cooperate with non-traditional partners, such as NGOs, local community groups, local governments and local entrepreneurs, when operating at the BoP (e.g. Hart 2005; Klein 2008; London and Hart 2004; Prahalad 2005). It is argued that non-traditional partners are the most likely partners to possess the local understanding and information on the local context, legitimacy, embeddedness, infrastructure and relationships (Klein 2008; Rondinelli and London 2003).

9.1.2 Partnerships with different actors in BoP business

Next we move on to discuss large companies' partnerships with different types of actors, including discussion of benefits of partnerships with various actors and the roles these actors can take in the BoP business models.

9.1.2.1 Partnerships with BoP individuals and communities

In BoP business, local micro-entrepreneurs can be engaged as either suppliers or distributors of products and services. In addition, the people at the BoP can collaborate in, for example, conducting market research, giving community-based training and co-creating innovations (UNDP 2008).

Engaging the people at the BoP as suppliers can benefit both the companies and the local communities. While the BoP micro-entrepreneurs can gain new skills, assistance in raising productivity, and perhaps better prices for their products, companies can gain benefits such as increased quality, traceability and sustainability of supply, which are increasingly important particularly in agriculture, forestry and apparel industry). Moreover, local content reduces the need for transporting raw materials and capital equipment, which can be prohibitively expensive, or simply impossible, because of the poor infrastructure in many subsistence marketplaces (Weidner *et al.* 2010).

Local micro-entrepreneurs appear relatively often engaged as distributors in the BoP business models. Distributing products and services through BoP micro-enterprises can be an effective strategy for reaching especially rural target markets at the BoP (Hoyt and Jamison 2007; Jenkins and Ishikawa 2009; UNDP 2008). In this context the word distribution does not refer only to distributing products, but rather to a broad spectrum of functions at the BoP customer interface. At the same time, BoP micro-entrepreneurs can be consumers for the products and services.

Microfranchising appears an increasingly popular way to engage BoP suppliers and distributors (Gibson 2007). Although the exact definition of the concept is still debated, it can perhaps be stated that the main characteristic of microfranchising is that operations are streamlined and replicated to scale through micro-enterprises (e.g. Christensen *et al.* 2010; Gibson 2007). However, very extensive control and standardization of processes may not be desirable, especially in distribution activities, since various BoP markets can be very heterogeneous (Christensen *et al.* 2010).

9.1.2.2 Partnerships with NGOs and microfinance institutions

Partnerships between companies and NGOs have been frequently promoted in the BoP literature (e.g. Chesbrough *et al.* 2006; Drayton and Budinich 2010). The power of company–NGO partnerships lies in the complementary strengths of the participants: businesses offer scale, expertise in manufacturing and operations, and financing, while social entrepreneurs and organizations contribute lower costs, strong social networks and deep insights into customers and communities (Drayton and Budinich 2010).

NGOs can advise companies on low-income communities' needs and potential opportunities (WEF 2009a) and their understanding of the local environment can help multinational companies (MNCs) develop initial ideas into valuable opportunities (Chesbrough *et al.* 2006; Webb *et al.* 2010;). Moreover, through their networks and relationships with the local societies, they can help companies overcome voids of formal institutions and build legitimacy and trust between the BoP community and the MNC (Webb *et al.* 2010), as well as assist in recruiting, organizing and training the BoP entrepreneurs (Chesbrough *et al.* 2006; London *et al.* 2010, WEF 2009a).

In addition, microfinance institutions (MFIs) have been promoted as potential partners in BoP business. While their obvious role is to provide credit to BoP consumers and BoP micro-entrepreneurs, making it possible for poor producers and consumers to finance investments or large purchases (UNDP 2008), they can also help companies in, for example, recruiting the micro-entrepreneurs (Dalberg 2009).

9.1.2.3 Partnerships with governments

In BoP literature, the role of governments in BoP business has typically been neglected, or companies have been advised to avoid dependency on governments altogether in order to avoid problems such as corruption and bureaucracy (Hart 2005; Klein 2008). On the other hand, other authors claim there can be a lot to gain from cooperation with governments as well, and, in some cases, government cooperation may be an essential condition for doing business at the BoP (UNDP 2008).

9.1.2.4 Partnerships with companies

Although the importance of non-traditional partners has been emphasized in the BoP literature, intercompany alliances may also be needed to reach synergies in

BoP business. The literature on these alliances—although limited—suggests that companies may benefit from aligning complementary investments, sharing supply and distribution costs, or joining forces to improve the business environment. Furthermore, companies may pool their resources to gather market information, take collective action to fill gaps in market infrastructure (such as cold chains, sewage treatment plants or processing and packaging facilities) or self-regulate through setting common standards for their industries (UNDP 2008; WEF 2009b).

9.1.2.5 Other partnerships

Reficco and Marquez (2009) found that the BoP ventures they examined had benefited from the contributions of organizations providing financial, intellectual or social "seed capital". These contributions were often short-lived but important to assure the viability of the enterprise. These kinds of supporting organization may be donors, intergovernmental organizations or research/academic institutions, all of which may have important roles to play in BoP business models (WEF 2009b). For example, they can undertake or fund research and development for new product development targeted to poor communities' needs; conduct research to identify pro-poor business and market development opportunities and communicate them to stakeholders; mobilize stakeholders around common priorities; fund the start-up phase of new business models to enable experimentation; conduct public education campaigns on key products or concepts; monitor, evaluate and assess impacts of business models; and share best practices and lessons learned, regionally and globally (ibid.).

External funding in particular may be crucial for BoP ventures since, as the business requires complex partnerships and may not immediately offer attractive rates of return, it might lose out to other more conventional business proposals in the competition for in-house funding (WBCSD 2004). External funding can be received from, for example, multilateral financial institutions, bilateral development agencies, private foundations, or social loan and venture funds (ibid.).

9.1.3 Data and methodology

The research was conducted as a multiple-case study of 20 BoP business models of both foreign and local companies from various sectors and countries. The research approach involved both deductive and inductive steps. In the beginning, previous research was reviewed in order to find out what were the main observations about companies' partnerships at the BoP (deductive step). The findings of the empirical study were used to complement and extend the suggestions of the previous literature (inductive element).

Potential cases were identified from various sources:

- Case study bank of the United Nations Development Programme (UNDP) Growing Inclusive Markets initiative
- Case study bank of the World Business Council for Sustainable Development
- C.K. Prahalad, *The Fortune at the Bottom of the Pyramid* (2005)

- Kandachar and Halme (eds.), *Sustainability Challenges and Solutions at the Base of the Pyramid* (2008)

- Fairbourne *et al.* (eds.), *Microfranchising: Creating Wealth at the Bottom of the Pyramid* (2007)

- World Economic Forum, *The Next Billions: Business Strategies to Enhance Food Value Chains and Empower the Poor* (WEF 2009a)

- Nokia's *Expanding Horizons* publications

- Various academic articles

The initial criterion was that a business enterprise should be the central actor in the business model. Identification of cases was followed by a search for data on partnerships used in the cases, first from the case studies and then from complementary sources. Finally, 64 potential cases were screened against the data needs and cases on which sufficient partnership data was missing were excluded, eventually leaving 20 cases for analysis. Nine of them were local and 11 were foreign companies, mainly MNCs. They represent altogether ten sectors (Table 9.1).

Table 9.1 **Cases by sector and country of origin**

Sector	Local company	Foreign company
ICT	1	4
Financial services		4
Energy/Water/Sanitation	2	1
Food		2
Agriculture	1	
Irrigation	1	
Forestry	1	
Artisanal goods	1	
Recycling	1	
Cosmetics	1	
Sum	9	11

The collected data included the name of the venture, type(s) of actor owning the venture, source, description of the BoP activities, country of operation, and descriptions of how different partners were engaged with under the categories of various types of partners (BoP individuals and communities; NGOs and MFIs; governments; companies; other). The data was collected mainly from existing case studies and company websites, and complemented with selected interviews. Case companies' sectors, short description of their main activity, organization type, key partners and countries of operation appear in Table 9.2.

Table 9.2 **Case data**

Case study	Sector	Description of BoP activities	Organization type	Key partners	Country	Sources
Amanco	Irrigation	Selling irrigation systems to farmers	Developing country MNC	Ashoka (INGO), RASA (NGO)	Mexico	UNDP 2008; IFC 2007
ANZ Bank rural banking in Fiji	Financial services	Providing mobile banking accounts and financial literacy training to rural communities	MNC	UNDP	Fiji	Liew 2005; ANZ website
Barclays Capital Susu collectors initiative	Financial services	Providing microfinance through the informal financial system of "Susu collectors" in Ghana combined with knowledge sharing with the end-customers	MNC	Ghana Susu Collectors Association (NGO), Ghana Microfinance Institutions Network (NGO)	Ghana	UNDP 2008
CocoTech	Artisanal goods	Engaging the BoP as suppliers in the making of cocofibre nets used e.g. for slope stabilization and erosion control	Local SME	National and local government, BoP suppliers	Philippines	UNDP 2008
Danone Poland Milk Start	Food	Developing and marketing a nutritious milk porridge for low-income families	MNC	Lubella SA (manufacturer), Biedronka (retailer), Institute of Mother and Child (public institution)	Poland	UNDP 2008

Case study	Sector	Description of BoP activities	Organization type	Key partners	Country	Sources
Freeplay Energy Weza project	Energy	Creating sustainable rural businesses that use a foot-powered portable energy source "Weza" to provide energy services for basic needs, such as communications and LED lighting	Foreign SME	CARE Rwanda (INGO), BoP micro-entrepreneurs, universities	Rwanda	Webb et al. 2010; Freeplay Energy website
Grameenphone Village Phone	ICT	Providing phone services via a network of village entrepreneurs	MNC/NGO joint venture	BoP micro-entrepreneurs, funders (IGOs and development agencies)	Bangladesh	WRI 2001
Grameen-Danone Shokti Doi	Food	Providing a fortified yoghurt to improve the nutrition of poor children in Bangladesh, while engaging the poor as suppliers, manufacturers and distributors	MNC/ NGO joint venture	GAIN (INGO), local NGOs, BoP micro-entrepreneurs, The John Hopkins University	Bangladesh	Danone website; Yunus Centre website; Social Innovator website
Huatai Paper	Forestry	Mobilizing local farmers to plant fast-growing trees, supporting them through technical assistance, irrigation services and direct subsidies, and making a contract to buy the lumber from them at protected prices	Large domestic company	Local government	China	UNDP 2008; Business and public policy blog
Integrated Tamale Fruit Company	Agriculture	Cultivating certified organic mangoes through an outgrower scheme through which the farmers get interest-free loan in the form of farm inputs and technical services	Local SME	Farmers' association and organizations providing funding for the association	Ghana	UNDP 2008

LYDEC	Energy/ Water/ Sanitation	Providing electricity, water and sanitation services to shantytowns	MNC	National and local public authorities, subcontractors, the World Bank	Morocco	UNDP 2008
Manila Water Company Livelihoods Program	Water	Developing supply-chain partners in local communities: created a pipe rethreading cooperative by training previously unemployed and unskilled employees, financing the cooperative and leasing them the equipment at an affordable rate	Large domestic company	Subcontractor cooperative	Philippines	UNDP 2008
Natura Ekos	Cosmetics	Sourcing ingredients of natural cosmetics from rural communities that extract raw material from the nature	Developing country MNC	Local NGOs	Brazil	UNDP 2008
Nokia Lifetools	ICT	Providing mobile services including Agriculture (information on seeds, fertilizers, pesticides, market prices, and weather), Education (learning English and preparing for exams) and Entertainment services	MNC	Content providers, operators	India	Interview; company material; Nokia press release
Nokia Microfinance	ICT	Selling phones in rural areas via a microfinance organization that also gives the low-income customers loans for buying the phones	MNC	SKS Microfinance (for-profit MFI), Airtel (operator)	India	Interview; Nokia Expanding Horizons publication

Case study	Sector	Description of BoP activities	Organization type	Key partners	Country	Sources
Nokia Money	Financial services	Providing a mobile banking service that does not require a bank account, enabling the payment of bills, transfer of money, and recharging of the prepaid account	MNC	Yes Bank, Obopay (payment platform provider)	India	Nokia website; Nokia blog
Nokia Siemens Networks Village Connection	ICT	Bringing voice and Internet connectivity to rural villages where traditional GSM network roll-out and operation would be too costly by implementing an IP-based network architecture and a business model of local village operators	MNC	Operators, BoP micro-entrepreneurs, microfinance providers	Tanzania	Skarp et al. 2008; NSN website
PETSTAR	Recycling	Constructing a bottle-to-bottle recycling facility and partnering with garbage sorting and recycling workers to improve their working conditions and livelihoods	Large domestic company	NGOs, companies (buyers), International Finance Corporation (IFC), Institute of Social Research of the Universidad Autónoma de Nuevo León	Mexico	UNDP 2008; IFC press release
Real Microcrédito	Financial services	Providing microfinance	MNC/ NGO joint venture	USAID	Brazil	Webb et al. 2010; ACCION website; WBCSD 2004
Tsinghua Tongfang Changfeng computer	ICT	Providing computers designed especially for rural consumers	Large domestic company	Municipal government agencies, software companies	China	UNDP 2008

As to data analysis, first within-case analysis was conducted in order to assess individual cases on how the partnerships operate in practice and what kinds of purpose they serve (see Eisenhardt 1989). Then the data on partnerships was categorized according to the types of actors collaborated with. Hence, the observed partnerships were listed under categories of different types of actors: BoP individuals and communities; NGOs and MFIs; governments; companies; and other. In the category of "BoP individuals and communities", the data was further subcategorized based on whether the entrepreneurs were organized into associations or not and whether the partners were existing entrepreneurs or new entrepreneurs created with the help of the company. In the category of "NGOs and MFIs", the partnerships were further subcategorized on the basis of size of the organization. The "government" partnerships were further subcategorized based on whether the partner was a local, regional, municipal or national government.

Next, on the basis of the observed roles that partners had in the cases, nine categories of partner roles were created. These were: co-developers, suppliers, distributors, complementors, customers, microfinance providers, brokers, funders and impact assessors. The creation of partner role categories involved a repeated iteration, and the categories had to be modified several times before the stage was reached when all roles manifested in the data were captured by them. Within each of these categories, the data was further analysed based on the type of actor engaged in the role. Hence, the end result was a list of the types of actors that may be engaged as partners in each of the nine partner roles (Table 9.3). Finally, a search for cross-case patterns was conducted by grouping the cases based on any variables that were thought to possibly have an influence on what kinds of partnerships companies engage in. Next we discuss which partner roles were identified, and which organizations typically fulfil these roles.

9.1.4 Findings: partner roles

While the previous literature on partnerships in business at the BoP has primarily addressed the prominent partners for companies operating at the BoP, the results of this study complement the existing body of knowledge by suggesting a comprehensive list of partner roles needed in BoP business models. In this section we present the identified nine categories of partner roles that emerged from the empirical data: co-developers, suppliers, distributors, complementors, customers, microfinance providers, brokers, funders and impact assessors. We also discuss which partners filled these different roles (Table 9.3). In the following we will refer to some examples from the 20 cases analysed as the space does not allow a more thorough discussion. For an overview of the analysed cases, a brief description of all cases can be found in Table 9.2.

Table 9.3 **Types of actors used in various partner roles**

Partner role	BoP micro-entrepreneurs	NGOs	Governments	Companies	Other
Co-developers	X	X	X	X	X
Suppliers	X			X	
Distributors	X	X		X	
Complementors				X	
Customers			X	X	
Microfinance providers		X		X	
Brokers	X	X	X		
Funders			X	X	X
Impact assessors		X		X	X

Co-developers are partners involved in the developing of the offering or the business model. The partners engaged as co-developers were NGOs, international governmental organizations (IGOs), other companies and governmental agencies, although according to the literature (e.g. UNDP 2008) BoP individuals and communities could also be engaged in this role. As companies may find it difficult to develop suitable business models and offerings for the markets alone because of insufficient knowledge and understanding of the BoP markets, partners with in-depth knowledge about the BoP can help companies to develop solutions that fit the markets. Congruently with the literature (e.g. Chesbrough *et al.* 2006; Drayton and Budinich 2010; Webb *et al.* 2010) in many of the examined cases, NGOs provided their expertise on the local environment to the ventures. However, when in need of technical or industry expertise, not only NGOs but also other companies, IGOs and government organizations came in as co-developers. For instance, PET-STAR, which aims at better recycling and improvement of scavengers' working conditions, is a joint venture between two companies, a leading environmental service firm (PASA) and the largest collector of post-consumer plastic in Mexico (Avangard). Sometimes, developing a business model together with governmental agencies is necessary because of the government's role in managing common resources or providing public services. For example, in its efforts to mobilize local farmers in tree growing, Huatai, the biggest newsprint manufacturer in China, needed the local government's involvement in developing its eucalyptus outgrower scheme because it has the rights over land. In Morocco, LYDEC, an energy, water and waste services company, engaged in a public–private partnership with the Moroccan authorities to provide electricity, water management and sanitation services in Casablanca.

The **suppliers** in the examined cases were BoP micro-entrepreneurs or companies. The micro-entrepreneurs were engaged as agricultural suppliers (CocoTech,

Integrated Tamale Fruit Company, and Grameen Danone's Shokti Doi), twiners and weavers for CocoTech's nets, and as service subcontractors in Manila Water's supply chain. Companies, in contrast, were used as suppliers of products or services requiring more advanced technological capabilities (for example, as component suppliers to Tsinghua Tongfang computers and subcontractors establishing LYDEC's electricity networks). Thus, although localization of value production is sometimes recommended in the BoP literature (e.g. Weidner *et al.* 2010) its applicability is very case-specific. It may often not be economically feasible to produce locally on a very small scale or to train BoP suppliers to produce technologically advanced products.

Distributors are referred to here as partners involved in the process of making a product or service available to the customer. Sometimes the distributor's role in BoP business may also include consumer training. The partners operating as distributors of products or services were most often BoP micro-entrepreneurs, although larger companies, NGOs and MFIs were also used as distributors in some cases. In service business, BoP individuals were engaged as loan collectors in Barclays' Susu Collectors Initiative and as service providers for their communities in Nokia Siemens Networks' (NSN) Village Connection, Grameenphone's Village Phone, and Freeplay Energy's Weza project. In product distribution, small BoP retailer shops as well as door-to-door distributors were used as rural distribution channels in the case of Grameen Danone's Shokti Doi yoghurt. NGOs were used in product distribution in the case of Amanco, and a commercial MFI acted as a distributor in the case of Nokia Microfinance.

Complementors are defined here as partners providing complementary offerings that are essential for the usefulness of a company's product or service. Many such examples were found from the information and communications technology (ICT) sector's BoP business models, in which the complementors were generally companies from complementary lines of business. For instance, content providers and operators were essential partners in the Nokia Life Tools service offering.

Customers can be regarded as partners in some cases. In BoP business models, they can be intermediate buyers of offerings targeted at the BoP, as in the case of Tsinghua Tongfang or NSN Village Connection or buyers of products sourced from the BoP, as in the case of CocoTech or PETSTAR. For CocoTech and Tsinghua Tongfang, the partner customers were governments: CocoTech's nets were purchased by the national government, while Tsinghua Tongfang's computers were bought by the municipal government to the rural information centres. For PETSTAR and NSN, the customers were companies: PETSTAR made sales contracts with companies such as Pepsi and Danone, while NSN sells its Village Connection solution to operators.

Microfinance partners were mostly needed in business models engaging BoP entrepreneurs in ways that required substantial new investment from them. Attaching the microfinance possibility to a specific business model may facilitate the BoP micro-entrepreneurs' access to a relatively large amount of credit. Microfinance partners may also be needed when selling relatively expensive products to the BoP. Microfinance could be provided by NGOs, or commercial MFIs.

Brokers, meaning the partners recruiting, coordinating and training BoP micro-entrepreneurs, were most often NGOs, but local governments and producers' organizations were also sometimes used in this role. In Grameenphone's Village Phone model, the non-profit partner Grameen Telecom took over the responsibility of coordinating and training the Village Phone ladies. PETSTAR partnered with small NGOs to build trust with the BoP scavengers, and Barclays partnered with the national MFIs' association, which brokered the relationship with the Susu collectors and trained them. In contrast, CocoTech used the help of a local government agency to organize the community partners. These tasks may in many cases be beyond the company's resources, since companies often lack embeddedness at the BoP.

Funders were bilateral development aid agencies, governmental agencies and IGOs, although various types of private actor could also be used in this role, as suggested by the literature (WBCSD 2004).

Finally, **impact assessor partners** were found in a few cases. It may often be important for companies to be able to show to funders or other stakeholders that their BoP ventures do, indeed, have positive development effects. However, the assessment of the impact of these ventures may be beyond the capabilities of the company, owing, for example, to the complexity of the social processes involved. Moreover, a point of view of an external evaluator is likely to increase the credibility of the results. Most often, the impact assessors were universities, but NGOs, IGOs and companies were also engaged in this role.

9.1.5 Discussion and conclusions

This study provides a systematic examination of the different kinds of partnerships that companies form with various types of actors when doing business at the BoP. Based on an examination of 20 companies' business models, nine partner roles were identified, and an overview of which actors and organizations tend to fulfil these roles was provided. This is an important contribution to the BoP literature, since although the importance of partnerships in BoP business has been repeatedly emphasized, a comprehensive overview has been missing.

The findings confirm that partnerships can be used to tackle many of the challenges of doing business at the BoP. For example, as suggested by Rivera-Santos and Rufin (2010), various gaps in the institutional environments could be filled through forming partnerships. In the case of missing traditional distribution channels, non-traditional partners, such as BoP individuals, NGOs or MFIs took on the tasks of distributors. In the case of missing complementary offerings, the offerings were developed together with partners in complementary lines of business. In addition, other types of challenges were tackled through partnerships. In many cases, the lack of resources needed for developing BoP business models, such as understanding of the BoP markets, was compensated for by collaborating with co-developers that had the necessary resources. Furthermore, the challenges of finding the BoP micro-entrepreneurs, coordinating them and building their capacity were tackled by engaging organizations close to the BoP as brokers. In some cases, the challenge of getting internal company funding was solved by external capital providers.

As suggested by the literature (e.g. Hart 2005; Klein 2008; London and Hart 2004; Prahalad 2005; Webb et al. 2010), the non-traditional partners, such as NGOs and local micro-entrepreneurs, were indeed collaborated with. However, somewhat contrary to the assertions of BoP literature, the more traditional partnerships with other companies and national governments played significant roles in many of the ventures analysed. In particular, partnerships with government agencies were found to be more extensive than the literature suggests. If governments are indeed significant partners for BoP ventures, why has their role been downplayed in the literature? A couple of reasons can be suggested. First, the significance of the government as a potential partner depends on the national context. While much of the early and most-cited BoP research stems from the Indian and South American contexts, where local self-help groups or other NGOs are salient players, this may have influenced the strong NGO emphasis regarding BoP partnerships. Yet the country of operation appears to be an important intervening factor. In some countries (e.g. China, Ethiopia, Russia or Vietnam) the government's role is so extensive that government partnerships may be necessary to set up any business. Second, the need to emphasize the salience of NGOs may have led to unintended underestimation of the role of different levels of governments.

Certain partner roles suggested in the literature did not appear in the present data. For example, the people at the BoP were not notably involved in doing market research, giving community-based training or co-creating innovations (UNDP 2008; Hart 2005). In addition, there were no observations of companies sharing costs of investments, setting common standards, or lobbying governments together. The lack of these kinds of observation can be explained by the limited number of cases analysed. Still, the lack of observations in 20 cases implies that those types of partnerships are at least not typical in BoP business.

One noteworthy finding of this study is that there were little significant differences in the partner needs of foreign and local companies. This is contrary to the assumption that local managers would by definition be close to the local BoP and rather supports the assumption that local companies may also face a great "psychic distance" from the BoP markets (Sánchez et al. 2005) and hence need to cooperate with actors that are close to the BoP. The only difference was that the local companies appeared to partner with smaller and more local NGOs than the MNCs. This may be because it may be easier for local companies to find local partners as they are likely to have better access to networks within their own countries. Another possible reason is that the foreign companies, which were mostly MNCs in the sample, want more scale to their business models, and thus prefer to work with larger organizations that can cooperate with the company when also replicating the business model in other locations.

9.2 Implications and future research

As to managerial implications, the findings of the study highlight the importance of partnerships for creating and maintaining business models for poverty alleviation. Companies can use these findings when planning their BoP business models to get an overview of what kinds of partners may be useful in BoP business, and non-profit actors designing their own operation models for the BoP may also benefit from the present findings. From the point of view of partners, for example, government agencies and NGOs can reflect on the possible roles they could take as partners of BoP ventures.

The wide perspective of this study was chosen to enable a comprehensive outlook of partner roles in BoP business models of large companies, and on the actors that typically fulfil those roles. Future research can build on the present findings of partners and their roles, and examine whether the different constellations have different impacts with regard to poverty alleviation. Additionally, conflicts of power and interest differences are bound to arise due to the twofold interests—business and poverty alleviation aims—that characterize these partnerships. These are further aggravated by the frequent complexity of partner networks and their challenging operating environments.

Bibliography

Chesbrough, H., S. Ahern, M. Finn and S. Guerraz (2006) "Business Models for Technology in the Developing World: The Role of Non-Governmental Organizations", *California Management Review* 48.3: 48-61.

Christensen, L.J., H. Parsons and J. Fairbourne (2010) "Building Entrepreneurship in Subsistence Markets: Microfranchising as an Employment Incubator", *Journal of Business Research* 63: 595-601.

Dalberg (2009) *Franchising in Frontier Markets: What's Working, What's Not, and Why* (A report by Dalberg Global Development Advisors with support from the John Templeton Foundation and the International Finance Corporation; Copenhagen/New York: Dalberg, http://www.dalberg.com/documents/Franchising_in_Frontier_Markets.pdf, accessed 30 November 2014).

Das, T.K., and B. Teng, B. (2000) "A Resource-Based Theory of Strategic Alliances", *Journal of Management* 26.1: 31-61.

Drayton, B., and V. Budinich (2010) "A New Alliance for Global Change", *Harvard Business Review* 88.9: 56-64.

Eisenhardt, K. (1989) "Building Theories from Case Study Research", *Academy of Management Review* 14.4: 532-50.

Eisenhardt, K., and C. Schoonhoven (1996) "Resource-based View of Strategic Alliance Formation: Strategic and Social Effects in Entrepreneurial Firms", *Organization Science* 7.2: 136-50.

Fairbourne, J.S., S.W. Gibson and W.G. Dyer (2007) *Microfranchising: Creating Wealth at the Bottom of the Pyramid* (Northampton, MA: Edward Elgar Publishing).

Gibson, S.W. (2007) "Microfranchising: The Next Step on the Development Ladder" in J.S. Fairbourne, S.W. Gibson and W.G. Dyer (eds.), *Microfranchising: Creating Wealth at the Bottom of the Pyramid* (Northampton, MA: Edward Elgar Publishing: 17-42).

Gulati, R., N. Nohria and A. Zaheer (2000) "Strategic Networks", *Strategic Management Journal* 21: 203-215.

Hahn, R. (2009) "The Ethical Rationale of Business for the Poor: Integrating the Concepts OF THE Base of the Pyramid, Sustainable Development, and Corporate Citizenship", *Journal of Business Ethics* 84, 313-24.

Hart, S.L. (2005) *Capitalism at the Crossroads: The Unlimited Business Opportunities in Solving the World's Most Difficult Problems* (Upper Saddle River, NJ: Wharton School Publishing.

Hoyt, M., and E. Jamison (2007) "Microfranchising and the Base of the Pyramid", in J.S. Fairbourne, S.W. Gibson and W.G. Dyer (eds.), *Microfranchising: Creating Wealth at the Bottom of the Pyramid* (Northampton, MA: Edward Elgar Publishing: 111-32).

IFC (2007) *Case Study: Amanco. An Excerpt from Market Movers: Lessons from a Frontier of Innovation* (Washington, DC: International Finance Corporation, http://www.ifc.org/wps/wcm/connect/233ac58048855812bed4fe6a6515bb18/MarketMovers_CS_Amanco.pdf?MOD=AJPERES, accessed 20 December 2014).

Jenkins, B., and E. Ishikawa (2009) *Business Linkages: Enabling Access to Markets at the Base of the Pyramid. Report of a Roundtable Dialogue March 3-5, 2009, Jaipur, India* (Washington, DC: International Finance Corporation/ International Business Leaders Forum/CSR Initiative at the Harvard Kennedy School, http://c.ymcdn.com/sites/www.gbsnonline.org/resource/collection/0814C059-1ABC-4D1F-B774-A01A9014CF79/BusinessLinkages_BaseOfPyramid.pdf, accessed 20 December 2014).

Kandachar, P., and M. Halme (eds.) (2008) *Sustainability Challenges and Solutions at the Base of the Pyramid: Business, Technology and the Poor* (Sheffield, UK: Greenleaf Publishing).

Klein, M.H. (2008) "Poverty Alleviation through Sustainable Strategic Business Models: Essays on Poverty Alleviation as a Business Strategy", PhD thesis, Erasmus University Rotterdam. http://repub.eur.nl/pub/13482/.

Liew, J. (2005) "Banking the Unbanked in Fiji: The ANZ Bank and UNDP Partnership", paper presented to the *ADB Regional Conference on Expanding the Frontiers of Commercial Microfinance*, Manila, Philippines, 14–15 March, http://www.ncrc.org/global/australAsia/documents/Fiji_Art_1_3-29-05.pdf, accessed 20 December 2014.

London, T., and S.L. Hart (2004) "Reinventing Strategies for Emerging Markets: Beyond the Transnational Model", *Journal of International Business Studies* 35.5: 350-70.

London, T., R. Anubindi and S. Sheth (2010) "Creating Mutual Value: Lessons Learned from Ventures Serving Base of the Pyramid Producers", *Journal of Business Research* 63: 582-94.

Prahalad, C.K. (2005) *The Fortune at the Bottom of the Pyramid: Eradicating Poverty Through Profits* (Upper Saddle River, NJ: Wharton School Publishing).

Prahalad, C.K., and S.L. Hart (2002) "The Fortune at the Bottom of the Pyramid", *Strategy + Business* 26: 1-14.

Reficco, E., and P. Marquez (2009) "Inclusive Networks for Building BOP Markets", *Business and Society* 51:3: 512-56.

Rivera-Santos, M., and C. Rufin (2010) "Global Village vs. Small Town: Understanding Networks at the Base of the Pyramid", *International Business Review* 19.2: 126-39.

Rondinelli, D.A., and T. London (2003) "How Corporations and Environmental Groups Cooperate: Assessing Cross-sector Alliances and Collaborations", *Academy of Management Executive* 17.1: 61-76.

Sánchez, P., J.E. Ricart and M.Á. Rodríguez (2005) "Influential Factors in Becoming Socially Embedded in Low-Income Markets", *Greener Management International* 51: 19-38.

Skarp, M., R. Bansal, R. Lovio and M. Halme (2008) "Affordable Communication for Rural Communities", in P. Kandachar and M. Halme (eds.), *Sustainability Challenges and Solutions at the Base of the Pyramid: Business, Technology and the Poor* (Sheffield, UK: Greenleaf Publishing): 307-25.

UNDP (2008) *Creating Value for All: Strategies for Doing Business with the Poor* (New York: United Nations Development Programme, http://www.undp.org/publications/Report_growing_inclusive_markets.pdf)

Uzzi, B. (1996) "The Sources and Consequences of Embeddedness for the Economic Performance of Organizations: The Network Effect", *American Sociological Review* 61: 674-98.

WBCSD (2004) *Finding Capital for Sustainable Livelihoods Businesses* (Geneva: World Business Council for Sustainable Development, www.wbcsd.org/web/publications/SL%20Finance%20guide%20August%2030.pdf).

Webb, J.W., G.M. Kistruck, R.D. Ireland and D.J. Ketchen Jr (2010) "The Entrepreneurship Process in Base of the Pyramid Markets: The Case of Multinational Enterprise/Non-government Organization Alliances", *Entrepreneurship Theory and Practice* 34.3: 555-81.

WEF (2009a) *The Next Billions: Business Strategies to Enhance Food Value Chains and Empower the Poor* (Geneva: World Economic Forum).

WEF (2009b) *The Next Billions: Unleashing Business Potential in Untapped Markets* (Geneva: World Economic Forum, http://www.weforum.org/pdf/BSSFP/NextBillionsUnleashingBusinessPotentialUntappedMarkets.pdf, accessed 20 December 2014).

Weidner, K.L., J.A. Rosa and M. Viswanathan (2010) "Marketing to Subsistence Consumers: Lessons from Practice", *Journal of Business Research* 63: 559-69.

WRI (2001) *What Works: Grameen Telecom's Village Phones* (Washington, DC: World Resources Institute, http://pdf.wri.org/dd_grameen.pdf, accessed 20 December 2014).

10

Access2innovation
An innovative BoP network partnership model

Jacob Ravn

Access2innovation, Denmark

Innovative partnerships between NGOs, universities and the private sector is gaining increased momentum as a means to ensuring poverty alleviation based on a market-driven approach. Knowledge is, however, scarce on how these partnerships are being formulated and implemented. This chapter sets out to identify the do's and don'ts in joint partnership innovation. This is based on the experiences gained by the access2innovation network, which in the period 2007–11 launched four partnerships that essentially show that cross-sector partnerships are not "business as usual" and hold a number of challenges for everyone involved.

10.1 Access2innovation as an example of innovative partnerships within relief and development aid

Over the last decades, cooperation across organizational borders has been seen as a defining premise when it comes to innovating products, services and business models in order to access new customers and markets. This development is also seen within aid work and long-term development projects, base of the pyramid (BoP) and corporate social responsibility (CSR) initiatives. In Denmark, this has led to a series of initiatives such as LifeStraw, Grundfos Lifelink, CleanStar Mozambique, Baisikeli and MYC4. On top of this, a string of publicly subsidized initiatives have been set up, for example, Innovative Partnerships for Development and the Danida Business Partnerships. These are all initiatives that derive from collaborations between companies, scientists and non-governmental organizations (NGOs) in order to reduce poverty in developing countries through a market-driven approach.

Despite the increased focus on this new partnership trend, relatively little knowledge exists on how the partnerships are developed and implemented. A situation that, in a worst-case scenario, could lead to mismanagement of partnerships; the same challenges being faced over and over again, leaving partners behind or resulting in end-users or producers ending up wasting their time and resources. These pitfalls must be addressed if poverty reduction is to be met effectively through partnerships; substantial knowledge is therefore essential to guide future initiatives.

This is the backdrop for this chapter, which aims to discuss some of the lessons learned from launching and implementing the access2innovation initiative,[1] where the NGO DanChurchAid (DCA), in collaboration with 21 companies and five research teams from 2007 to 2011, has launched four partnerships that innovate market-driven solutions targeting needs within relief and development aid:

- **Sky-Watch.**[2] A small drone providing on-site real-time geo-referenced pictures and HD video for NGOs and other international organizations within humanitarian relief and development activities

- **ViewWorld (VW).**[3] Smartphone app and back-office data-handling system optimizing information handling, surveys and project management for NGOs and UN organizations leaving pen, paper and inefficient administration behind

- **The Green Generator**. A portable generator aiming at substituting the widespread use of polluting diesel generators with photovoltaic (PV) panels, fuel cells and low-tech wind turbines as energy providers for off-grid energy supply

- **Community-based biogas projects** for rural electrification in Bangladesh

1 www.access2innovation.com.
2 www.sky-watch.dk.
3 www.viewworld.dk.

Initiated partnership from the access2innovation network demonstrating that cooperation between NGOs, companies and researchers can facilitate better relief and development, as well as providing access to new markets for businesses and new areas of research for academia.

At the same time, it is evident that these cross-sector partnerships are not "business as usual" and hold a number of challenges for everyone involved. The development and implementation have in no way been running on autopilot. The partnerships within the access2innovation network have continually found themselves facing a number of challenges and opportunities that were impossible to spot when the initiative was launched in 2007, ruling out classic innovation models as effective planning tools.

Thus, this chapter aims to unveil some of the key lessons drawn from the access2innovation initiative by focusing on the possibilities and limitations when developing and implementing partnerships that target needs with relief and development aid.

Despite the fact that the process behind access2innovation is probably best illustrated by a bowl of spaghetti, the following will—to ensure a certain rigour—be organized in the following sections:

- Setting the methodological and theoretical platform for studying access2innovation

- The story of access2innovation—from idea to action

- Lessons learned from launching access2innovation partnerships

- Building up cross-sector partnerships

- Setting the stage for commercialization

- From pilot project to innovation hub

- Lessons learned from launching network-based partnerships

10.2 Setting the methodological and theoretical platform for studying access2innovation

As founder and head of secretariat of access2innovation I have studied the access2innovation initiative from an action-research approach (O'Brian 2001; Reason and Bradbury 2006) that has allowed close interaction with the field and created a thorough understanding of the processes that the founding network and following partnerships (Sky-Watch, ViewWorld, etc.) have gone through. The analysis and theoretical discussion of the implications of setting up partnerships between NGOs, researchers and companies is available in my PhD thesis (Ravn 2012), but the following sections will tell the story behind access2innovation. A story that in a number of respects can provide inspiration on the **do's** and—in particular —the **do nots** when launching and implementing commercial partnerships as a means for poverty reduction.

The study of access2innovation is based on the underlying theoretical understanding that network-based innovation in essence is about connecting knowledge from different organizational domains, for example, companies in different industries, researchers, NGOs or public institutions (Hargadon 2002). These domains hold knowledge, practices, competences and networks that enable innovation when combined or implemented in new settings. However, the domains also hold a number of limitations because new initiatives need to be able to fit into the already established norms, knowledge and organizational strategies.

Based on the experiences from access2innovation, this has motivated a series of enquiries into network organization, facilitation and the development of network-based business models due to the commercial goal of the access2innovation initiative. We shall return to some of these aspects in the closing discussion, but in the following introduction it is worthwhile paying attention to how:

- The access2innovation network and initiated partnerships have been **organized**, as the organizational framework has a direct impact on the operational activities (for inspiration see Provan and Kenis 2007).

- **Facilitation** of the network and partnerships has played a crucial role in initiating, developing and maturing the concepts, as the process of networks and partnerships have developed in a very non-linear way (for inspiration see Dhanarj and Parkhe 2006; Hargadon 2002; Rothwell 1994).

- **Business models** have matured and changed depending on the partners' ability to develop the connections between product, market, customer relations, production, business partners, etc. (for inspiration see Chesbrough and Schwarts 2007; Kolk 2013; Osterwalder *et al.* 2002; or www.businessmodel generation.com).

These crucial focal points help shed some light on the experiences from the access2innovation network and the initiated partnerships, thereby deepening the understanding of why the initiatives have been marked by a number of iterations, partnership reformulations, changes in solution proposals and the addition of new partners.

To sum up, the lessons learned from access2innovation draw a picture of network-based innovation as an extremely dynamic process, challenging the often-used Stage-Gate models, logical frame approaches and incremental innovation strategies. These experiences can provide a benchmark for further investigations into the opportunities and challenges when launching BoP targeted initiatives.

10.3 The story of access2innovation: from idea to action

As Anders Ladekarl, Head of the International Department at the Danish Red Cross, concluded in January 2007 (pers. comm.): "NGOs are ten years behind in integrating new knowledge or technical solutions that are already available in developed countries." The primary reason for this is that the role of most NGOs is to be operational. As an illustration, Danish Red Cross at that time employed only one doctor at its headquarters whose responsibility it was to coordinate and assist 25 health programmes globally. This meant that there was very little time to innovate or engage in lengthy development processes with researchers and companies. In other words, NGOs could be much more efficient and perform better if they had the ability and strategy to continuously integrate new knowledge from researchers and companies. Companies, on the other hand, could access new potential markets if they were able to meet the demands from an apparently under-served market, and academia could gain access to new research in areas that were often overlooked.

Based on this finding, the idea of formulating an innovation platform emerged to link existing resources, skills and network from NGOs, researchers and companies based on the following reasoning:

- NGOs have insight into the needs and opportunities in developing countries but lack the resources to develop and produce the needed solutions. By entering into a partnership with researchers and industry, NGOs could potentially provide better relief and the basis for more effective poverty reduction

- Companies have skills, resources and production tools to provide solutions but lack insight and understanding of the opportunities within relief and development aid. Through active collaboration with NGOs and researchers, companies can gain access to new markets as well as positive branding opportunities

- Universities have access to state-of-the-art technology and are experienced in user involvement and documentation. However, they often lack practical experience and an NGO/business network that focuses on developing countries. By partnering with NGOs and companies, researchers are able to gain access to new fields of research and expand their contact with the industry

The basic idea was, therefore, that knowledge, resources and network in facilitated partnerships between NGOs, companies and researchers could form the base for a range of new innovations, ensuring better relief and development activities and—as an equally important incentive for the companies—open up new markets. This would take a bottom-up approach, where the NGOs at the centre of the stage should act as mediators to the end-users' need in relief and development activities. A process that would voice the needs and possible business opportunities to researchers and companies who would be gaining access to knowledge, testing grounds and potential "blue ocean" markets that otherwise would be difficult to enter. An apparent win–win–win situation for all parties involved.

The idea was picked up by two Danish offices for small and medium-sized enterprises (SMEs) and the Confederation of Danish Industry (DI) as they saw new market and financing opportunities for the businesses they represented; Aalborg

University (AAU) was looking for new research areas and DanChurchAid (DCA) spotted opportunities in cooperating with businesses to develop new appropriate technologies that could support their existing activities within relief and development.

Based on this organizational framework and legitimacy from institutional partners, the access2innovation network was launched in the autumn of 2007 with the ambition of building three to four partnerships deriving from the operational activities of DCA and its more than 100 partner organizations in developing countries. The idea was to use a bottom-up-driven approach in order to gain direct access to end users through DCA's partners who were responsible for the actual planning and execution of water, food and educational projects. The process was kick-started by a series of workshops in Denmark and abroad in combination with direct contact with DCA representatives from Asia and Africa in order to map out potential challenges within energy, information and communications technology (ICT) and food security.

The bottom-up approach was challenged immediately, because concrete ideas were quite difficult to obtain from DCA headquarters staff and local partners. Innovation and cooperation was not a strategic priority and to some seemed outside the scope of the NGO's operational activities. For the few who were interested, it turned out to be a major challenge to describe the needs, possibilities and wishes for products or services that would attract the interest of researchers and businesses. This information was crucial, because companies were asking for specific technical specifications and market data before they would even consider investing in new and relatively unclear business initiatives.

The development was therefore grinding to a halt in the spring of 2008 when DCA on its side found it difficult to visualize the needs due to lack of technical expertise. At the same time, businesses were not interested in throwing resources into partnerships before concrete ideas had been described and documented more thoroughly. Despite the fact that a number of challenges obviously exist within relief and development aid, they need to be communicated in a way that the private sector understands.

By chance, an alternative approach materialized during a talk with Sam Christensen, Head of DCA's Humanitarian Demining Department (HDD). Unlike other departments, HDD is active in a large number of field operations in countries such as Albania, Sudan, Angola and Congo. The team provided direct access to specialists with the necessary technical knowledge and operational experience. This was a stark contrast to the other departments and resource people in DCA, whose primary focus was either on fundraising or managing projects that were implemented by sister organizations in partnering countries.

Coupled with a single innovation project from DCA's sister organization RDRS in Bangladesh, this changed approach resulted in a revised focus: from the needs of end-users in developing countries to instead building on the NGO's own operations where market data existed and technical expertise was available. The revised strategy led to the required specifications and knowledge that resulted in formulating the four specific ideas already mentioned:

- The Eye in the Sky, which focused on the use of small helicopters to fly over de-mining sites, ensuring more effective mine clearing through geo-referenced still pictures and HD video recordings

- An ICT solution to optimize the information-gathering process in mine clearance work in order to avoid administrative duplication and incorrect entries

- The Green Generator, aimed at developing a generator based solely on renewable energy sources for use in humanitarian demining. This would lower the costs, minimize the risks when transporting diesel and prevent operations from shutting down due to lack of energy

- A biogas project in Bangladesh based on already existing initiatives, focusing on community-based installations where expert knowledge was required to ensure sustainable and efficient production

The ideas were going to be implemented within an organizational structure where the network partners (DCA, DI, AAU and SME offices) would meet two or three times a year to set the framework for the strategic development of the start-up phase. Jointly allocated staff from the founding network members would facilitate the launch and implementation of the initiatives. And so, by the spring of 2008, the foundation for launching and implementing the initiatives was in place and ready to build up partnerships with researchers and companies and start the joint innovation that would lead to the final commercialization. The reality, however, turned out to be quite different.

10.4 Lessons learned from launching access2innovation partnerships

Retrospectively, the four initiated partnerships kick-started by the access2innovation network have largely gone through the same processes, which gives good indications of some of the challenges and opportunities arising when launching and implementing cross-sector commercial partnerships in a network setting. Figure 10.1 summarizes this process, and the following sections will highlight some of the lessons learned. It should, however, be stressed that the phases did not become visible until after four years of work, and that Figure 10.1 does not include the number of iterations that have been the hallmark of the project.

The starting point for the initiated partnerships in Phase 1 was a close dialogue and several meetings with DCA HDD, ending up with the formulation of four concept notes on 5–7 pages (see excerpt in Box 10.1). The concept notes provided short contextual introductions to the challenges that, based on the DCA staff's technical expertise, provided the platform for drawing up existing knowledge and recommendations for solutions: to be robust, easy to use, affordable, possible to integrate with existing tools/databases, etc. within a humanitarian mine-clearing market of US$475 million per year.

Box 10.1 **Extract from the DCA concept note on ICT solutions**

In order to try to lighten the administrative burden of the field personnel in DanChurchAid's humanitarian de-mining operations and to facilitate the flow of data through the DCA system, the idea of supplying field personnel with purpose-programmed PDAs has been raised.

Currently, all daily reporting in the field is done on paper and then later when opportunity arises (i.e. returned to main camp) the report is transferred to computer and stored in the main database. Besides the obvious duplication of work described here there is always the risk of papers getting lost or damaged while in the field or during transport; furthermore, these reporting procedures are slow and prevent headquarters staff from getting a thorough day-to-day outline of the progress achieved in the field (field work can last up to several weeks).

With the concept notes in hand, the stage was set to map out existing academic knowledge, typically through direct contact with one or more researchers who either were working within the areas of interest or could pin-point relevant resource persons within the academic environment.

The researchers turned out to be interested in the presented initiatives, and the insight gained was very valuable in the early screening stages because of their neutral position and knowledge of existing solutions that could potentially assist in filtering through technologies and methodologies to match the identified needs. Due to existing research cooperation with the business community they were even able to identify potential partners in the industry.

Thus contact with companies came through recommendations from researchers at the universities and partly through a snowball effect, where the SME offices could pin-point companies or clusters that might have interest in the initiatives, or assist in identifying other possible stakeholders. In addition, we used newsletters from the network partners, but the feedback from these efforts was limited. Despite this explicit use of existing contacts, it was, however, a "cold canvas" approach with direct contact and personal networking that eventually formed the foundation for relations with companies.

This approach was further challenging as the solutions outlined by DCA turned out to be far from off-the-shelf solutions. This meant that technologies, competences and resources from different companies and researchers had to be pieced together to develop the platform for the solutions needed, thereby making it difficult to communicate what was in it for the individual company:

Figure 10.1 **Phases in implementation of access2innovation partnerships**

	Launch of projects				Implementation
Phase 1. Idea formulation	**Phase 2. Match making**	**Phase 3. Funding**	**Phase 4. Formulation**	**Phase 5. Test**	**Phase 6. Commercialization**
Identification of needs based on input from DCA DDC and sister organizations. Ideas are formulated on concept notes that briefly outline needs, existing practices and possible ideas for solutions	Identification of researchers and companies having interest in participating in workshops	Developing applications to public donors	Conducting needs analysis and specification of products demands. Identification of entrepreneurs and business model	Establishment lead company based venture funding and public donor funding. Re-evaluation and formulation of partnerships and technology basis. Hiring of employees (Sky-Watch and ViewWorld)	Test of prototype, identification of parallel markets, developing distribution, sales channels, start-up of parallel markets and formulation of new partnerships. (Sky-Watch and ViewWorld)
Stakeholders: DCA and sister organizations coordinated from the access2innovation secretariat	**Stakeholders:** EU offices and researchers coordinated from access2innovation	**Stakeholders:** EU offices and researchers coordinated from access2innovation	**Stakeholders:** Partnerships in collaboration with DCA and support from EU offices and a2i secretariat	**Stakeholder:** Lead Entrepreneur in interaction with partners. A2i providing sparring on business model development as well as network to Danish and international network	**Stakeholder:** Lead company engaging with new suppliers A2i supporting with network

- The Eye in the Sky helicopter solution should consist of a flying unit, wireless communication for control and download of images, a simple user interface and tools for image management.

- The ICT solution demanded both an understanding of users' existing collection and use of information in humanitarian de-mining situations, as well as state-of-the-art insight on existing technological platforms that could collect data in remote and harsh environment—and back-office information handling and integration with existing systems.

- The Green Generator should be able to connect to a number of existing technologies such as fuel cells, small wind turbines, PV panels, etc. but was challenged by understanding the end-users' needs and adaptability of low-cost technologies to very rough and diverse operational scenarios.

- The biogas project in Bangladesh was based on existing technologies, but the challenge lay in adapting the technologies to the local context and uncovering how a sustainable business model could be established for both local users and the private sector in Denmark.

In sum, the existing technologies needed to be combined in new settings.

10.5 Building up cross-sector partnerships

Based on the developed concept notes it was, however, possible to identify a number of relevant companies and host the first workshops between June 2008 and February 2009. Companies and researchers were introduced to the partnership approach behind access2innovation and the identified needs from DCA. This was the starting point for a discussion that typically focused on technology, where companies had the opportunity to present existing expertise to DCA and obtain a better understanding of the concept notes presented. A very open process gave room for discussion and clarification of different opportunities but eventually ended up with companies asking for further descriptions of technical functionalities that DCA would then seek to clarify before the next meeting.

The initiating workshops had between 10 and 20 participating companies per initiative, but a number of companies later decided to pull out. This was mainly because they did not see the business opportunities, or the opportunities did not fit with their existing business strategies, or because of the realization that access2innovation was not simply about selling existing solutions, but about joint development based on partnership—a rather odd construction to many companies.

A clarifying process resulted in two to five companies participating in the follow-up workshops for each initiative. The remaining companies were motivated by the learning and business opportunities when entering into cooperation with the end-users from DCA, and, not least, by a range of identified public donor funding opportunities that could minimize the financial risk associated with participating in the still maturing initiatives.

But the companies would not simply jump on board and start innovating. More information and knowledge was needed; therefore, the goal in the third phase was to access donor funding to further describe the technical specifications, identify markets, and so on, in partnerships between the interested stakeholders.

The network partners from the SME offices and DCA therefore started preparing and developing the applications to get the initiatives off the ground. Companies and researchers participated in this process to a limited extent, arguing that they still lacked knowledge about what solutions DCA was looking for—if or when the project obtained financing.

On top of this, the usage of donor funding as the vehicle for launching the partnerships meant that the initiatives virtually stopped until there was money on the table. It was a very long and time-consuming process to gain funding, and the network partners were essential in keeping up the momentum in a process that would have otherwise stalled. Luckily, the cooperation between NGOs, companies and researchers attracted interest from a wide range of donors and resulted in the initiatives receiving pledges of support of US$2.7 million to kick-start the initiatives.

Despite the fact that the partnerships were now in place and the financing for narrowing down technical specifications and market information was available, the activities in phase four turned up yet a new string of challenges:

- Due to the emerging financial crisis, participation and involvement was channelled to other tasks within the existing operation, reducing attention to the partnership, despite the funding already gained of up to 50% of the cost to be incurred in the upcoming activities.

- Despite their interest, the researchers had other research and tuition tasks that delayed participation and their ability to engage with the companies when needed.

- Businesses wanted a clear statement of interest for the purchase of services from the DCA prior to starting their work. Obviously, it was difficult for the NGO to make this commitment before the solution was developed and tested.

These constraints eventually left the SME offices and DCA with the project management of collected funds, but without the necessary technical management skills or resources to implement a product and business development.

In addition, two underlying issues in the ongoing activities of the partnerships emerged: companies that engaged in the initiatives did not necessarily have the organizational framework to develop the product and take it to the market. The technologies and products might materialize within the partnerships, but setting up distribution channels, sales forces and capital for investment proved to be a very serious challenge.

On top of that, the rapid technological development meant that new doors were opening. As an example, the ICT solution was originally based on using small, hand-held, very rugged computers (personal digital assistants—PDAs), which, however, proved too expensive. Use of relatively low-cost smartphones, development of apps and focus on the development of a back-office solution began, but only after a major change in the group of affiliated companies.

10.6 Setting the stage for commercialization

Despite these challenges, needs, market and technical specifications were outlined through a series of trips with DCA to Albania in 2009 (testing the Eye in the Sky), identification of needs for generator solutions in Angola in February 2010, identification of needs for biogas partnerships in northern Bangladesh in April 2010 and testing ICT solutions during the winter of 2011. This was based on two different lead strategies:

- Testing and developing ICT solutions and Eye in the Sky was handed to two entrepreneurs who were interested and willing to take the lead and the financial risk to establish two companies; ViewWorld ApS (www.viewworld.net) and Sky-Watch A/S (www.sky-watch.dk), which would continue on the ICT solution and the Eye in the Sky.

- Implementation of field trips and special design of the prototype of the Green Generator was carried out in cooperation between network partners led respectively by South Denmark and EU (SDEU) office and DCA. The status of these activities is that the Green Generator exists as a prototype and a business network with an interest in following the project onwards, possibly as subcontractors.

The biogas project culminated with a final report highlighting the potential needs and business opportunities of making semi-commercial urban biogas by collecting waste to ensure the needed scale. This was opposed to the desired focus on community-based facilities involving the vulnerable groups that DCA's local sister organization RDRS is working with.

Where the activities in phases one to three were primarily facilitated by access2innovation network, the handover to the lead entrepreneurs in phase four ensured that the needed ownership materialized through concrete business strategies, access to venture capital and companies dedicated to the task at hand. This was based on the close collaboration with DCA, which was now showing interest in procuring upcoming solution. This meant that venture funds gained confidence in the proposed Sky-Watch solutions. Adding to this, DCA provided access to Danish Red Cross and CARE Denmark who entered as partners in the development and test of the ViewWorld solution in phases five and six.

Joint activities based on the established partnership have paved the way for accessing a number of parallel markets where Sky-Watch, for example, is now working with visual inspection of wind turbines, thermal images of buildings to reduce energy consumption, patrolling refugee camps, etc.—established markets with private and public capital that has further ensured the profitability of the developed businesses.

During this process, the access2innovation secretariat and the SME offices retracted to the role of advisers on the business model development and as network partners who were able to open up new possibilities for the partnerships.

Though it was not part of an explicit strategy at the time, the access2innovation network dialogue was maturing further with a number of stakeholders at home and abroad as the interest was rising in the partnerships already established. Thus, the access2innovation network turned out to be a marketing platform, leading to interest from Unicef, Grundfos, International Woodland Company, Danish Sewage Association and others, which are now showing commercial interest in the Sky-Watch and ViewWorld solutions.

In other words, the access2innovation gained legitimacy from new institutional partners by being able to demonstrate newly developed solutions ready for use, while the launched partnership and small companies gained access to customers who would have otherwise been out of their reach.

As the above tale of access2innovation briefly demonstrates, the activities have been characterized by technologies, business strategies, business partners, market focus, and so on, undergoing a number of iterations and fundamental reformulations. In other words, cross-sector partnership was needed to gain access to the necessary knowledge, resources and networks, but the final product and business cases ended up in a new "born global" company. This has been the outcome for Sky-Watch and ViewWorld, whereas the Green Generator and biogas projects have not got an organizational platform from which to be implemented.

10.7 From pilot project to innovation hub

Despite the evident challenges in launching and implementing the initiated initiatives, the lessons learned and the apparent potential led to the idea of establishing a nationwide access2innovation platform in order to scale up the bottom-up partnership innovation approach. This was to be a platform that could hold the resources to facilitate the process of building cross-sector partnerships and act as a framework for developing new solutions targeting the vast opportunities within relief and development in the BoP market space.

This was to have a specific focus to develop an infrastructure that minimizes the risks that the partnerships potentially hold throughout the process—from facilitation of requirements, gathering and identifying market opportunities in collaboration with Danish NGOs and UN agencies, to launching the partnerships through workshops where companies, researchers and NGOs can select interesting project initiatives together. Based on the experiences gained from the pilot projects, the platform should:

- Be organized around a small secretariat with seed funds that can support the proper maturing of new business cases

- Have a network and overview of experts to build up teams with the resources to initiate the processes and the skills to kick-start organizations into the process

- Have a clear thematic focus to ensure early involvement of the companies' own priorities

Based on a broad base of institutional stakeholders from NGOs, researchers and the private sector,[4] the access2innovation platform is now up and running with a budget of US$4.3 million that can ensure a dedicated and fast launch and test of new initiatives. By the end of 2012, 13 new initiatives had been formulated, directly targeting identified needs with access to sustainable energy and agro-business as well as water and sanitation mainly in East Africa.[5]

10.8 Lessons learned from launching network-based partnerships

Access2innovation has evolved from being a small pilot project to a well-established network consisting of a range of stakeholders with an interest in creating market-driven solutions to the challenges in developing countries. The above story of access2innovation has addressed several challenges and opportunities that have emerged to strengthen knowledge on how commercial partnerships between NGOs, researchers and companies can be a means for poverty reduction. The main focus has been on network and partnerships within relief and development aid, but recent access2innovation activities addressing the BoP markets provides experience that is equally important when addressing the needs of customers and producers in developing countries.

Taking a step back, the tale of access2innovation provides a number of indications of why the private sector and innovative commercial partnership—despite the evident market opportunities—still remain reluctant to engage in innovation that targets needs within emergency and development. The risk associated with entering the markets appears to be too high, and the required knowledge and resources are often only found outside the existing organization. The technologies very often exist, but the challenge is to fully comprehend the end-user needs and

4 Danish Red Cross, WWF, MS Action Aid, CARE Denmark, Confederation of Danish Industry, Renewable Energy Innovation Network, Danish Water Forum, North Jutland Food Network, University of Copenhagen, Copenhagen Business School, Aalborg University and North Denmark EU Offices managing the secretariat.
5 For more information, see www.access2innovation.com.

market opportunities and constraints, to identify potential and to develop and test the business models in a new and relatively unknown market setting for the private sector. This requires skill and resources beyond most individual NGOs' or companies' organizational capacity.

If we are to move from single-case-based initiatives to a strategic level, support is needed to enforce the interplay between skill, resources and networks across businesses, academia and NGOs that are otherwise too dispersed to be merged.

A number of initiatives are working on this endeavour globally, with which access2innovation has worked intensively with a bottom-up partnership approach; an approach calling for a network that needs institutional legitimacy to facilitate the mapping of potential needs and business opportunities together with local stakeholders in order to kick-start the initiatives. A clear, commercial goal is essential to attract entrepreneurs that, in partnership with NGOs, researchers and relevant companies, can ensure successful implementation and prove the network's value and legitimacy.

Returning to the theoretical constructions briefly introduced above, this overall realization has led to a number of findings from creating innovative partnerships between NGOs, researchers and companies targeting the relief and development aid.

First, a key finding is that the organization of the network and partnerships has been characterized by a fluid set-up where roles, responsibilities and invested resources have changed as the concepts have matured. The network between DCA, AAU, DI and the SME offices provided the platform and facilitation of the initial stages of the partnership from where the concepts were handed over to companies, leaving the network and facilitator as sparring partners without any direct say on the implementation. NGOs play a part as potential customers and researchers are left behind once they have provided their state-of-the-art knowledge. In contrast to a classic organizational governing structure, network and partnerships are therefore emerging in a setting without hierarchal structure and control. In that sense, the access2innovation network has been a "partnership incubator" based on the ability to identify needed knowledge and resources, facilitate the formulation of partnerships and access new networks. This has happened within an organizational setting where it is crucial to understand that:

- The initial network provided legitimacy for kick-starting an innovation platform aimed at a relatively unclear market setting.

- Establishing a network secretariat in a joint effort with the SME offices and DCA has been crucial to ensuring the coordination and progress of the network and, not least, launch of and support to the implementation of the partnerships.

- The ability to build trust, share information and develop a common goal that fits with the individual partners' own interests is central in relation to launching and implementing successful networks and partnerships.

- Participating partners *must* realize and accept the changing organizational nature, as the joint value created is handed over from the NGO to the network facilitator to the lead entrepreneur who holds the final responsibility for the commercialization.

- Initially created partnerships are changing with new partners coming in and others leaving, as the maturing of the concept calls for new knowledge, resources and technologies.

- Network initiatives depend on delivering concrete outputs from the partnerships between NGOs, companies and researchers.

Second, facilitation of the process in the network and partnerships has provided the "glue" for initiating, developing and maturing the concepts; a role that has proven crucial for ensuring ownership, access to information and funding that the participating companies otherwise would not have been able to obtain. The following lessons learned have emerged from facilitating the partnerships:

- Dedicated financial and human capital is needed to ensure ongoing coordination between network members and facilitation of the partnership process, from identification of needs to final commercialization.

- Facilitating innovation partnerships is very much about coping with uncertainties, leaving elaborately detailed action plans behind and calling for more dynamic and iterative process planning. This is because the implicit co-creation process between NGOs, researchers and the private sector must be open to new knowledge and change the strategy to a learning-by-doing process.

- The role of the facilitator is constantly changing shape, from being the initiator and game master who identifies needs and builds up the partnerships in the first phases to taking a supporting role in the following activities. A role in which the lead entrepreneurs from the private sector take ownership and develop their business strategy but still need support in gaining access to funding, identifying new partners and resource persons from academia and NGOs.

All in all, it is a process that is characterized by the ability of both network facilitators and partnerships to navigate unknown waters with no clear rules of engagement and emerging strategy planning. A problem-based explorative innovation process that will often challenge both NGOs, companies and researchers, and all the more reason why the facilitator's ability to set the direction in an uncharted territory is central in setting the stage for successful partnerships.

Third, the partnership business models have matured and changed, depending on the partners' ability to develop the connections between product, market, customer relations, production, business partners, etc. For instance, the View-World solution was originally based on heavy-duty PDAs from a well-established company, but turned out to be commercialized in a new company selling an integrated reporting system based on smartphones designed to suit the NGO's needs; a process in which the initial models were formulated on a partnership formation, but ended up being driven by one company where previous partners have left the initiative, invested in the newly established company or have been engaged as a sub-supplier. Whereas a lot of changes occurred with the companies' partnership and by changing the business model design, it is interesting to note that the developed business models have integrated the capabilities and resources of mainly the NGOs, and to some extent the researchers, in relation to:

- Access to the potential customers/markets when defining features and pricing
- Testing and developing in collaboration with end-users both in Denmark and by visiting NGO field operations
- Building legitimacy in the market by working closely with the Red Cross, DanChurchAid, CARE, etc.
- Researching knowledge and gaining access to university students when building up the companies' core competencies
- Networking with international NGOs and UN organizations through the access2innovation network
- Gaining access to venture funding, as the NGOs/customers were participating in development of the solution, and thereby providing reassurance of the market demand

Despite these positive aspects, the companies have, however, been challenged in developing the needed business models because:

- Cooperation with several NGOs and other relevant stakeholders has been essential in order to validate product ideas—the reason why upcoming partnerships should involve several end-users/organizations in the screening and product development phase.
- It is difficult to base sales solely on NGO and UN organizations as they have a long penetration time. Parallel market opportunities should be addressed at an early stage.
- Core competences need to be built up to ensure the necessary knowledge skills for developing product/service, sales and marketing. These competences are often not available within the founding partnership.
- Access to donor and venture funding has been critical in order to build production, sales, service and distribution.

The above case findings have had a main focus on managing networks and partnerships and should, of course, be accompanied by tools for user-driven innovation, understanding of local culture, regulatory framework and product development. This is not for the sake of academia, but is due to the underlying understanding that successful partnership-driven innovation is essentially about the ability to connect knowledge, competencies and resources across organizational boundaries—a growing realization among both practitioners and academics that calls for the need to fully comprehend the possibilities and challenges in the process of developing commercial partnerships between NGOs, researchers and companies as an effective and sustainable market-driven path towards poverty reduction.

Bibliography

Chesbrough, H., and K. Schwarts (2007) "Innovation Business Models with Co-Development Partnerships", *Research Technology Management* 50.1.
Dhanaraj, C., and A. Parkhe (2006) "Orchestrating Innovation Networks", *Academy of Management Review* 31.3.
Hargadon, A. (2002) "Brokering Knowledge: Linking Learning and Innovation", *Research in Organizational Behaviour* 24: 41-85.
Kolk, A., M. Rivera-Santos and C. Rufín (2013) "Reviewing a Decade of Research on the 'Base/Bottom of the Pyramid' (BOP) Concept", *Business and Society* 53.3.
O'Brien, R. (2001) *An Overview of the Methodological Approach of Action Research*, in R. Richardson (ed.), *Teoria e Prática da Pesquisa Ação (Theory and Practice of Action Research)* (João Pessoa, Brazil: Universidade Federal da Paraíba).
Osterwalder, A., M. Rossi and M. Dong (2002) "The Business Model Handbook for Developing Countries", IRMA 2002 Information Resource Management Association International Conference 2002, Seattle.
Provan, K.G., and P. Kenis (2007) "Modes of Network Governance: Structure, Management, and Effectiveness", *Journal of Public Administration Research and Theory* 18: 229-52.
Ravn, J. (2012) "Access2innovation: Network Based Innovative Business Models Targeting Relief and Development Aid", PhD thesis, Aalborg University.
Reason, O., and H. Bradbury (2006) *Handbook of Action Research* (London: Sage).
Rothwell, R. (1994) "Towards the Fifth-generation Innovation Process", *International Marketing Review* 11: 7-31.

Part VI
Inclusive business models as a response to environmental sustainability challenges

11

Urban agriculture as a strategy for addressing food insecurity of BoP populations

María Alejandra Pineda-Escobar
Politecnico Grancolombiano University, Colombia

The aim of this chapter is to analyse urban agriculture as a strategy for addressing the food insecurity of urban dwellers in emerging and developing countries, with a particular focus on the implications for populations at the base of the pyramid (BoP). The first part provides a succinct definition of the concepts of food security and urban agriculture, exploring the magnitude of both on a global scale. The Colombian context is then examined, presenting the case of the "Mutualitos y Mutualitas" initiative in Bogotá, sharing its success as a local experience of urban agriculture that has turned a dumpsite into an organic farm, improving the living conditions of the urban poor. The third section looks into issues of contaminants, water and land tenure as the main perils that have been associated with the practice of urban agriculture. The chapter concludes by exploring the role of policymakers in creating an enabling environment for urban agriculture as a valid alternative for responding to the nutrition needs of BoP populations in urban areas.

History has witnessed the production of food in urban settings ever since the existence of native indigenous civilizations in the Americas, such as Mayas or Incas, or the plantation of "victory gardens" during war times, for example. But since the last decade of the 20th century, we have experienced a resurgence of urban agriculture in alignment with a world need to alleviate urban poverty and increase food security.

This chapter will focus on analysing urban agriculture as a valid alternative for responding to the nutrition needs of urban dwellers in emerging and developing countries, with a particular focus on the implications it has for lower-income households at the base of the pyramid (BoP). It starts by briefly defining the concepts of food security and urban agriculture and exploring the magnitude of both on a global scale. It then moves on to understanding the Colombian context in general, and that of Bogotá (its capital city) in particular, in relation to food insecurity of the urban poor. This provides the framework for studying a BoP successful and promising case of urban agriculture in Bogotá with the potential to both alleviate urban poverty and increase food security on a local scale. The chapter continues by looking into the main risks that have been associated with the practice of agriculture in urban settings. To conclude, the last section of the chapter is devoted to analysing the role of public policy for creating an enabling environment for urban agriculture that minimizes the risks associated with its practice and enhances its potential for bringing food security to urban populations at the BoP.

11.1 Contextualizing urban agriculture and food security

In 1996, the Rome Declaration on World Food Security and World Food Summit Plan of Action (FAO 1996) declared it intolerable and unacceptable that "more than 800 million people throughout the world, and particularly in developing countries, do not have enough food to meet their basic nutritional needs", placing the issue of food security at the top of the international development agenda. As a result, the Declaration's commitment to halve the number of undernourished people no later than 2015 was restated on the United Nations Millennium Declaration (UN 2000), becoming the third target (i.e. target 1C) of the first Millennium Development Goal (MDG), which aims to eradicate poverty and hunger by 2015.

The Food and Agriculture Organization (FAO) defines food security as a "situation that exists when all people, at all times, have physical, social and economic access to sufficient, safe and nutritious food that meets their dietary needs and food preferences for an active and healthy life" (FAO, IFAD and WFP 2014). Given the above, it follows that poor populations at the BoP are more likely to face a chronic, seasonal or transitory situation of food insecurity, as their socioeconomic conditions might lead them to face fluctuations in the supply of food, being unable to secure access to sufficient amounts of safe and nutritious food to adequately cater to their needs and those of their families.

By 2010, the UN Development Group Task Force on the MDGs presented a set of thematic papers in an effort to clarify the road towards the achievement of the MDGs by 2015. The Task Force believes that target 1C has been one of the worst performing MDG targets, particularly due to a regression in progress as a consequence of the global economic crisis, which led to an upsurge in food prices. They calculate that the proportion of the global population below the minimum level of dietary energy consumption grew by 2 points between 2004 and 2009, rising from 13% to 15%. In absolute terms, this means that as of 2009 there were more than 1 billion undernourished people in the world (UNDG 2010).

Recent FAO estimates provide more optimistic results but still calculate that at least 12% of the world population lacks food security. According to the 2014 *State of Food Insecurity in the World* report, although progress has been made in the reduction of global hunger, about 805 million people are still estimated to be chronically undernourished in 2012–14 (FAO, IFAD and WFP 2014). On a regional basis, Latin America and the Caribbean has shown the greatest progress in reducing hunger, being in fact the only region that has already reached MDG target 1C; whereas western Asia and sub-Saharan Africa have shown minimal progress, since the former has actually experienced an increase in the number of undernourished people and the latter presents the worst indicators of all regions in the world, with one out of four inhabitants living in hunger.

These numbers ought to be considered together with growth in urban population. The year 2008 marked a historic landmark as more than half of the world population was, for the first time in history, living in urban areas. Trends also show that most of the urban growth will take place in developing and emerging countries. By 2030, 80% of urban areas are expected to be located in the developing world, housing a population of around 5 billion. Particularly challenging is the fact that a significant portion of this urban expansion will be composed of poor people (UNFPA 2007). Thus, guaranteeing food security for urban dwellers at the base of the pyramid becomes central to development efforts.

In this scenario, the practice of urban agriculture is gaining increased attention as a promising response to the challenge of securing food for the urban poor. The Canadian International Development Research Centre (IDRC) is recognized as a strong advocate for urban agriculture, having produced significant theoretical and practical work on the subject. It defines urban agriculture as:

> An industry located within (intra-urban) or on the fringe (peri-urban) of a town, a city, or a metropolis, which grows or raises, processes, and distributes a diversity of food and nonfood products. It (re)uses on a daily basis human and natural resources, products, and services largely found in and around that urban area and, in turn, supplies on a daily basis human and material resources, products, and services largely to that urban area (Mougeot 2006).

Thus, urban agriculture not only encompasses the production of food in urban settings but also includes other agricultural systems such as floriculture, aquaculture and livestock breeding. In addition, the practice of urban agriculture is likely to be environmentally sound, as it is often based on re-using and recycling resources available in urban areas, making it potentially helpful as a waste management alternative for BoP contexts. This is particularly important when taking into consideration that most of the urban waste produced in developing countries is biodegradable, such as in Nairobi, where at least 70% of its solid waste is biodegradable and potentially useful (Lee-Smith 2010).

From a poverty perspective, urban agriculture is also considered to have a double impact on the living conditions of the poor as it not only represents a direct source of food but also reduces food-related expenditures, freeing income for alternative expenses. Considering that poor people spend between 50% and 70% of their income on food (von Braun 2008), this impact is significant, as families are able to allocate this freed income to other essential non-food items such as housing, clothing or personal hygiene. Similarly, multiple examples show how low-income households involved in urban agriculture may also increase family income with the sale of surplus production from their domestic farming activities (Dubbeling 2013). Although the benefits of additional income are evident, a word of caution should be raised about the need for guiding the poor to avoid misuse of the extra income by the head of household.

11.2 The case of urban agriculture in Colombia

Colombia is a country with abundant natural resources, currently regarded as one of the most solid and dynamic economies in Latin America (OECD 2013). It is, for instance, ranked by the World Bank as a medium–high income economy, and is among the countries with high human development according to the Human Development Report for 2014, which with an index of 0.711 ranks Colombia in 98th place among 187 countries included in the index (UNDP 2014).

However, despite this seemingly glowing picture, Colombia continues to have high rates of poverty and inequality. According to estimates by the National Bureau of Statistics (DANE) the country's population by 2013 was 47 million. Of this number, DANE estimated that by June 2013 more than 15 million people were in poverty, that is, 32.2% of the total population. For the same period, an estimated 10.1% Colombians were living in extreme poverty, which means that about four and a half million people in Colombia survive on less than $1.25 a day. These figures confirm that Colombia remains a country with one of the highest Gini coefficients, not only in Latin America but also worldwide (OECD 2013), reaching 0.539 as measured by the year 2012.

This should be analysed parallel to the employment situation, an area in which Colombia also shows some of the worst figures in the region. DANE estimated an unemployment rate of 9.3% by August 2013, which, although it represents a constant decrease from the levels of the early 2000s, remains one of the highest rates in Latin America, with an average rate for the region of 6.4% for 2012 (CEPAL and

OIT 2013). These figures should be viewed together with the alarming levels of informality in the country, which according to DANE estimates for July 2013 corresponded to almost 50% of total occupations in the country.

In addition, particularly worrying for Colombia are the figures of internally displaced people due to the decades-long internal violent conflict in the country. With nearly 5.4 million internally displaced persons by the end of 2013, Colombia continues to be one of the countries facing the largest internal displacement problem in the world, second only to the Syrian Arab Republic (UNHCR 2014). A significant portion of these people migrate to urban areas and in particular to Bogotá, where they end up adding to the urban poor at the base of the pyramid.

The latest census estimates that Bogotá has a current population of about 7.4 million, of which close to 40% are migrants and more than 20% are living in poverty (Wurwarg 2014). The National Survey on the Nutritional Situation in Colombia for the year 2005 reported that 33% of Bogotá's inhabitants were undernourished at a minor, moderate or severe level (Álvarez and Estrada 2008). In 2011 the Ministry of Social Protection published an update of this national survey revising the figures with a special focus on the situation of the poor. The survey calculates that 50% of children between the ages of 1 and 4 in Bogotá have zinc deficiencies and 28% lack proper vitamin A levels. The Inter-American Development Bank considers that although acute undernourishment is not a public health problem in Colombia anymore, chronic undernourishment is still present, prevailing among the poor, the rural population and in households where the mother lacks formal education (Neufeld, Rubio and Gutiérrez 2012).

The institutionalization of urban agriculture as a response to the nutrition needs of the BoP population in the city of Bogotá took place in 2004 with the administration of Mayor Luis Eduardo Garzón, who incorporated urban farming as part of the "Bogotá Without Hunger" programme. The initiative is implemented by the Botanical Garden of Bogotá Jose Celestino Mutis, which provides training and advisory services to the BoP population in the city for the practice of urban agriculture (Barriga and Leal 2011; Jardín Botánico José Celestino Mutis 2011). As of 2014, it is estimated that there are about 10,000 urban farmers in Bogotá who, thanks to their urban agricultural practice, have access to safe and organic food and have monthly savings of between US$5 and US$25 (Gómez 2014).

Alongside these public efforts, various initiatives have arisen in civil society aiming to incorporate urban agriculture into people's daily activities as a way to improve their living standards and help in their own processes of stepping out of poverty. That is the case of "Mutualitos y Mutualitas" (which can be translated as mutual support), a BoP initiative in Bogotá that has successfully turned a dumpsite into an organic urban farm and is promoting the practice of urban agriculture by the urban poor (see Box 11.1 for details).

Box 11.1 **Turning a dumpsite into an organic garden: the case of "Mutualitos y Mutualitas" initiative in Bogotá**

Rosa Evelia Poveda Guerrero, known to her friends and acquaintances as Rosita, is an inspiring and tireless woman who believes in the power of urban agriculture for solving the feeding needs of the urban poor. A native of Boyaca, one of the 32 departments of Colombia and an agricultural hub to the north of Bogotá, Rosa Poveda is a peasant who, like many more in rural Colombia, was a victim of internal displacement and ended up living in one of Bogotá's shanty neighbourhoods.

In 2003, Rosa found a dumpsite of 1,800 m, which was inhabited by homeless beggars and was located in the eastern hills of Bogotá in the Perseverancia neighbourhood in central Bogotá. This neighbourhood is mostly populated by low-income people and is known to be home to multiple crimes with frequent cases of robbery, burglary and homicide and constant confrontations between gang groups. Having dreamt about the opportunity of having an urban farm, Rosa decided to look for the owner of this site and received it as a *commodatum* (gratuitous loan). She then moved into the dumpsite, setting up a provisional camp, and started, together with her sons, a process of cleaning waste that had been piling up during the last 40 years.

Figure 11.1 **Rosa Poveda at "Mutualitos y Mutualitas" organic urban farm**

Photo credit: Daniel Barbosa, July 2014

Clearing up tons of waste was not an easy task, especially for a single woman aided only by two teenagers and without any access to financial resources, let alone machinery or equipment to speed up the process. This is why, in 2005, Rosa decided to organize the first *minga* (indigenous word referring to collective work to the benefit of the entire community) as a community gathering offering a lunch in exchange for a day of work cleaning the dumpsite. The call was a success, and about 250 people showed up at her doorstep bringing tools and willingness to work. In the end, more than 2,500 bags of waste were taken out of the dumpsite. Materials were classified and whatever was useful was either sold to recyclers or re-used as construction material for the improvement of the site.

Nearly a decade has gone by since that first *minga* took place, and those 1,800 m have now turned into a green and ecological urban farm where more than 100 different crop varieties are grown, next to farm animals such as hens, rabbits and quail. The construction of the farm has been done entirely with recycled material. Chemical fertilizers are completely avoided. Manure is produced from organic waste from various sources including waste that is collected and given by local families, excreta from the ecological toilet, horse dung obtained from a neighbouring military base, sawdust discarded by carpenters, and grazing. With all these resources, six different types of manure are obtained and used on the farm.

Besides producing organic food for her own consumption and that of her relatives, Rosa participates at peasant markets, where barter is the main means of exchange, and provides catering services for socially conscious events that hire her. She is currently working on the creation of a collection centre at her farm to receive organic products from urban farmers and set up a commercialization and distribution chain.

But Rosa is convinced that through education and awareness-raising she can make a bigger change in respect to food security, particularly among younger generations. That is why she has opened the doors of her urban farm to children and youngsters with an interest in what she does. She started by inviting children from the neighbourhood to come and work at the farm after school hours, offering them an alternative for using their free time and learning skills for their future, while moving them away from the environment of crime and gang groups that surround them.

After some time, Rosa started receiving visitors from schools, universities and community organizations from Bogotá and peripheral towns. She teaches them how to grow organic food in urban settings, and shows them how it is possible to effectively cater for the nutrition needs of the poor in a natural, healthy and sustainable way. If they are keen to grow their own crops Rosa will go to the schools and universities and give them advice on setting up their plantations. Rosa has also taken her experience across borders and has been invited to share her views on organic urban agriculture in Bolivia, Ecuador, Panama, Peru, France and Italy, among others. Altogether, Rosa estimates she has reached out to more than 20,000 people with her message, and she is eager to sensitize many more.

11.3 Urban agriculture and its risks

Academics and practitioners involved with urban agriculture have called attention to several risks and constraints related to its practice among the poor. On one side, low-income people at the BoP generally live in informal settlements, slums or shanty neighbourhoods, where they lack basic services such as sanitation. This environment leaves them potentially exposed to multiple environmental risks, including biological and chemical contaminants (Lee-Smith 2010). As a consequence, farmers can be exposed to potential health risks through the soil they use for their plantations, which frequently comes from near railways or industrial areas and may be polluted with heavy metals, or through the water they use for irrigation, because it comes from non-purified sources and may have pathogenic or chemical contaminants (Gallaher *et al.* 2013). Lack of proper drainage systems and inappropriate waste-water management can also generate potential risks for the practice of urban agriculture.

Together with the health risks of untreated waste-water, water availability has also become a matter of concern around urban agriculture. As water scarcity and the depletion of water tables is becoming more evident and increasingly alarming, some academics have argued against the practice of agriculture in urban settings, as they believe it will only impose greater stress on already depleted urban reservoirs (Stewart *et al.* 2013).

Land tenure has also been identified as a significant constraint for the practice of urban farming by the poor. Often, the BoP population may lack clarity about the title to the land where they live, and this increases the uncertainty around the possibility of actually been able to harvest what they grow, and hinders their possibilities of formalizing their farming activity (Mougeot 2000).

11.4 What policymakers can do: the role of public policy in urban agriculture

To conclude we will briefly touch on the role that public policy may have for the improvement of urban agriculture in cities in the developing world. As pointed out by Gupta and Gangopadhyay (2013), food insecurity, together with urban hunger and unemployment, is among the major factors that create unsustainable cities. Therefore, policymakers in urban settings should incorporate the challenge of guaranteeing food security into their urban planning.

One of the most significant contributions from policymakers can come from a well-structured work in education and empowerment of the urban poor, to enhance their capacities for practising urban agriculture. Urban farmers need to be aware of the potential health risks associated with the soil, water and waste they are using. If they are better informed, farmers will understand how their farming practices may need to be adapted in order to minimize their exposure to contaminants. Similarly, training can be provided for the proper implementation of organic farming techniques and for exploring other alternatives for growing food when key resources such as water and soil are scarce. Common alternatives include hydroponics, aeroponics, and sack and vertical gardening.

Additional support from policymakers can come through regulating and supporting the creation of special markets for the commercialization of products obtained by urban farmers. Accompanying and guiding the commercialization of production surplus may increase the chances that urban farmers have of actually selling their products in the market.

Urban agriculture is not the magic bullet that can solve all the challenges of food security in urban areas, but it can surely make a significant input, especially for the urban poor (Gupta and Gangopadhyay 2013). In Latin America, lessons from cities such as Curitiba (Brazil), Havana (Cuba) and Rosario (Argentina) provide practical and sound evidence of the benefits that the incorporation of urban agriculture into city policy-making can have for improving the quality of life of the urban poor at the base of the pyramid.

Bibliography

Álvarez, M., and A. Estrada (2008) "Inseguridad alimentaria de los hogares colombianos según localización geográfica y algunas condiciones sociodemográficas", *Perspectivas en Nutrición Humana* 10.1. 23-36.

Barriga, L., and D. Leal (2011) *Agricultura Urbana en Bogotá: Una evaluación externa participativa* (Bogotá: Universidad del Rosario).

CEPAL and OIT (2013) *Coyuntura Laboral en América Latina y el Caribe: Avances y desafíos en la medición del trabajo decente* (Santiago de Chile: ONU).

Dubbeling, M. (2013) *Scoping Paper Feeding into the Development of UNEP's Position on Urban and Periurban Agriculture* (Leusden: RUAF Foundation).

FAO, IFAD and WFP (2014) *The State of Food Insecurity in the World 2014: Strengthening the Enabling Environment for Food Security and Nutrition* (Rome: Food and Agriculture Organization).

FAO (1996) "Rome Declaration on World Food Security and World Food Summit Plan of Action", *World Food Summit*, Rome, 13–17 November 1996.

Gallaher, C., D. Mwaniki, M. Njenga, N. Karanja and A. WinklerPrins (2013) "Real or Perceived: The Environmental Health Risks of Urban Sack Gardening in Kibera Slums of Nairobi, Kenya", *EcoHealth* 10: 9-20.

Gómez, S. (2014) "Bogotanos crean sus propias huertas en las terrazas de la *Tiempo*, 23 June 2014.

Gupta, R., and S. Gangopadhyay (2013) "Urban Food Security Through Urban Agri and Waste Recycling: Some Lessons for India", *Perspectives* 38.3: 13-21.

Jardín Botánico José Celestino Mutis (2011) *Unidades Integrales de Agricultura Urbana Bogotá D.C.: Cartilla para el manejo integrado de la fertilización, las plagas y las enferme-dades* (Bogotá: Jardín Botánico José Celestino Mutis).

Lee-Smith, D. (2010) "Cities Feeding People: An Update on Urban Agriculture in Equatorial Africa", *Environment and Urbanization* 22.2: 483-98.

Mougeot, L. (2000) *Achieving Urban Food and Nutrition Security in the Developing World: The Hidden Significance of Urban Agriculture* (Focus 3, Brief 6 of 10; Washington, DC: International Food Policy Research Institute.

Mougeot, L. (2006) *Growing Better Cities : Urban Agriculture for Sustainable Development* (Ottawa: International Development Research Centre [IDRC]).

Neufeld, L., M. Rubio and M. Gutiérrez (2012) *Nutrición en Colombia II: Actualización del estado nutricional con implicaciones de política* (Washington, DC: Banco Interamericano de Desarrollo).

OECD (2013) *Estudios Económicos de la OCDE Colombia: Evaluación Económica* (Paris: Organisation for Economic Co-operation and Development).

Stewart, R., M. Korth, L. Langer, S. Rafferty, N. DaSilva and C. van Rooyen (2013) "What are the Impacts of Urban Agriculture Programs on Food Security in Low and Middle-income Countries?" *Environmental Evidence* 2.7: 1-13.

UN (2000) *United Nations Millennium Declaration* (A/RES 55/2; New York: United Nations).

UNDG (2010) *Thematic Paper on MDG1, Eradicate Extreme Poverty and Hunger* (New York: United Nations Development Group).

UNDP (2014) *Human Development Report 2014. Sustaining Human Progress. Reducing Vulnerabilities and Building Resilience* (New York: United Nations Development Programme).

UNFPA (2007) *The State of World Population 2007. Unleashing the Potential of Urban Growth* (New York: United Nations Population Fund).

UNHCR (2014) *War's Human Cost: UNHCR Global Trends 2013* (Geneva: UN High Commissioner for Refugees).

Von Braun, J. (2008) *Food and Financial Crises: Implications for Agriculture and the Poor* (Washington, DC: International Food Policy Research Institute).

Wurwarg, J. (2014) "Urbanization and Hunger: Food Policies and Programs Responding to Urbanization, and Benefiting the Urban Poor in Three Cities" *Journal of International Affairs* 67.2: 75-90.

populations 189

casas", El

culture

12

The triple leap
Addressing poverty and environmental challenges both at home and abroad

Tokutaro Hiramoto and Shusuke Watanabe
Nomura Research Institute, Japan

Since the Great East Japan Earthquake which struck on March 11, 2011, Japanese companies have realized the importance of adaptation to address climate change issues. Some Japanese companies that implement BoP in developing countries have consequently shifted their focus on harmonizing their BoP and adaptation businesses with the aim of expanding the market and creating social impact. The next challenge is to create the "triple leap" that can contribute to three improvements: raising BoP income; preventing a decrease in BoP income caused by climate change; and halting the progress of climate change through clean technology. All three improvements are important for the creation of a sustainable world. If companies are contributing to only one of these improvements, they have huge potential to evolve towards the other two.

12.1 Growing BoP business in Japan after the tsunami

On 11 March 2011 in Japan, the Tohoku Pacific Ocean earthquake, also called the Great East Japan earthquake, caused great damage to many people, not only through the direct impact caused by the earthquake but also from the considerable damage from the tsunami it unleashed. Such huge damage takes a long time to restore, but Japan has begun to achieve new developments in various fields through the reconstruction after the earthquake. The base of the pyramid (BoP) business of Japanese companies has also evolved in this process.

Innovative products and technologies used in BoP business are often typically provided to developing countries from industrialized countries. On the other hand, as shown in the "Green Leap" of Professor Hart (2010) and the reverse innovation by General Electric (Immelt *et al.* 2009), in order to create a sustainable world, innovative products and technologies also need to be provided by developing countries to developed countries. This trend is taking place in Japan in the wake of the earthquake. Specifically, the products and technologies that are deployed in the BoP business of Japanese companies in developing countries have been used in the earthquake-affected areas after the tsunami. There are several examples of this:

1. Panasonic has provided the Life Innovation Container for the affected areas. The container is a facility for a region without electricity to mount a solar-powered system with storage battery and solar panels and also the Solar Lantern made by Sanyo Electric. In areas without electricity in Kenya, Tanzania, Uganda, India and Indonesia, these techniques have already been used for BoP business and related activities.

2. Nissin Foods has provided one million Cup Noodles (instant noodles) and seven kitchen cars with hot water provision to the affected areas. The kitchen car has already been used to provide instant noodles with increased nutrients to people living in the areas of Kenya where safe water is difficult to find.

3. Nippon Poly-Glu has provided a water purification agent for the affected areas. This agent is a product that has been sold through local women entrepreneurs to people living in countries such as Bangladesh who are not able to get safe water.

In addition, there is a reverse flow from the above in the reconstruction process. Products and technologies that have been developed for the reconstruction of the affected areas are now used in BoP business in developing countries. For example, NEC is promoting BoP business in India to take advantage of hydroponic cultivation technology developed by GRA Co. Ltd. located in Yamamoto-cho, Watari-gun, Miyagi Prefecture, which was damaged by the salt caused by the tsunami in the Great East Japan Earthquake. In addition to using GRA's technology, NEC tries to stabilize the power supply required for hydroponic cultivation by managing grid power and private power generator system using NEC's energy management technology. In addition, by partnering with a local agricultural college in Pune, India, on-the-job, hands-on training in hydroponics technology has been provided for students. Through this training, NEC is fostering local production managers for hydroponic cultivation.

Owing to the impact of climate change, social issues in developing countries, such as salt damage, have increased. New products and technologies that were born in the wake of the earthquake recovery have the power to solve these social issues.

In this way, after the earthquake in Japan, a new innovation cycle has occurred due to a two-way flow of innovative products and technologies between developed and developing countries (see Fig. 12.1).

Figure 12.1 **New innovation cycle after the tsunami**

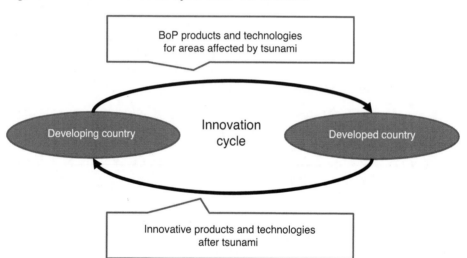

12.2 New business for Japanese companies through the integration of climate change and BoP business

This new innovation cycle that has occurred in Japan is an important countermeasure to the global issues of climate change. Dealing with climate change involves two areas: one is mitigation and the other is adaptation.

Mitigation is the concept of reducing greenhouse gases (GHGs) such as CO_2, and also continuing to reduce climate change itself. In this concept, "clean" technology is believed to be an important solution. Professor Hart believes that it is important to integrate clean technology with the BoP business, and has called this fusion "the Green Leap" in *Capitalism at the Crossroads* (2010).

Adaptation, on the other hand, is the idea that people will continue to try to solve the social problems that have already been increased by climate change by leveraging technology. Social problems increased by climate change take a wide variety of forms. For example, there are the issues such as floods and tsunami disaster already stated, deterioration of agricultural production, water shortages due to changes in temperature and climate, spread of disease, increase of refugees, and lack of energy. A new innovation cycle occurring in Japan is recognized as a fusion of this idea and BoP business. In this chapter, this is referred to as the "Resilience Leap" (see Fig. 12.2).

Figure 12.2 **The double leap for climate change issues**

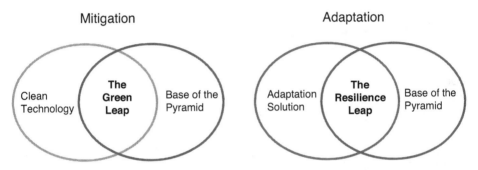

Through the concept of the Resilience Leap, humanity can continue to solve not only the current global issues but also the growing challenges. Since social issues are increased by climate change, and the resources to solve those issues, such as people and money, are increased as well, business opportunities are also expected to grow for companies through the Resilience Leap. BoP business improves market access for BoP people and achieves an increase in income for them. And adaptation measures will prevent a decrease in income due to climate change. It is possible to achieve continuous growth of potential customers and also loyal customer retention.

In fact, there are many similarities between climate-change adaptation measures and BoP business. Therefore, it can be said, as a next step, companies that are promoting BoP business are in an environment already conducive to the Resilience Leap. The following four points are examples of those similarities.

1. Activities are deployed for the people who live in places where basic social services such as medical services, electric power and safe water are lacking.

2. Continued support is needed.

3. Products and services that are tailored to local needs have to be provided.

4. Respect for the voluntary activities and intentions of the local people will be needed so that those people can live autonomously.

Owing to these common points, the innovation cycle emerged in Japan to achieve the Resilience Leap in the wake of the earthquake.

In addition, the Japanese government aggressively promotes BoP business, and after the earthquake it reviewed existing policies and created new measures for BoP business to take advantage of the new technologies that were born in the earthquake reconstruction process.

The next section shows the trend of these public–private partnerships operated by the Japanese government as an example of a policy framework for producing the Resilience Leap.

12.3 Rising BoP business in Japan and new policy after the tsunami

As mentioned above, many Japanese corporations that had already been implementing BoP business provided their products to the affected area. That means that Japanese corporations have made the Resilience Leap with their experiences in BoP business. This section describes the Japanese situation related to BoP and the Resilience Leap from the aspect of public support by Japanese governmental organizations.

In 2009, which is considered to be the first year of BoP business in Japan, Japanese government organizations such as the Ministry of Economy, Trade, and Industry (METI), the Japan International Cooperation Agency (JICA) and the Japan External Trade Organization (JETRO), as well as international organizations such as the United Nations Development Programme (UNDP), all either began or expanded initiatives to promote BoP business. In particular, a scheme of providing funds for feasibility studies and a programme of providing support for finding potential local partners are thought to have led to a significant increase in the number of Japanese corporations making the first move to enter the BoP markets (Table 12.1).

Specifically, in 2009, the METI invited proposals for projects through the scheme of the Survey for Feasibility Studies on BoP Business, which was conducted by Nomura Research Institute (NRI) at the request of METI. As a result, ten projects were selected. In 2010, in JICA's programme 20 projects were provisionally selected and 19 survey projects were implemented. In 2011, JETRO launched the BoP Business Partnership Support Project and 19 projects were selected. From its second to its fifth public announcements, JICA provisionally selected 56 projects in 2011–13.

Beside these moves, there are also related projects that have been undertaken by the Ministry of the Environment, the Ministry of Internal Affairs and Communications and the Japan Bank for International Cooperation (JBIC). If we include support programmes provided by international organizations such as the UNDP, we find that 166 organizations have undertaken 113 projects under the initiative of the public sector. (Projects having similar themes for the same region are counted as a single project. Because there are many cases of multiple organizations taking on a single project, the number of projects is less than the number of organizations.)

Furthermore, when we consider the number of applications made to JICA's publicly announced programme, we see that there are even more businesses that are considering engaging in BoP business, with more than 200 Japanese corporations either making full-scale studies of BoP business or actually going ahead and promoting these efforts.

The earthquake happened at a time when BoP business was already rising because of public support. A lot of Japanese corporations have been finding a way to leverage their technology in their existing BoP business to the restoration of the affected area.

Other Japanese corporations have been contributing to the restoration of the affected area and have been developing various new technologies there. The Japanese government is aware of this situation and has made opportunities for leveraging their new technologies as solutions to global issues.

In particular, JICA has improved its "Preparatory Survey for BOP Business Promotion" framework. In its third call for proposals, JICA recommended both these new technologies and attendance of corporations whose headquarters were in an affected area.

In another case, METI has established a new feasibility study (F/S) support policy for the acceleration of adaptation solutions through global business by Japanese corporations. As a result, 13 business studies by Japanese corporations have started F/S of their adaptation business under the support policy (see Table 12.1). In this group Yamaha Motor, Sanyo Electric and Yukiguni Maitake have already used JICA's F/S support policy for BoP business. These examples show the compatibility between BoP business and the adaptation solution.

Table 12.1 **Selected projects from a new METI feasibility study support policy for the acceleration of adaptation solutions**

Source: Ministry of Economy, Trade and Industry.

Company	Products/services	Project objective	Country	Year
Sharp	Electrolysis water purification system	To increase access to safe water, which is reduced by climate change	Kenya	2012
Toray	Desert greening promotion	To prevent desertification by PLA (polylactic acid) sand-tube and convert desert to farmland	South Africa	2012–2013
Yamaha Motor	Water purification system	To increase access to safe water, which is reduced by climate change	Côte d'Ivoire Ghana	2012
Ajinomoto	Amino acid contained fertilizer	To make crops durable to higher temperature and increase yield amount	Tanzania	2012
Kawasaki Geological Engineering	Slope disaster prevention	To prevent slope disaster triggered by increasing torrential rainfalls and storms	Vietnam Thailand	2012–2014
Sanyo Electric	Solar lantern	To increase the safety of refugees due to drought by providing them with solar lanterns	East Africa	2012

Company	Products/services	Project objective	Country	Year
Yukiguni Maitake	Bean production in salinized area	To produce mug beans in salinized area which is increased by climate change	Bangladesh	2012–2013
Euglena	Bean production in salinized area	To produce mug beans in salinized area which is increased by climate change	Bangladesh	2014
Yamaha Motor	Water purification system and drip irrigation system	To increase access to safe water and irrigation for agriculture, which is reduced by climate change	Tanzania	2013
Maruha Nichiro Foods	Nutrient-rich food	To improve nutrition by fish sausage	Ghana	2013
Mitsubishi UFJ Morgan Stanley	Water purification system	To increase access to safe water, which is reduced by climate change	Vietnam Myanmar	2013
Kaiho Sangyo	Recycled agricultural machinery	To solve food security issue by rental business of recycled agricultural machinery	Ghana	2014
from far east	Additive-free shampoo and soaps	To reduce flood damage by recovery of agricultural land and forests through cultivating raw materials of additive-free shampoo and soaps	Cambodia	2014
PEAR Carbon Offset Initiative	Composting organic waste	To prevent damage by sea level rise with compost as embankment	Maldives	2014

In March 2013, METI and UNDP hosted an international symposium "Inclusive businesses and adaptation solutions in African markets" in Tokyo, in which sessions were held by Sharp, Toray, Sanyo Electric, Yamaha Motor and Wellthy Corporation, which had been studying the feasibility of their Resilience Leap. METI also hosted similar symposium in 2014. Through these symposiums, many companies must now be aware of importance of the Resilience Leap.

12.4 The next challenge for creating the "Triple Leap" to address climate change with a BoP focus

So far, BoP businesses by Japanese corporations have been developing the Resilience Leap. The next step is the "Triple Leap". The Triple Leap means business innovation that combines the Green Leap with the Resilience Leap. This business is made up of three components: base of the pyramid, clean technology and adaptation solution (see Fig. 12.3). We can contribute to three improvements through this business: to raise BoP income, to prevent a decrease in BoP income caused by climate change and to prevent the progress of climate change. In Japan, some Japanese corporations have already established a renewable energy system in the tsunami-affected area and the Triple Leap is the new innovation that has been expanded after the tsunami.

Figure 12.3 **The Triple Leap**

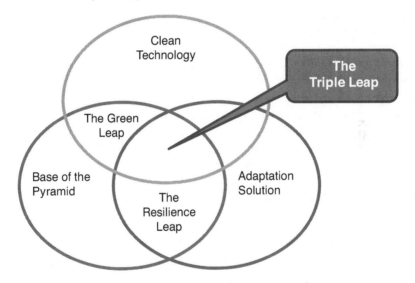

What is the benefit of the Triple Leap for various sectors?

First, for **multinational corporations** (MNCs) the benefit is increasing external resources that they can leverage in developing countries. One of the differences between BoP business and normal business is that it is easy to leverage external resources that are high quality and low cost. When MNCs implement BoP business they can leverage F/S support policies by government, pro bono work by high-level professionals, and so on. When MNCs implement the Triple Leap they can leverage three times external resources in poverty reduction, mitigation and adaptation.

For example, Sanyo Electric leverages various support policies of the Japanese governmental organizations for growing its solar lantern business. First, Sanyo Electric leveraged F/S support policy for mitigation from the Ministry of Environment for its business in Uganda. Second, it leveraged F/S support policy for BoP business from METI for its business in India. Third, it leveraged F/S support policy for inclusive business from UNDP for its business in Kenya. Fourth, it leveraged F/S support policy for BoP business from JICA in Kenya. Fifth, it leveraged F/S support policy for adaptation solution by METI for its business in Somalia and Kenya. The spread of solar lanterns as replacement for kerosene lamps decreases GHGs, and it improves BoP livelihoods through education in non-electrified areas. It also contributes to improving livelihoods in times of disaster such as the tsunami in developed countries. Finally, it improves refugees' livelihoods that are damaged by drought. Sanyo Electric could prove these various social efficiencies from the above five F/S projects. And they could establish their operating base in various markets.

MNCs can scale up their business by leveraging external resource through the implementation of the Triple Leap. And they can increase business opportunities for governmental organizations in developing countries if they can prove the social efficiency of their business.

Second, for the **public sector**, such as governments and multilateral development organizations, the benefit of the Triple Leap is leveraging private resources by public–private partnership (PPP) for the achievement of social aims such as poverty reduction, mitigation and adaptation. At present, the flow of private capital to developing countries largely exceeds the flow of public capital. It is important for the public sector to do a lot of PPP projects to achieve its social mission. For that, it needs to share the result of different projects for poverty reduction, mitigation and adaptation by avoiding the government's vertically structured administration.

Finally, the **base of the pyramid** populations can acquire sustainable financial security through the Triple Leap. To do that they should learn from the experiences of the MNCs and merge them with their own experiences. That effort will make a sustainable stable growth of markets in developing country and will also create a win–win situation between MNCs, the public sector and the BoP. Table 12.2 summarizes these benefits and challenges.

Table 12.2 **Benefits and challenges for companies and organizations making the Triple Leap**

	Benefits	Challenge
Private corporations	Corporations can leverage external financial and human resources for BoP, clean technology and adaptation solutions for their business.	Corporations need to prove the social efficiency of their products/ technologies and demonstrate them extensively.
	Corporations can retain potential loyal customers through sustainable stable growth of local markets.	Corporations should clarify how to measure the social efficiency of their products/technologies.
	In various governmental projects, opportunities for procurement of their products must increase.	
Public sector	The public sector can leverage resources of private corporations for poverty reduction, mitigation and adaptation.	The public sector needs many PPP projects to achieve their social mission.
		The public sector needs to share the results of different projects on poverty reduction, mitigation and adaptation circumventing the government's vertically structured administration.
BoP	BoP can acquire a sustainable wealthy lifestyle.	BoP should learn MNCs' various experiences and merge them with theirs.

Japanese corporations now need to leverage various experiences and new technologies that have accrued after the tsunami to increase the Triple Leap. That effort must contribute to the solution of various global issues.

The tsunami has wreaked enormous damage in Japan. But the tsunami has also triggered recognition of the importance of the Triple Leap for the Japanese. And we are actually implementing it in small steps. We should share our precious experiences and new technologies all over the world in the hope that we will be able to create a sustainable world as quickly as possible through this new innovation.

12.5 The three perspectives for new business from the Triple Leap

From the experience of the Triple Leap in Japan, we can extract three perspectives for new business as the solution to social issues by private corporations. These three perspectives can also release successful businesses' potential (see Fig. 12.4).

Figure 12.4 **The three perspectives for new business from the Triple Leap**

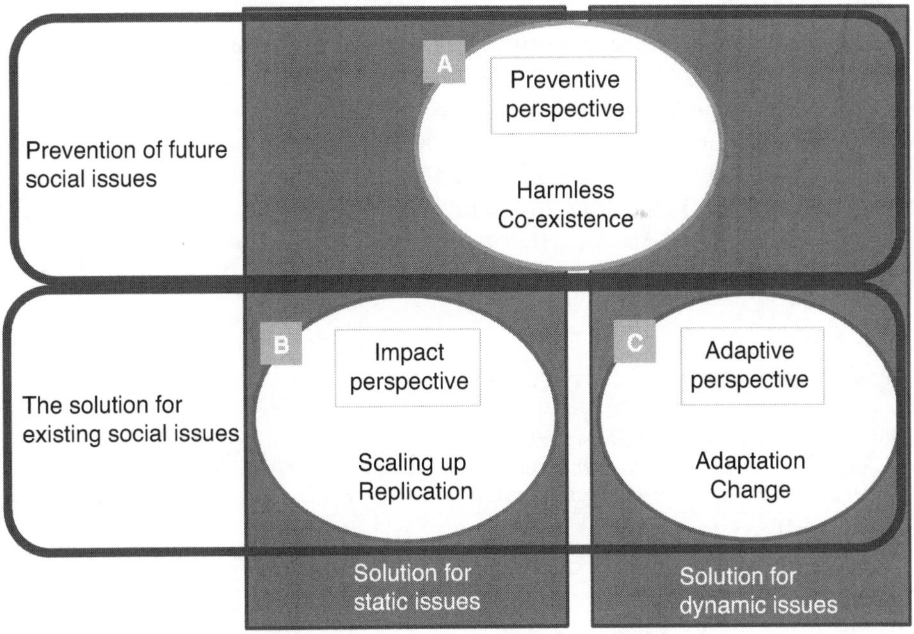

These three perspectives are arranged along two axes. The first axis relates to the dimension of social issues, divided into "Solution for static issues" and "Solution for dynamic issues". The second axis relates to time, and business solutions are divided into "Prevention of future social issues" and "The solution for existing social issues". These two axes create three perspectives.

1. From the **preventive perspective**, new business as the solution to social issues should be harmless for our world and also focus on co-existence with nature. Most existing businesses lack this perspective. Corporations should be always trying to improve business from a preventive perspective. In the Triple Leap, clean technology solution involves the preventive perspective.

2. From the **impact perspective**, new business as the solution to social issues should focus on the biggest existing social issues such as the Millennium Development Goals. Corporations determine if their business has capacity to face such a huge issue. They should always be trying to find the best way of scaling up and replicating for their business. In the Triple Leap, the base of the pyramid solution involves the impact perspective.

3. From the **adaptive perspective**, new business as the solution to social issues should focus on the social issues that face the biggest changes. Exploding social issues arising from a big change break up traditional lifestyles and values. Corporations should create and introduce renewed lifestyle and values with new business that fit the new world after a big change. In the Triple Leap, the adaptation solution involves the adaptive perspective.

All three perspectives are important for the creation of a sustainable world. Now there are already many successful businesses that can hold the solution to social issues. If they depend on only one perspective at present, they have huge potential for evolution to the other two perspectives. Or they can collaborate with other business from the other two perspectives. These three perspectives can remind us of the potential of the existing successful business and the multifaceted nature of social issues.

Bibliography

BoP Global Network (2013), *Raising the Base of the Pyramid Through Enterprise: Innovative Case Studies of BoP Ventures and Initiatives* (Barcelona: Global CAD/ESW/BoPGlobal).

Hart, S.L. (2010) *Capitalism at the Crossroads: Aligning Business, Earth, and Humanity* (Upper Saddle River, NJ: Prentice Hall, 3rd edn).

Immelt, J.R., V. Govindarajan and C. Trimble (2009) "How GE Is Disrupting Itself", *Harvard Business Review* 87.10: 56-65.

Japan Ministry of Economy, Trade and Industry (2012) *Study on Sustainable Contribution by the Japanese Private Sector to Developing Countries' Adaptation Needs* (Tokyo: Ministry of Economy, Trade and Industry).

Japan Ministry of Economy, Trade and Industry (2014) *Projects to Contribute Overseas to Countermeasures Against Global Warming Caused by Carbon Dioxide from Non-Energy Sources (Project For Visualization Of Contributions by Japanese Companies Relating to Countermeasures Adopted and the Prevention of the Decline and Degradation of Forestry in Developing Nations) in FY 2014* (Tokyo: Ministry of Economy, Trade and Industry).

Koike, J., T. Hiramoto and T. Izumi (2013) *Strategy to Develop Frontier Markets with Emphasis on Adaptation to Climate Change* (NRI Papers 191; Tokyo: Nomura Research Institute).

Prahalad, C.K. (2004) *The Fortune at the Bottom of the Pyramid: Eradicating Poverty Through Profits* (Upper Saddle River, NJ: Wharton School Publishing).

Prahalad, C.K., and S.L. Hart (2002) "The Fortune at the Bottom of the Pyramid", *Strategy + Business* 26: 1-14.

UNFCCC (2014) "Adaptation Private Sector Initiative (PSI)", http://unfccc.int/adaptation/workstreams/nairobi_work_programme/items/4623.php, accessed 30 November 2014.

Watanabe, S., T. Hiramoto and N. Tsuzaki (2012) *Developing BoP Business as the Principal Strategy in Emerging and Developing Economies (Volume 1): Paving the Road to a New Market that is Expected to Reach 5.5 Billion People and 70 Trillion Dollars by 2030* (NRI Papers 172; Tokyo: Nomura Research Institute).

Watanabe, S., T. Hiramoto and N. Tsuzaki (2012) *Developing BoP Business as the Principal Strategy in Emerging and Developing Economies (Volume 2): Improving the Profitability of BoP Business in India and South Africa* (NRI Papers 175; Tokyo: Nomura Research Institute).

About the authors

Edgard Barki is an Assistant Professor of Marketing and Social Business at Fundação Getulio Vargas, Escola de Administração de Empresas de São Paulo (FGV-EAESP) from where he holds a PhD and master's in Business Administration. He is an Adviser of Instituto Coca Cola Brasil and Artemisia, Associate Dean of the Master's in International Management at FGV-EAESP, leader of the BoP Lab Brazil at GVcev (Center for Retailing at FGV-EAESP) and Coordinator of the Center for Social Impact GVcenn (Center for Entrepreneurship and New Business). He is the author of several articles in national and international journals on social business and base of the pyramid, co-editor of the books *Business with Social Impact in Brazil* (Peirópolis, 2013) and *Retail for Low Income* (Bookman, 2008) and co-author of *Retail in Brazil* (Atlas, 2014).

Fernando Casado Cañeque is the founder and director of CAD. He is a PhD economist and journalist specialized in projects related to economic and sustainable development. He worked for seven years for the UN and as senior consultant in the Department of Sustainable Development at PricewaterhouseCoopers. He specializes in managing projects promoting the achievement of development goals and cross-sectoral partnerships. He is the author of several books on CSR and development and director of social documentaries. He holds a PhD from the Central University of Barcelona in Economic and Social Sciences, a master's from the School of International and Public Affairs (SIPA) of Columbia University and a postgraduate degree in Environmental Management from the University of Barcelona's Institute for Public Economics. Fernando is a certified Master Trainer of the IFC-SME Toolkit of the World Bank and professionally accredited partnership broker (Partnership Brokers Accreditation Scheme). He is also the Associate Director of the BoP Global Network.

Nicolas Chevrollier is a passionate social innovator with over 15 years of experience on the intersection of innovation, entrepreneurship and development in Africa, South Asia and the USA. He is currently a programme manager at the BoP Innovation Center (BoPInc) facilitating the acceleration of entrepreneurship in low-income markets. Prior joining BoPInc, he was the deputy manager of the programme "Innovation for Development" and the co-founder and leader of the ICT for Development innovation team at TNO, the Dutch Organization for Applied Scientific Research. Adding to his international experience, Nicolas has been a guest researcher at the National Institute of Standards and Technology (NIST), USA, to carry out his PhD work and an international volunteer for the international organization Agence Universitaire de la Francophonie in Madagascar. He holds a PhD and engineering degree from the National Institute of Telecommunications (France). He completed his education with executive training on social entrepreneurship at INSEAD.

Myrtille Danse is the Founding Director of the BoP Innovation Center (BoPInc) and is an internationally recognized expert on the intersection of business strategy and sustainable poverty alleviation. She has more than 20 years' experience on value-chain development and inclusive business strategies with multinational enterprises and local private sector in transition and developing economies. This experience was obtained as a project leader of numerous international business development initiatives in Europe, Africa, South East-Asia and Latin America. Her experience as a private sector adviser, including more than eight years in Central America, as policy adviser and trade attaché of the Dutch Ministry of Foreign Affairs, and adviser on local private sector development for an international NGO on development cooperation, enables her to mediate between the private sector and vital societal actors required to develop successful pro-poor market-based innovations.

Chiropriya Dasgupta is the Director of Strategic Initiatives at Enterprise for a Sustainable World. She has over ten years' experience in technology, management consulting and business development for the corporate sector and for social enterprises working with the rural and urban poor. Priya joined ESW from the World Bank where she served as a private sector development specialist. Her experience at the BoP includes fund management and advisory services for microfinance in Africa, enterprise creation for the informal waste sector in the Philippines, Brazil and Peru, design and implementation of a pilot ultra poor initiative with the largest tribal group in India, design and implementation of a ranking system for indigenous groups in the Latin America and Caribbean region among others. Priya holds an undergraduate degree in Electronics and Telecommunications from University of Pune and an MBA from Cornell University's Johnson Graduate School of Management.

Markus Dietrich is an inclusive business specialist with extensive experience in consulting, research and project development on base of the pyramid (BoP) and renewable energy based in the Philippines. He founded Asian Social Enterprise Incubator (ASEI) Inc. in 2009 to apply his broad knowledge on the nexus of business, policy and sustainable development to ASEI's clients, which include the Asian Development Bank, World Bank, GIZ, Frankfurt School, BCI Asia and other corporates. He authored the ground-breaking ADB Inclusive Business (IB) Country Study Philippines that triggered the development of IB in the country. He has a BSc in Business Studies from CASS Business School and an MS in International Community Economic Development from Southern New Hampshire University. He also participated 2011 in INSEAD's Social Entrepreneurship Programme in Singapore. In 2012 he co-founded Hilltribe Organics, a social enterprise producing high-value organic products, initially focused on free-range and organic eggs, which improves the livelihoods of hill-tribe farmers in northern Thailand.

Minna Halme, PhD, is professor of management at Aalto University School of Business, Helsinki, Finland. Her research focuses on inclusive business for poverty alleviation in low-income emerging markets and business models for sustainability. Minna works with a number of European research consortia and leads national research projects on sustainable business and consumption. Minna teaches sustainability management on master's, doctoral and executive MBA courses in Finland and South Korea, and cooperates with the industry in research projects. She is a member of the editorial board of the journal *Business Strategy and the Environment, Scandinavian Journal of Management* and *Organization and Environment* and has published in, e.g., *Ecological Economics, Journal of Management Studies* and *Journal of Business Ethics*, and authored two international books. She has served as an adviser in the UN Secretary-General's High-level Panel on Global Sustainability and is frequently interviewed by news media. In October 2008 she received an award from the Academy of Finland for the societal impact of her research.

Stuart L. Hart is Professor and the Steven Grossman Endowed Chair in Sustainable Business at the University of Vermont Business School and the Samuel C. Johnson Chair Emeritus in Sustainable Global Enterprise and Professor of Management Emeritus at Cornell University's Johnson School of Management. He is also Founder and President of Enterprise for a Sustainable World and Founder of the Base of the Pyramid Global Network. Professor Hart is one of the world's top authorities on the implications of environment and poverty for business strategy. With C.K. Prahalad, Hart wrote the pathbreaking 2002 article "The Fortune at the Bottom of the Pyramid", which provided the first articulation of how business could profitably serve the needs of the four billion poor in the developing world. With Ted London, Hart is also the author of a book entitled *Next Generation Business Strategies for the Base of the Pyramid*. His best-selling book, *Capitalism at the Crossroads*, published in 2005 was selected by Cambridge University as one of the top 50 books on sustainability of all time; the third edition of the book was published in 2010.

Marjo Hietapuro graduated in 2011 with an MSc (Econ) from Aalto University, Helsinki, Finland, where she majored in economics and international business. During her studies, she worked at Aalto University as a project researcher and teacher in the Corporate Environmental and Social Responsibility research group examining BoP business models while writing her master's thesis on partnerships in BoP business. Since graduation, she has been involved in building cross-sector partnerships in various projects related to sustainability and emerging markets. For example, she was a project manager at Helsinki Business and Science Park in a cross-sector project aimed at exporting Finnish food safety know-how to emerging markets. Prior to that, in the Environment Centre of the City of Helsinki, she participated in designing a new platform for companies and other actors that enables better collaboration in fighting against climate change in Helsinki. Currently, she works as a management consultant at EY (Ernst & Young) in Finland focusing on strategy and performance improvement consulting.

Tokutaro Hiramoto joined NRI in 2004 as a consultant. He also works for Meiji University as a guest professor and at Miyagi University as a part-time professor. His specialties include business development in Africa, BoP business, developing management systems for CSR, public–private partnership, and reforming business management through balanced scorecard method. He provides consulting services for companies from a wide range of industries and for Japanese governmental agencies. He has worked with several dozen Japanese companies such as Ajinomoto, Sumitomo Chemical and Panasonic for developing their African business/BoP strategies. He has also supported Japanese Ministry of Economy, Trade and Industry (METI) initiatives for familiarizing BoP Business since 2008. He launched the Japan Inclusive Business Support Center (http://www.bop.go.jp/en) in 2010 and was leader of its operational projects (commissioned by METI) in 2010–11. Since 2012 he has been a member of the Center's Steering Committee. He has a strong partnership with the Tokyo offices of AfDB, ADB, IDB, IFC, USAID, UNIDO, UNDP and UNICEF.

Tashmia Ismail is a fellow at UNU Maastricht Economic and Social Research Institute on Innovation and Technology and is a Lecturer at the Gordon Institute of Business Science (GIBS) where she teaches innovation on core programmes and works on strategies for low income markets across the school and in her consulting practice. She heads and manages the GIBS Inclusive Markets Programme which offers a collaborative platform for stakeholders interested in developing and executing developing market strategies. Tashmia published a book in 2012 titled *New Markets, New Mindsets* (over 2,000 copies sold) and has also published multiple articles and case studies. She is regularly invited as a speaker and panellist at conferences and forums both local and international.

Urs Jäger. As an Associate Professor of INCAE Business School and Associate Professor (Privatdozent) of the University of St Gallen, Urs Jäger supports students to learn effective entrepreneurial practices at the interface of developing countries (base and top of the pyramid) and developed countries. As Research Director of the Center for Knowledge Exchange of VIVA TRUST (Centro de Intercambio de Conocimiento de VIVA TRUST) he develops new teaching methods to create and spread knowledge on sustainable strategies and social entrepreneurship, to connect sustainability experts and to support entrepreneurs in creating and executing their business plans. Urs has published a number of articles in leading journals of third-sector research (e.g. *Nonprofit and Voluntary Sector Quarterly, Voluntas, Nonprofit Management and Leadership*) and five books, of which the latest is *Managing Social Businesses: Mission, Governance, Strategy and Accountability* (Palgrave Macmillan). He is a reviewer for leading journals, has advised over 40 national and international non-profits and business organizations and has three years of working experience within Deutsche Lufthansa AG (Germany).

Claudia Knobloch is one of the directors of Endeva and an expert in realizing inclusive business models in collaboration with companies. Claudia has 15 years of experience in project management and management consulting. She has supported around 80 companies to enter new markets in Europe, South America and Asia, worked in strategic consultancy projects for foundations and organizations such as GIZ and has worked intensively on research projects and publications on inclusive business and international CSR. She recently did market research for an inclusive energy business in Madagascar and is currently researching customer needs at the BoP housing market. She holds a master's degree in International Business and Cultural Studies.

Aline Krämer is an expert on inclusive business. As a founder and managing director of Endeva, she has developed and directed research and consulting projects on the topic for more than seven years. Aline co-authored several studies on inclusive business models—all aiming at understanding how to make these models work for both companies and the target group: people living in poverty. Most recently, she led as well as co-authored a study on "Multiplying Impact: Supporting the Replication of Inclusive Business Models". Her field experience lies in understanding and assessing the needs of low-income consumers through participatory methods and integrating them into the development of suitable solutions.

María Alejandra Pineda-Escobar is a consultant and researcher in inclusive business and corporate social responsibility, working with the Center of Partnerships for Development (CAD) in Latin America. She has been a consultant to the Colombian Business Council for Sustainable Development (CECODES), documenting cases of inclusive territorial development and evaluating the adoption of sustainability principles by financial institutions in the country. She is also Regional Coordinator for the Towards the Human City Project in Latin America and is Associate Professor at Politecnico Grancolombiano University, Colombia, where she lectures on sustainability, globalization and competitiveness in business. She is the author of several articles, papers and book chapters on CSR and sustainability at the BoP and is a member of the National Committee of Inclusive Business of Colombia (CONNIC). She graduated in International Business and has a Bachelor of Commerce in small business and retail management, an MSc in Public Policy and Human Development from Maastricht University in The Netherlands, and an MA in Sustainability and CSR (Spain).

Jacob Ravn has initiated and managed the access2innovation network since 2007. The network has established the platform for launching 16 partnerships between NGOs, academia, the private sector and recently central and local government through a commercial network-based innovation approach. The partnerships launched have focused on relief work, sustainable energy, agri business, and water and sanitation and have so far led to seven new spin-off companies and new workplaces in developing countries and in Denmark. From his previous five years working at the Danish Red Cross, Jacob possesses in-depth knowledge of the Danish and international NGO sector. Based on his work with access2innovation 2007–11 he holds a PhD in network-based business model innovation aimed at aid and relief work from Aalborg University. He has an MA in International Politics from Ceris (Centre Européen de Recherches Internationales et Stratégiques) in Belgium and an MSc in Public Administration from Aalborg University in Denmark.

Vijay Sathe is the C.S. & D.J. Davidson Chair and Professor of Management in the Peter F. Drucker and Masatoshi Ito Graduate School of Management at Claremont Graduate University, California. He was previously on the faculty at the Harvard Business School for ten years and has also taught at IMD, the International Institute for Management Development in Lausanne, Switzerland. Professor Sathe received the Bachelor of Engineering degree from the University of Pune, India; an MS in Mechanical Engineering from the University of Wisconsin; and the MBA and PhD in Business Administration from The Ohio State University. He has published numerous articles and six books: *Controller Involvement in Management* (Prentice-Hall, 1982), *Culture and Related Corporate Realities* (Irwin, 1985); *Organization* (with John Kotter and Leonard Schlesinger, Irwin, 1992); *Corporate Entrepreneurship: Top Managers and New Business Creation* (Cambridge, 2003); *Manage Your Career: Ten Keys to Survival and Success When Interviewing and on the Job* (Business Expert Press, 2008), and (co-edited with Urs Jäger), *Strategy and Competitiveness in Latin American Markets: The Sustainability Frontier* (Edward Elgar, 2014) .

Christina Tewes-Gradl is an expert on inclusive business. As a founder and managing director of Endeva, she works with partners from all sectors to identify and implement market-based solutions to poverty. Christina has more than 12 years' experience in research and advising on sustainability, strategy and development issues. She is a Research Fellow at the CSR Initiative of the Harvard Kennedy School. In her PhD research, she developed a stakeholder view of the business model concept. Christina holds master's degrees from the University of Passau and the London School of Economics. Previously, Christina worked as a strategy consultant with McKinsey and Co. and with rice farmers in Madagascar.

Jun Tibi is an entrepreneur who focuses on micro, small and medium-sized enterprises and the development sector. He also devotes time to working with other organizations that share his entrepreneurial interests and passion. Currently, he is a co-founder of a Manila-based design and communications agency and a tour operating company in the historic island of Culion, Palawan, which has been recognized as one of the accomplished youth organizations in the Philippines. Tibi completed his degree in Business Management (Honours) in Ateneo de Naga University in 2008.

Shusuke Watanabe is a senior consultant in NRI's Consulting Division. His specialties include planning business strategies and supporting the launch of new businesses, as well as planning alliance and partnership strategies and providing support, principally in the fields of healthcare, BoP business, information and communications. His consulting services cover a wide range of private industries such as electronics, telecommunication and medical field. He also has considerable experience in supporting Japanese government agencies. In the field of BoP business, he supported several Japanese companies to expand their business in emerging countries. Those activities included marketing research, partnership arrangement and business strategy making for the sales of newly developed products such as solar panels, water purification powder and medical equipment. Since April 2014, he has been a senior staff member of NRI's Corporate Strategy Department.

Index

99designs 75

access2innovation 161-78
  building up partnerships 170-2
  business models 164, 169, 170, 173, 176-8
  commercialization 172-3
  facilitation of network/partnerships
        164, 172, 173, 176
  history of 164-7
  implementation phases 167, 169
  organization of networks/partnerships
        164, 166, 167, 175-6
  study of 163-4
Accion Venture 93
Affordable value innovations 40
Ajinomoto 195
Alpaca breeders 24-5
Alpina 25
Amanco 149, 155
Animal-bite clinics 132, 134-6
ANZ Bank 149
Aravind 120
Aravind Eye Hospital 16-17
Artha Venture Partners 105
Ashoka 69, 82, 105, 149
Asia-Pacific National Innovation Systems
        Online Resource Centre 66
Asogragan 25
Asopoleche 25
Atizo 75

Bangladesh
  bean production 196
  biogas project 162-3, 167, 170, 172, 173

Grameen Danone 11, 14, 16, 17, 18, 111,
        114, 150, 155
  water purification 191
Bank of America Merrill Lynch 97, 107
Banking
  community banking 37
  correspondent banking 113
  low-income consumers 31-2, 33,
        34-5, 37, 41
  mobile banking 32, 36, 64, 113, 149, 152
  rural banking 84, 149
  skunkworks operations 37
  Standard Bank Access banking model 41
Barclays Capital 149, 155, 156
Benefit corporation (B Corp) 17, 19
Biofuels 67, 84, 97, 98, 107
Biogas project, Bangladesh 162-3, 167, 170,
        172, 173
BipBop programme 91-2
Blue Label Telecoms 41-2
Bolivia 24-5
BoP Innovation Centre (BoPInc)
        82, 92
BoP space 13
  capabilities in 23-7
  cross-sector collaboration 25
  failure to access 14-15
  formal markets 23-4
  global standards 26
  innovation 26-7
  insecure environments 25-6
  motivation for business in 21-3
  perceptions of 20-1
  recommendations for success in 14

BoP vision   27-30
    ambition and capability   27-9
    creating   27-30
    dreamer vision   29
    dropout vision   29
    sleeper vision   29
    winner vision   29
Brazil   26-7, 151
    correspondent banking   113
    door-to-door distribution   114
    Geekie   121
    microfinance   152
    Nestlé até Você   114
    participatory market research   46-57
    Projeto Coletivo   115
    Social Technologies Bank   68
    Social Technologies Network   68
    Sorridents   121
Bureau of European Policy Advisers
        (BEPA)   64
Business models   8, 15-17
    access2innovation   164, 169, 170,
        173, 176-8
    moving from closed to open models   40-1
    private sector   6
    shared-channel distribution   132-7
    transformational   39-40

CAD (Centro de Alianzas para el
        Desarrollo)   69-70
Canadian International Development Research
        Centre (IDRC)   182
Capitec Bank   31, 32, 33, 34-5, 42
Casas Bahia   47
Cassava   52-3, 67, 97, 98, 107
Cell phones *see* Mobile phones
Cemex   13, 36, 42
Center for Technology Licensing, Cornell
        University   105
Centre of Science for Villages (CSV)   67
Challenge.gov   75
Charcoal   97, 107
Charles, Prince of Wales   119
Chetty, Mechell   40, 41
China   124, 150, 152, 157
China Innovation Network (CHIN)   67
chotuKool fridge   63
Christensen, Clayton   35
Christensen, Sam   166
CleanStar Mozambique (CSM)   97-8, 107-8
Climate change
    adaptation
        definition   193
        Resilience Leap   193-4, 196, 197

    solutions   195-6, 197
    Triple Leap   196-200
    Japanese companies   192-6
    mitigation   192
    social problems   93
Clinton, Hillary   96
Closed innovation   49, 73
Cluster developments   16, 17
Coca-Cola   13, 115, 124
CocoTech   149, 154, 155, 156
Coffee producers   13
Collaborative lifestyles   74
Colombia
    Mutualitos y Mutualitas   184, 185-7
    urban agriculture   181, 183-8
Committee for Democratization of
        Information Systems (CDI)   115
Community banking   37
Confederation of Danish Industry (DI)   165-6
Cooaprisa   25
COPROCA   24-5
Corporate volunteering   16, 17
Correspondent banking   113
Coupled innovation   72
Cross-sector collaboration   25
Crowdfunding   93
crowdSPRING   75
Customer expectations   22

Dabbawalas, Mumbai   118-19
Dairy industry   26
DanChurchAid (DCA)   162-78
Danish Red Cross   164-5
Danone   13, 14, 90-1
    see also Grameen Danone
Danone Poland   149
DataStation   75
De-mining operations
    ICT solution   167, 168, 170, 171, 172
Deforestation   97, 107
Development Innovation Ventures (DIV)   89
Disruptive innovation   6, 35, 36, 37, 102,
        103, 125
Distribution   110-22
    access to basic service   120-1
    BoP penalty   126-8
    challenges   110-11, 124-8
    commercial policies   117-19
    cost structure   113, 117
    credit   117-18
    dabbawalas, Mumbai   118-19
    door-to-door   111, 114, 155
    education services   121
    efficiency in   116-19

flexibility   113, 118-19
franchising   120-1
innovation   113-14
last mile   3, 9, 39, 111-12, 124
logistics   113, 116
multinational corporations   112-13
partnerships   114-15, 116, 145-6
the Philippines   125-8, 132-8
retail as a platform   119-20
sales structure   116-17
shared channel *see* Shared-channel
      distribution
slums   112
Drucker, Peter   12, 15, 61

Economic innovation   61
Ecuador   26
Embrace   120
Emergent Institute   9, 100
   action research   105
   Cluster Networks   103
   ecosystem evolution   101-5
   Emergent Accelerator   102-3, 105-6
   Emergent Seed Fund   104
   entrepreneur network   104
   green leap Technology Bank   103-4
   resource commitments   107
   successes and failures   105-7
   Udyogini   101-2
   vision for   100-1
Enabling ecosystems   9, 65, 69-71
   see also Innovation ecosystem
ENAP (Empresa Nacional de Petróleos)   13
Endeva   48
Enviu   93
Ericsson   37
Essilor   14
Ethiopia   41, 82, 157
Euglena   196
European Sharing Economy Coalition   73-4
Exploitation of the poor   15
Eye in the Sky   167, 170, 172
Eyeglasses   14
eYeka   75

Fairtrade   13
Family Vaccine and Specialty Clinics, Inc.
      (FVSC)   132, 134-6
Fiat Mio   75
Fiji   149
Fischer, Carl   33
Floralp   26
Food and Agriculture Organization
      (FAO)   181, 182

Food security   181-2, 196
   definition   181
Franchising   92, 120-1
Freeplay Energy   150, 155
Fringe stakeholders   22-3
from far east   196
Frugal innovation   35-6, 43, 62
FUNDES   25

GDF Suez   90-1
Geekie   121
General Electric (GE)   23, 35, 191
Ghana   149, 150, 195, 196
Ghosn, Carlos   35
GIZ (Deutsche Gesellschaft für
      Internationale Zusammenarbeit)
      69-70
GlaxoSmithKline (GSK)   39-40, 43
Global standards   26
Godin, Benoît   60
Gordon Institute of Business Science
      (GIBS)   9
GRA Co. Ltd   191
Grameen   14
Grameen Danone
   door-to-door distribution   111, 114
   fortified yoghurt   14, 16, 17, 18, 111, 114,
      150, 155
Grameenphone   115, 150, 155, 156
GrandPa headache powder   39-40
Grassroots innovation   3, 62, 65
   networks   66-9
Grassroots Innovation Augmentation Network
      (GIAN)   67
Grassroots Innovations, UK   68
Green Generator   162, 167, 170, 172, 173
Green Leap   191, 192, 197
Green leap ventures   100, 101
   Technology Bank   103-4
Grupo Bimbo   41-2

Hapinoy   132, 136-7
Head Held High   105
HealthStore Foundation   120-1
HERi Madagascar   48
Hindustan Lever (HUL)   35, 114
Hollard Insurance   37
Honey Bee Network   66, 67
HSSi   132-4
Huatai Paper   150, 154
Hughes, Nick   36
Hybrid enterprises   16, 17
Hydroponic cultivation   191-2
Hypios   75

ICCO   82, 92, 93
ICM   97, 107
Idea Bounty   75
Idea Crossing   75
IdeaConnection   75
ideaken   75
IFU   97, 107
Immelt, Jeffrey   23
Inclusive Business Fund   92, 93
Inclusive innovation   62, 80, 82-3
  definition   83
  financing
    case studies   82
    corporate impact finance   90-1
    dedicated early-stage BoP investment
      firms   93
    Development Innovation Ventures   89
    duration of funding   86-7
    finance needs   83-5
    financial instruments   88-93
    food and nutrition sector, Africa   84
    impact investing   81, 87, 88-9
    inadequate granularity of funding   87
    inadequate types of funding   86-7
    Inclusive Business Fund   92
    India Inclusive Innovation Fund   90
    Innovation Against Poverty   89-90
    investment constraints   86
    Schneider Electric BipBop
      programme   91-2
  pioneer gap   81
    as barrier to high-volume investing
      87, 88
    definition   87
    position in investment cycle   88
Inclusive markets
  accessibility   34
  affordability   34
  banking   31-2, 33, 34-5, 37, 41
  building   31-43
  costs and benefits   36-7
  disruptive innovation   35
  frugal innovation   35-6, 43, 62
  insurance   32-3, 35
  local capacity building   40, 41, 43
  low-income consumers   31-2, 33, 34-5, 37
  metrics and reporting   38-9
  micro-enterprises   39-40
  partnerships   41-2, 43
  reorganizing the organization   37-8, 43
  reimagining products   42
  skunkworks operations   37
  South Africa   8, 31-43
  transformational business models   39-40

India   14, 16-17, 35, 100, 151
  corporate social responsibility law   106-7
  dabbawalas, Mumbai   118-19
  door-to-door distribution   111, 114
  Emergent Institute *see* Emergent Institute
  hydroponic cultivation   191-2
  Nokia   151, 152, 155
  Shakti Project   114
India Inclusive Innovation Fund (IIIF)   90
Indonesia   191
Informal markets   21, 22, 116
Information technology   26
Inkling Markets   75
Innocentive   75
Innoget   75
Innovation
  affordable value innovations   40
  in BoP space   26-7
  closed innovation   49, 73
  coupled innovation   72
  defining the implications of   61-2
  definitions   60
  disruptive innovation   6, 35, 36, 37, 102,
    103, 125
  in distribution   113-14
  Drucker's seven opportunities for   61-2
  economic innovation   61
  ecosystem *see* Enabling ecosystems;
    Innovation ecosystem
  frugal innovation   35-6, 43, 62
  grassroots innovation   3, 62, 65, 66-9
  history of concept   60
  imitation   60
  inclusive innovation *see* Inclusive innovation
  integrated innovation   72
  market pull   72
  open innovation   3, 39, 41, 53, 72-5
  participatory market research   46-57
  partnerships   41-2, 43, 73
    see also access2innovation
  Prahalad's 12 principles of innovation   62-3
  reimagining products   42
  reverse innovation   23, 113-14, 121, 191
  sharing economy model   73-4
  social innovation *see* Social innovation
  technology push   71-2
  value-chain phases   75
Innovation Against Poverty (IAP)   89-90
Innovation ecosystem   3, 74, 96
  building   99-101
  CleanStar Mozambique (CSM)   97-8, 107-8
  concept   99-100
  ecosystem innovation platforms   69-71
  Emergent Institute *see* Emergent Institute

green leap ventures   100, 101, 103-4
see also Enabling ecosystems
Innovation Exchange   75
Innovation labs   6, 37, 40
Insecure environments   25-6
Insurance   129
   low-income consumers   32-3, 35
Integrated innovation   72
Integrated Tamale Fruit Company   150, 155
Inter-American Development Bank   17
International Network on Appropriate
      Technology   66
International standards   22
Intrade   75
Investment constraints   86

Jaipur Foot   120
Jaipur Leg   63
Japan   190-200

Kaggle   75
Kahneman, Daniel   64
Kaiho Sangyo   196
Kawasaki Geological Engineering   195
Kennedy, John F.   18
Kenya   32-3, 36, 37, 191, 195, 197

Ladekarl, Anders   164-5
Land tenure   187
Last mile   3, 9, 39, 111-12, 124
Legitimacy   22-3, 144, 146, 166, 173, 175, 177
Leopold, Aldo   99
   A Sand County Almanac   99
LG   13
Life Innovation Container   191
Llama breeders   24-5
Local capacity building   40, 41, 43
Low-income markets *see* Inclusive markets
Low-profit limited liability company (L3C)
      17, 19
LYDEC   151, 154, 155

Madagascar
   participatory market research   46-57
Magazine Luiza   26-7, 47
Manila Water Company   151, 156
Market research *see* Participatory market
      research
Markets
   formal markets   23-4
   inclusive *see* Inclusive markets
   informal markets   21, 22, 116
   redistributing markets   74
Maruha Nichiro Foods   196

Massachusetts Institute of Technology (MIT)
   D-Lab   69
   Grassroots Invention Group (GIG)   69
Merck   40
Metrics   38-9
Mexico
   Grupo Bimbo   41-2
   PETSTAR   152, 154, 155, 156
Micro-enterprises   39-40, 70, 83, 101-2, 120,
      146
Microfinance   64, 81, 132, 146, 149, 155
   Nokia Microfinance   151, 155
   Real Microcrédito   152
Millennium Development Goals (MDGs)
      181, 182, 200
Mine clearance *see* De-mining operations
Mitsubishi UFJ Morgan Stanley   196
Mobile banking   32, 35, 36, 64, 113, 149, 152
Mobile phones   14, 16, 34, 42, 100, 113
   Grameenphone   115, 150, 155, 156
   Nokia   151, 152, 155
   smartphones   162, 172, 176
   Vodafone   35, 36
Monitor Group   125
Moreno, Israel   36
Morocco   151
MTN   42
Murray, Greg   97
Myoo Create   75

Nairobi   33, 183
Narayana Health   36
Narayana Hrudayalaya heart hospital   16-17
National Grassroots Innovation Databank,
      Malaysia   67
Natura Ekos   151
NEC   191-2
Negro Women for Tomorrow Foundation
      (NWTF)   132-4
Nespresso   13
Nestlé   13, 38, 114
Network on Technologies for Social
      Inclusion   68
NewFire Africa   98
NewsFutures   75
Next-practice strategies   100-1
NICE International   92
NineSigma   75
Nippon Poly-Glu   191
Nirma detergent   14, 15
Nissin Foods   191
Nokia   124, 148
Nokia Lifetools   151, 155
Nokia Microfinance   151, 155

Nokia Money   152
Nokia Siemens Networks   152, 155
Novartis Foundation for Sustainable
        Development   20
Novo Nordisk   102
Novozymes   97, 98, 107

One Billion Minds   75
Open innovation   3, 39, 41, 53, 72-5
OpenIDEO   75
Over-the-counter (OTC) medicines   136-7

Palm oil   25-6
Palmas del Espino   25-6
Panasonic   191
Participatory market research   46-57
    benefits   48-51
        creation of trust   50
        empowerment   50
        enhanced understanding   50
        identification of practical user
            innovations   51
    briefing participants   55
    case studies   48
    constructivist epistemology   49
    focus   54
    focus groups   48, 51, 52-3, 54, 56
    history of participatory approaches   49
    identifying key players   57
    implementation   55-6
    incentives for participants   55
    lessons learned   53-7
    limitations   56-7
    methods   51-3
        perceptions   52-3
        selection of methods   54
        solutions   53
        use context   51-2
    paparazzi method   51, 52, 54
    participatory interviews   52
    preparation   54
    selecting participants   55
    triangulating results   56
    understanding the context   54
    use   56-7
    visual material   55-6
Partnering Initiative   71
Partnerships   41-2, 43
    co-developers   154
    companies   146-7
    cross-sector partnerships   161-78
    in distribution   114-15, 116, 145-6
        see also Shared-channel distribution
    embeddedness   114-15, 145

enabling ecosystem   71
external funding   147
government's role   146, 157
individuals and communities   145-6
innovation   41-2, 43, 73
    see also access2innovation
NGOs and microfinance institutions   146
open innovation   73
partner roles   153-6
    brokers   153, 156
    co-developers   153
    complementors   153, 155
    customers   153, 155
    distributors   153, 155
    funders   153, 156
    impact assessors   153, 156
    microfinance partners   153, 155
    suppliers   153, 154-5
for poverty alleviation   142-58
public–private partnerships   25
resource gain   144-5
Patagonia   16, 17, 18-19
PDVSA (Petróleos de Venezuela sA)   13
PEAR Carbon Offset Initiative   196
Pep Stores   37
Peru   25-6, 69
Petrobras   13
PETSTAR   152, 154, 155, 156
Philippines
    CocoTech   149, 154, 155, 156
    distribution in   125-8, 132-8
    Manila Water Company   151, 156
Phillips   37, 40
Poland   149
Poveda, Rosa Evelia   185-7
Practical Action   68
Prahalad, C.K.   1, 5, 13, 20, 62-3, 117
PRESANS   75
Procter & Gamble   14, 35
Product-based systems   74
Prolinnova   66
Public–private partnerships   25, 71, 154, 194,
        198
Puma   13
PuR   14
Purpose
    concept of   18
    decoding the real purpose   18-20

Rabobank Foundation   82, 92, 93
RDRS   166, 172
Real Microcrédito   152
RedesignMe   75
Redistributing markets   74

RedTISA 68
Resilience Leap 193-4, 196, 197
Reverse innovation 23, 113-14, 121, 191
Rice to Riches 119
Roche 40
Rome Declaration on World Food
      Security 181
Rural Relations 105
Rwanda 150

Samhita 105
Sanyo Electric 191, 195, 196, 197-8
Saxena, Segun 97
Schneider Electric BipBop programme
      91-2
Schumpeter, Joseph Alois 61, 100
Sehgal, Vikram 37
Shakti Project 35, 114
Shared Channel Assessment Framework
      (SCAF) 128-9, 137, 138
  alignment dimensions 129-30
  business location 130
  customer awareness 131
  financing support 130
  geography 131-2
  market access 131
  market development dimension 131-2
  market readiness 131
  organizational skills and values 130
  products and services 129
  supply-chain management 130
  value-add dimensions 130-1
Shared-channel distribution 123-8
  as business model 132-7
  case studies 132-8
  emergence of 125
  global perspectives 124
  opportunities and challenges 132-7
  the Philippines 125-8, 132-8
Sharing economy model 73-4
Sharp 195, 196
Shining Path guerilla movement 25-6
Sierra Leone
  participatory market research
      46-57
Skunkworks operations 37
Sky-Watch 162, 163, 169, 172-3
Smartphones *see* Mobile phones
Social innovation 62-4
  definition 62
  social challenge perspective 64
  social demand perspective 64
  social system innovation 60
  systemic changes perspective 64

Social media 26, 34, 40, 42, 100
Social Technologies Bank, Brazil 68
Social Technologies Network, Brazil 68
Solar lanterns
  Madagascar 48
  Sanyo Electric 191, 195, 196, 197-8
  shared-channel distribution model 132-4
Soros Economic Development Fund
      97, 107
Sorridents 121
South Africa 66, 69, 195
  inclusive markets 8, 31-43
Standard Bank 37, 41, 42
  Access banking model 41
Starbucks 13
Susu collectors initiative 149, 155, 156
Swedish International Development
      Cooperation Agency (SIDA)
    Innovation Against Poverty (IAP) 89-90
Symbid 93
Syrian Arab Republic 184

Tanzania 191, 195, 196
  Nokia Siemens Networks 152, 155
Tata 13, 16, 17, 35
TekScout 75
Telenor 115
Tetra 13
Thinking like a mountain 99
Thomas, Dave 39
Toray 195, 196
Traditional Knowledge Digital Library
      (TKDL) 67
Triple Leap 196-200
Tsinghua Tongfang Changfeng
      computer 152
Tunisia 69-70

UAP 32-3, 35
Udyogini 101-2
Uganda 191, 197
UMATA (Unidad Municipal de Asistencia
      Técnica Agropecuaria) 25
Unilab 132, 136-7
Unilever 35, 40-1, 111
  Hindustan Lever (HUL) 35, 114
United Nations
  Development Group Task Force 182
  Development Programme (UNDP) 194
  Industrial Development Organization
      (UNIDO) 48
  Millennium Declaration 181
  Millennium Development Goals
      (MDGs) 181, 182, 200

Unitus Seed Fund   93
Urban agriculture   180-8
  Colombia   181, 183-8
  definition   182
  food security   181-2
  household income   183
  land tenure   187
  Mutualitos y Mutualitas   184, 185-7
  risks   187
  role of public policy   187-8
  waste management   183, 186
  water contamination   187
  water scarcity   187
Uruguayan Center for Appropriate
      Technology   68
USAID (United States Agency for International
      Development)
  CleanStar Mozambique   97-8, 107-8
  Development Innovation Ventures   89

Value-chain efficiency   24-5
Vietnam   157, 195, 196
ViewWorld (VW)   162, 163, 169, 172, 173, 176-7

Visão Mundial   115
Vision 2050 report   12
Vodafone
  M-Pesa   35, 36
  Safaricom   36

Walmart   13
Water purification   10, 14, 191,
      195, 196
Water scarcity   187
Wellthy Corporation   196
Weza project   150, 155
World Food Summit Plan of Action   181
World Resources Institute   97, 126
World Vision   17

Yamaha Motor   195, 196
Yet2.com   75
Yukiguni Maitake   195, 196
Yunus, Muhammad   17

Zambales War Against Poverty (ZWAP)
      132, 134-6